Screening America

American University Studies

Series IX
History

Vol. 42

PETER LANG
New York · Bern · Frankfurt am Main · Paris

Marlette Rebhorn

Screening America

Using Hollywood Films
to Teach History

PETER LANG
New York · Bern · Frankfurt am Main · Paris

791.43
R291s

Library of Congress Cataloging-in-Publication Data

Rebhorn, Marlette
   Screening America : using Hollywood films to teach history /
Marlette Rebhorn.
   p.   cm.—(American university studies. Series IX, History ;
vol. 42)
   1. Historical films—United States—History and criticism.
2. United States in motion pictures.   3. Moving-pictures—United
States—History.   4. Moving-pictures and history.   5. American
history—Study and teaching—Audio-visual aids.   I. Title.
II. Series.
PN1995.9.H5R43   1988   87-26078
791.43′09′09358—dc19   CIP
ISBN 0-8204-0726-7
ISSN 0740-0462

CIP-Kurztitelaufnahme der Deutschen Bibliothek

Rebhorn, Marlette:
Screening America : using Hollywood films to
teach history / Marlette Rebhorn. – New York;
Bern; Frankfurt am Main; Paris: Lang, 1988.
   (American University Studies: Ser. 9,
   History; Vol. 42)
   ISBN 0-8204-0726-7

NE: American University Studies / 09

89-3398

Printed by Weihert-Druck GmbH, Darmstadt, West Germany

For Wayne, Matthew, and Rebecca

Table of Contents

Preface

The idea of using Hollywood films to teach history first occurred to me in 1978, in the middle of a hot Texas summer, as I struggled to interest students in a history survey course. Perhaps, I thought, they might be more eager to write the papers I was assigning if the subject came from a film they had seen recently. Although the idea sounded simple enough, however, carrying it out proved more difficult than I expected. Students had a hard time setting a film in context, or even determining when it took place. They also seemed to accept everything in the film as historically correct. Finally, they found it difficult to make connections between what they read in the textbook and the material in the film. I decided I would need to write introductory essays, therefore, setting each film in context, critiquing it for historical accuracy, and relating material they knew to specific action in the film. Thus were born the essays which make up this book.

But students still had trouble doing the assignment even after reading the essay. Told to find a topic to write on addressed by the film, some chose "mega-topics" more suitable for a doctoral dissertation, while others picked some rather insignificant subject. I wanted to allow them the greatest possible freedom to choose topics they were really interested in, but, on the other hand, I had to admit that some guidelines were required, and especially necessary would be a bibliography where students could begin their search. I prepared a list of topics for each film, running the gamut from traditional research papers, to book reports, to biographical sketches, to essay questions. Over the years, I added topics students had developed themselves which produced good work, and I provided the essays and the instructor's guides to my colleagues to experiment with. The Instructor's Guide which follows each essay in this book is the result of that process.

The results were very gratifying. While at first some students tended to regard the entire film project as an excuse for sloppy work, over time, the quality of the projects improved. Students who were more visually than print oriented to begin with enjoyed the opportunity to use viewing skills they already possessed to develop a topic. Many used the prepared topics in the instructor's guides, but many more created their own, investigating, under my supervision, aspects of American history they were intrigued with. Moreover, not only were they generally willing to work harder to find information, but the quality of their writing improved as well. My colleagues discovered similar results in their classes. Why not, I thought, collect the essays and instructor's guides, and make them available to others who might also want to interest students and improve their research and writing skills at the same time?

As this discussion indicates, I owe a debt of gratitude to many people. To my students and colleagues who shared their ideas with me, I extend my thanks. Specifically, I wish to acknowledge the help and support of William E. Montgomery and Roger Griffin, then co-chairs of my department, whose enthusiasm for the project bouyed up my sagging spirits more than once. I would also like to thank Steve Kinslow and Gwen Rippey, the deans on my campus, who helped me get a grant to prepare the original three essays, and to Mimi Valek, who heads the Austin Community College Instructional Development Office, go my thanks for shepherding the right forms through the right channels to obtain that grant. Finally, I want to thank my husband, Wayne A. Rebhorn, for reading, rereading, and then rereading again the manuscript, for offering his astute comments, and for understanding that when I was watching Hollywood movies at night, I really was working.

Introduction

I teach history, and I have a problem. Actually, I have two problems. For one thing, my students tend to think of history as something dull, far away, and fundamentally irrelevant. In addition, my students frequently have poor writing and research skills which they must improve if they are to succeed in the world outside the academy. These problems are nothing new, of course, nor am I the only instructor to struggle with them. Rather than continue complaining about them, however, I have developed a film project to enhance student interest in the basic American history survey, and to provide students with an opportunity to write about subjects which engage their attention. This book is the result.

The fact is that, increasingly, students are more visually than print oriented, and react more favorably to visual materials than to the printed page. Films, therefore, seemed a natural lure to increase student interest in events from the past. The films I chose had to meet three requirements, however. First, they all deal with a major historical event, or have such an event as background. This book is not a history of film *per se*, and so does not concern itself, except incidentally, with directorial styles, camera angles, or technological innovations. Rather, it uses films to explore major themes or events in American history from the Civil War to the present. Therefore, *All the President's Men*, which deals with Watergate, and *Birth of a Nation*, which deals with Reconstruction, are included, while Alfred Hitchcock's *Rear Window* is not.

Second, the films I have chosen are available on videocassettes which are cheaper to buy than reel-to-reel films are to rent. Moreover, the videocassette format allows maximum flexibility for instructors and students alike. Students can watch videocassettes outside of class, at home, or in the library, and so instructors do not have to sacrifice valuable classtime to show a film. If an instructor should choose to show a film "clip" to illustrate a point in lecture, however, it is relatively easy to fastforward the cassette to the appropriate point before coming to class, slip it into the machine, and push "Play." Likewise, videocassettes are easier to use than reel-to-reel film strips, and since video technology has become so widespread, both instructors and student feel quite comfortable using it.

Third, the films I have chosen all reflect a wide variety of topics and events from 1865 to the present. Some may disagree with my choices, preferring *Platoon* to *Deer Hunter*, for example, as an entré into the Vietnam experience. Some people have special favorites which they would prefer included; one of my colleagues argued strenuously in favor of *Citizen Kane*, and suggested dropping *Top Hat*. Ultimately, I suppose, personal prejudice may have triumphed (I like *Top Hat*), but I think a dispassionate reader will agree that, given limitations of space, the films chosen do deal with a wide cross-section of the American experience, from world war to the depression, from scientific theories to the development of American dance. Finally, I admit that some films originally included were later dropped because many students over many years found them boring. Trying to engage student interest in the past by showing films which put them to sleep is obviously counterproductive.

Having chosen the films with care, I have provided essays on each one, setting it in historical context, critiquing it for historical accuracy, and introducing students to the major themes in American history it addresses directly or indirectly. Students need these essays, I have discovered, because they frequently have trouble identifying the events being depicted. Most students know that *Casablanca* has something to do with World War II, for instance, but what the French have to do with it, or why the film is set in French Morocco remains a mystery to many of them. Likewise, students assume that everything in a film is accurate historically, since producers obviously paid someone a great deal of money to insure that this is so. Explaining how some films confuse dates or facts encourages students to be more sensitive and critical viewers. Finally, students need to know how the events they see in the film relate to major developments in American history.

How, then, can this book be used? In my classes, students are instructed to view the film outside of class, either on videocassettes in the library or by renting their own, and next to read the essay. They then have to do a paper on a subject raised by the film. I provide them with a list of suggested topics, which are contained in the instructor's guide which accompanies each essay. To insure maximum flexibility for a wide variety of teacher preferences and teaching situations, I include here many different kinds of assignments, from traditional book reports, to interpretive essays, to research papers, to biographical sketches. Students choose one of these topics, or develop a new one with me tailored to the requirements of the specific course they are taking. Most important, the guides provide students with a bibliography to launch them on their research.

Instructors grading these student assignments do not have to be film critics, nor even familiar with the film, for the essays and papers deal with historical events about which they are familiar and can be graded, therefore, the way instructors would grade any other piece of historical writing. The assignment can, moreover, be tailored to emphasize those concerns most important to individual instructors. For a course which emphasizes individualized research, for instance, essay topics might be preferable, while for a course which emphasizes teaching library skills, finding and analyzing reviews of a single book recommends itself. Those instructors who wish to improve student writing skills might keep the assignment relatively short, but insist students rewrite papers for credit. In short, the number of ways instructors can use this book is limited only by their imagination.

The films chosen to be included in this book are arranged in four groups of five each. The first group deals with events from the late nineteenth century to World War I, and includes, *Fort Apache, Ragtime, Birth of a Nation, Reds,* and *Sergeant York. Fort Apache* introduces students to the reality of the Old West, from the poorly paid, unglamorous horse soldiers to the indians trying to survive against an aggressive foe, and it also shows how the Jeffersonian yeoman farmer myth was transposed to the frontier to give it renewed meaning. *Ragtime* explores the profound changes which were occuring beneath the veneer of pre-World War I innocence, changes whose full meaning would become clear only after the war was over. The essay introduces readers to the pervasive racism both north and south of the Mason-Dixon line, a theme which *Birth of a Nation* picks up, showing how the first Ku Klux Klan accomplished its work of intimidation after the Civil War, died out, and was resuscitated in the World War I period to deal with increased black pride--and to express hostility to Jews, Catholics and immigrants as well. *Reds* gives students a brief history of the Russian revolutions of 1917, and relates events in Russia to the development of leftist thought in this country. Finally, *Sergeant York*, explores the reasons for American entry into the Great War, and how the War changed forever the yeoman farmers of Tennesee.

The second group of films deals with the period between the two world wars, and includes *City Lights, Inherit the Wind, Scarface, The Grapes of Wrath*, and *Top Hat*. *City Lights*, directed by and starring Charlie Chaplin, portrays the glamorous new urban culture which developed following the war, and the widespread flaunting of Prohibition. This new urban culture provoked a rural attack upon "city-slicker" ideas like evolution. The resulting conflict produced the Scopes trial, the subject of *Inherit the Wind*. Its essay introduces students to the rural attack on this new urban culture, and explores some new refinements of Darwin's theories proposed by the punctuationalists. *Scarface* portrays the crime wave Prohibition produced, and shows how gangsters adopted methods first pioneered by the robber barons of the nineteenth century to make their crime empires more efficient. The inefficiency of sub-marginal farmers is the subject of *The Grapes of Wrath*, which presents a searing portrait of dust bowl America; its essay sets the plight of the "Okies" into the context of the growth of agro-business from the late nineteenth century on. Finally, *Top Hat*, a Fred Astaire/Ginger Rogers vehicle, introduces students to major developments in American dance as well as to the escapism of the early depression years.

The third group of films deals with World War II and the immediate post-war period, and includes *Casablanca, Judgment at Nuremburg, Adam's Rib, Rebel Without a Cause*, and *On the Waterfront*. *Casablanca* introduces students to the early stages of the war, exploring why and how France fell, and how and why America entered the fight in 1941. *Judgment at Nuremburg* deals with the trials of Nazi war criminals following the war, and the essay discusses the Holocaust and Hitler's anti-semitic legislation, finding uncomfortably close relationships to events in the United States during the 1930's. *Adam's Rib* explores the new role for women the war produced, and how Hollywood struggled, usually unsuccessfully, to adapt its earlier heroine types to take account of the new women living outside the silver screen palaces. *Rebel Without a Cause*, starring James Dean, explores the deep unease many Americans felt in the post-war economy of abundance when the American dream threatened to become the American nightmare with the growth of juvenile delinquency and the blighting conformity of Levittowns. Finally, *On the Waterfront* shows how criminal elements had infiltrated labor unions, and offers comforting, if unrealistic solutions, to the problem.

The last group of films deals with the 1960's and 1970's, and includes *Dr. Strangelove*, *The Autobiography of Miss Jane Pittman*, *Deer Hunter*, *All the President's Men*, and *Fort Apache, The Bronx*. *Dr. Strangelove* portrays with black humor the discovery of the so-called "missile gap," and the essay introduces students to the early development of the arms race, especially Kennedy's massive build-up of the American nuclear arsenal. *The Autobiography of Miss Jane Pittman* deals with the early stages of the civil rights movement, and the essay indicates what happened after the date the film ended. *Deer Hunter* explores the devastating effects of the Vietnam war on a trio of steelworkers, suggesting close parallels between their experience before they left and their conduct during the war, and the essay briefly recounts the history of the conflict from 1945 onward. *All the President's Men* portrays the aggressive journalism which uncovered the Watergate scandal, and the essay sets the scandal in historical perspective. Finally, *Fort Apache, The Bronx* portrays the grim new American frontier within its aging cities, and suggests that the War Against Poverty, like many of Lyndon Johnson's Great Society programs, had at best mixed results.

Fort Apache - The Indians and the New Yeoman Farmer

Fort Apache, directed by John Ford, was made in 1948, and is the first of our series on the films of the United States. It is part of a trilogy, a three part epic of the Old West which includes *Fort Apache, She Wore a Yellow Ribbon* (1949), and *Rio Grande* (1950). Of the three, *Fort Apache* deals most sympathetically and accurately with the life of the average horse soldier and the indians he was supposed to control. Nonetheless, what the film leaves unsaid about the indians of the southwest is as interesting as what is left in. Along with the other films of Ford's triology, *Fort Apache* created an enduring, almost mythic image of the American frontier West, and in so doing rescued western films from the second class status to which they had fallen in the 1930's and 1940's. Finally, this new grandiose myth of the Old West contrasts strikingly with the image of life presented in *film noir*, or "dark film," a group of films made immediately following World War II. *Film noir* explores a nightmarish, indoor urban world whereas *Fort Apache* literally goes back to the land, in this case the starkly beautiful Monument Valley where nature's rock formations dwarf both indian and soldier alike. Closely attuned to an earlier nineteenth century, American, romantic love of the land, Ford redefines Jefferson's yeoman farmer myth in terms acceptable to the post-World War II generation.

In watching *Fort Apache*, the viewer is struck by its historical accuracy. There was, of course, a real Fort Apache in the northeast corner of Arizona, but we do not have to know that to accept the film's gritty reality. The fact was that, following the Civil War, officers were drastically demoted as more than one million volunteers were mustered out of the army in one year. Sgt. O'Rourke, the love-interest's father, could indeed have been a highly decorated Union officer during the war only to be dropped to sergeant's rank once the peace was signed. Moreover, in an economy move, Congress cut the pay of soldiers from a pitiful $16 to a scandalous $13 per month in 1871. Poorly paid, the horse soldier did not enjoy a glamorous life either. On their long marches under the glaring Arizona sun which bleaches the landscape in the film, the soldiers are covered with sweat and dust--and precious little glory unless they happen to die in a massacre. Finally, there was a rigid class system in the army which forbade the intermingling of officers and enlisted men except in structured situations like the enlisted men's ball, and this rigid class system was kept in force even on long marches when fewer than 50 men were involved. Thus, though Colonel Thursby might be a pompous, hard-hearted fool, he was correct in pointing out to his daughter, Philadelphia, that marriage between the colonel's lady and the son of an enlisted man might endanger her reputation and his career.

The film is accurate not only in what it portrays but also in what in scrupulously leaves out. Indians, for example, do not speak in the pidgin English made famous by Tonto, the Lone Ranger's sidekick, and any number of other indians from B-grade westerns. Neither do the indians dress in buckskin and live in tipis. Such dress and living accommodations were appropriate to the Great Plains indians like the Sioux and northern Cheyenne who operated around Colorado and Nebraska, for instance, where buffalo herds were abundant until the end of the nineteenth century. True to historical reality, in *Fort Apache*, which is set in Arizona, Cochise wears a variation of the white man's costume and his Chiricahua Apaches live in wickiups, a kind of lean-to. The indians of the southwest, of course, had been in contact with whites for over 200 years and had adopted many of their ways.

Another example of what the film carefully leaves out can be seen in the appearance of the fort itself. The fort is not a stockade made of logs set vertically next to one another. In fact, such stockades were relatively rare anywhere in the United States, in part because forts themselves were usually not permanent: as the frontier moved west, the soldiers moved with it and rapidly threw up a few rough buildings which became another fort for the time being. In the southwest, moreover, stockade forts were almost non-existent, because timber sufficient in quantity, size and shape was impossible to find. Imagine trying to make a stockade out of mesquite trees! Indeed, soldiers in most forts spent much of their time doing contruction work, building and repairing their quarters, and considerably less time fighting.

When the soldiers did fight, they generally rode out four-abreast as they do in the film, and on occasion they did ride into ambushes like the one presented in *Fort Apache*. The most famous of these ambushes, of course, was the massacre of Custer's men at Little Bighorn which, in a sense, is recreated in the film. Custer, like Colonel Thursby, was trained in the set piece battles of the Civil War and found it difficult to adapt to the guerrilla tactics of indian warfare. For example, a cavalry charge with sabers drawn makes a fine painting, but just as in Colonel Thursby's case, the picture will be painted posthumously if the commander tries this tactic on indians. Moreover, neither Custer nor Thursby took the time to reconnoiter the enemy, and as a result, both men's thirst for victory over a vaunted enemy led to annihilation.

For both Thursby and Custer, of course, there had been a history of annihilation of indians before they themselves were massacred. At Sand Creek in 1864 and at Washita in 1868, indian villages had been attacked without warning and huge numbers of Indians, including women and children, murdered.

The murdering of indians, however, was not isolated in the campaign against the Sioux and Cheyenne on the northern Great Plains. Cochise, Thursby's foe, certainly remembered the 1871 execution of his relatives by an American lieutenant. Cochise had been captured and held prisoner when the American army wrongfully accused the Chiricahua Apaches of stealing and kidnapping when in point of fact the crimes had been committed by the Coyotero Apaches who were not under Cochise's control. Cochise had escaped but his family was killed. Cochise and later Geronimo found it difficult to control various bands of Apaches who did, in fact, occasionally engage in terrorism for which they as chiefs were blamed.

Nonetheless, neither the Apaches nor the other indians ever posed much of a threat against the white settlers. Between 1840 and 1860, for example, approximately 316,000 people traveled the Oregon trail to the west. During that period, Indians killed 362 travelers, while by their own admission, American emigrants during the same period killed 426 indians. More would-be settlers died of dysentery, starvation, or accidents like drowning than were killed by indians. Even the classic pose of "circling the wagons" had less to do with warding off indian attack than it did with corraling the animals to keep them from wandering off.

Far from a blood-thirsty warrior, historically, Cochise had repeatedly tried to make peace with the whites who, however, insisted upon confining him and his people to reservations like the Bosque Redondo where they received inadequate rations and which were miles away from their ancestral homeland in the Chiricahua Mountains. Moreover, the Bosque Redondo reservation included other indian bands with whom Cochise's had traditionally been at war, and these rival groups made relations on the reservation very tense indeed. Cochise's son-in-law, Geronimo, who succeeded to the chieftaincy of part of the tribe after the death of Cochise in 1875, finally fled the American reservations to return to the Sierra Madres in Mexico in an attempt to secure the Apaches' well-being.

The fact of infighting among various indian groups, which *Fort Apache* ignores, is significant for it should remind the viewer that indians were no more a monolithic group than were "whites." On the contrary, there were many indian tribes who struggled with one another, and whose struggle made it easier for whites to control and exterminate them. One of the most famous such antagonisms is that between the Apaches of the film and the Comanches.

The Apaches, who originally came from the Mississippi River area around present day Missouri, had migrated into the southwest in the mid-seventeenth century, fleeing pressure from more warlike indians. These Apaches had been farmers, but on their long migration they returned to a hunting-gathering lifestyle. Desperate for food, when they first encountered the horses of the Spanish, they ate them, but soon they learned to domesticate them and became, as Captain York so rightly explains, the "best light cavalry in the world." The Spanish, however, had strict laws against trading guns to the indians, so the Apaches, though excellent horsemen, were armed only with stone arrowheads which were primitive, though deadly and the occasional metal knife. Nonetheless, because they could cover vast areas quickly and because the Spanish and the other indians of the southwest, like the Pueblo indians, were stationary, the Apaches ran havoc with their settlements, and earned an enduring reputation as savage fighters. By 1700, the most feared indian tribe in the New Mexico territory was the Apache nation.

At about this time, however, a new group of Indians was migrating into the same area from their homeland in the Great Basin between the two major western mountain ranges. These were the Comanches, who, like the earlier Apaches, had not been warriors, and who were contemptuously referred to as "jack-rabbit-catchers." Like the Apaches before them, they learned to use the horse, but unlike the Apaches, the Comanches had access to guns which they acquired from the Caddo tribe, which in turn had gotten them from the French. Although the Spanish forbade trading guns to the indians, the French did not; they gave guns to help produce more pelts for the profitable fur trade. In 1700, the Apaches had been the most powerful tribe in the southwest, but by 1725, the Comanches, armed with both horses and guns, had become the terrors of the area, spreading stark warfare from Texas to the Great Plains.

The Apaches had by then settled down to farming for at least part of the year, and so they were easy prey for Comanche attacks. Their "rancherias" were raided and many were sold into slavery to the Spanish. When the Spanish attempted to stop this trade by refusing to buy any more slaves, the Comanches slaughtered 200 prisoners in cold blood. As a result, the Spanish agreed to buy whatever Apaches the Comanches could bring to them, at least in part for humanitarian reasons. Ironically, however, in Spanish folklore, the Apaches maintained the reputation as vicious warriors, and the Spanish still refused to give them guns to protect themselves from the Comanches.

In the mid-eighteenth century, however, the Comanches raided San Antonio which was then experiencing a small pox epidemic. Without any natural immunity to the disease, the indians suffered a high mortality rate, and what is worse, because they raided throughout the middle part of the country, they spread the devastating disease elsewhere. At least 50% of the Plains indians died as a result, perhaps more.

The role of disease in controlling indian populations, weakening their social structure and undermining their religious beliefs is just beginning to be understood by historians. For example, recent ereearch shows clearly that the population of indians in New England had been reduced by perhaps as much as 90% following a disastrous plague epidemic which raged between 1616 and 1618; engaged in the fur trade with French outposts, these indians encountered this European disease to which, like small pox, they had no natural immunity. By the time the *Mayflower* sailed into Plymouth in Massachussetts in 1620, the English settlers encountered a severely weakened indian community. Indeed, this weakness may have contributed substantially to the Pilgrims' ability to survive.

Indians, therefore, not only struggled among themselves as much as the Spanish, French, and English did, but they engaged in vast migrations as significant as those which brought the Spanish to Mexico or the English to the American colonies. Moreover, they were not wandering savages, but sophisticated farmers, whose main crop, corn, which produced 80 kernals to every one sown, was considerably more efficient than European wheat, which produced barely five grains to every one sown. In fact, the growing of corn, especially in southern Europe, permitted Europeans to reduce and eventually end the periodic famines which plagued that continent, and in the process permittted a larger European population which could begin the industrial revolution.

Nonetheless, indians were regarded by white Americans as savage, and in 1887, the Dawes Act attempted to "civilize" them by destroying tribal life. The reservations were broken up into small plots which were given out to individual indians in order to turn them into yeoman farmers. In return, they would receive American citizenship. All extra land not given to indians would be sold to land hungry white settlers, with the proceeds going to indian schools. The small plots they received were frequently on sub-marginal land from which they could scratch a living only with great difficulty. Worse, further division of the land among the children of the original recipients created farms too small to work productively. While the white farmer, under the influence of the grangers, was coming to realize that the small, self-sufficient farms of myth could not produce enough profit, and so went into debt to buy ever larger farms and labor saving machinery, the indians were being forced to live up to the yeoman farmer myth which may never have been accurate, but which was certainly not true in the late nineteenth century as farmers increasingly adapted to "agro-business." Most indians were accustomed to tribal control of the land, and frequently did not even have a concept of private property. Moreover, the methods of intensive farming used by white settlers since Jamestown were totally alien to indian culture which regarded land as an integral part of a religious system, where whites saw land as a resource to be exploited. When, not surprisingly therefore, indians failed as small farmers, their lack of success was used to reenforce the idea that indians were heathen savages, racially inferior to whites, and dangerous if provoked.

By contrast, in *Fort Apache*, indians are not regarded as savages, but rather as noble, brave warriors who have been cheated and lied to by the likes of Thursby. Indeed, Captain Kirby York, played by John Wayne, is an admirer of Cochise, and while he admires Thursby's heroism and protects the colonel's reputation after his death, he condemns Thursby's high-handed tactics which led to an unnecessary massacre. York's attitude, however, is far removed from that prevailing in most westerns which dealt with indian threats. The last film before *Fort Apache* to allude to Custer's last stand was the 1942 movie starring Errol Flynn entitled *They Died With Their Boots On* which presented the indians as blood-thirsty savages and the soldiers as high-minded idealists.

With a few exceptions like *They Died With Their Boots On*, western films in the thirties and forties had been low budget quickies when they were made at all. By contrast, in the silent era, there had been westerns of high stature like *The Virginian* of 1914, but with the coming of sound, most studios abandoned the genre. The outdoor sets westerns demanded left little room to conceal a microphone, and the entire scene could be ruined by the unwanted sound of an airplane droning overhead or the whistle of a train moving in the distance. Studios, therefore, preferred gangster movies, like *Scarface* (1932), which could be shot on the back lot, or indoor costume comedies, like *Top Hat* (1935), where the acoustics were easier to control. When westerns returned, they were generally shot in indoor studios where the sets were painfully artificial, and these scenes were intercut with a few outdoor chase sequences where there was no dialogue and the sound of thundering horse hooves could be added later. Under these circumstances westerns were reduced to B-grade movies, the fillers on the double feature so popular during the depression thirties. With improvements in sound technique, filming in the open became possible once again in the late thirties. John Ford's *Stagecoach* of 1939 showed what the western could become in the hands of a skilled director. But with the advent of war in Europe in 1939, studios turned their attention to foreign locales instead of the Old West of America.

The western was not resuscitated quickly after World War II either. Following the war, American film was dominated by *film noir*. Translated directly, film noir means "dark film," and it explored the deep unease many American felt in the post-war, atom-bomb-dominated world. Movies in the *film noir* genre present an urban, night-time, interior world where violence is apt to explode at any moment and where human life is cheap. The *film noir* universe is a nightmarish, corrupt place full of every kind of sexual and emotional perversion in which nothing is quite what is seems. A close, perverse relationship exists between the corrupt law enforcers, the power brokers who by ruthless trickery control the city, and the criminal element which provides its seamy pleasures for a price.

Moral confusion reigns in *film noir*. Many movies in the genre are detective stories, but there is little difference between the detective and the criminals he tracks down. For example, the gangster Scarface of 1932 might have been a killer, but he was in many ways more humane than the cops who gun him down in the end. By contrast, in *The Big Sleep*, an example of *film noir* from 1946, Tony Canino, another gangster, is a sly, vicious hit man who kills for pleasure and who even uses poison, traditionally considered a "female" method, to murder a man in cold blood. But if Canino's behavior is despicable, so is that of Philip Marlowe, played by Humphrey Bogart, and supposedly the hero of the film, who watches but does nothing while Canino's victim is killed. In *film noir*, the confusion extends so far that the viewer is rarely sure of what he or she is seeing. In *The Big Sleep*, for example, even after we see the film to the end, we still are not sure "who did it" or even what "it" really was.

The bright, sundrenched open spaces of the Arizona frontier in *Fort Apache* are a world away from the night-time, interior scenes which characterize *film noir*. Moreover, while *film noir* presents a nightmarish, paranoid world filled with self-serving corruption, *Fort Apache* presents a world in which self-sacrifice, honesty and decency are virtues practiced by men who never benefit financially and who are slaughtered in the end. The commanding officer is a pompous fool, and he is accordingly punished for his many breaches of decorum. For example, Colonel Thursby insists Captain York welch on his promise to

Cochise because there can be no question of honor between an officer of the United States army and a man Thursby dismisses as an "illiterate, uncivilized murderer and treaty breaker." It is therefore Thursby who breaks the honor code of always keeping your promise and it is he who dies for it. By contrast with Thursby, the men in the doomed regiment exhibit an extraordinary sense of self-sacrifice: knowing that Lt. O'Rourke's life will be saved because Thursby has contemptuously ordered him to the rear with the supply wagons, the men nobly wish him luck instead of griping about the unfairness of it all. Moreover, the common soldiers who accompany Captain York to the corrupt indian agent Meachum's store condemn him for selling the indians whiskey and cheap trinkets. The soldiers may drink to excess occasionally, and show blatant favoritism, but their fundamental decency remains intact in Ford's western.

The closing scenes make clear that the decent horse soldier and not the glory hungry commander is the hero of the film in *Fort Apache*. York praises the individual soldier who exist on $13 a month and a diet of beans and hay while York's face is superimposed on a never ending troop of cavalry riding out to martial music. York's decency extends even to the now dead Thursby's reputation. At no point does York criticize the man who led his men to disaster. Rather, he diplomatically replies to a newspaperman's comment that Thursby was a great man, saying, "No man died more gallantly or with more honor for his regiment." York even accepts as "correct in every detail" an obviously inaccurate painting of Thursby's charge showing Cochise in a feather war bonnet and war paint.

It is with York's defense of Thursby's reputation that post-Watergate audiences have the most trouble. Most of us would have preferred a congressional investigation or, at the very least, a revealing newspaper exposé of Thursby's less than ideal motives and tactics. York's defense smacks of a whitewash. Yet to York, it is the average horse soldier rather than the occasional vain-glorious leader like Thursby or Custer who really matters, and if defending Thursby makes the enormous sacrifice of the average soldier worthwhile, to York that would appear to be a sufficient rationale.

In defending the average horse soldier, John Ford's *Fort Apache* redefined the Jeffersonian yeoman farmer myth in terms acceptable to post-World War II America. The sturdy independence of the yeoman farmer *as a farmer* had been permanently destroyed by the demands of twentieth century agro-business. A film like *The Grapes of Wrath* (1940), for example, portrays a battered farm family, the Joads, who may indeed be decent, but who suffer enormously in the depression and who are never independent. Small yeomen farmers became sharecroppers like the Joads, and were eventualy driven off their land. Ford, however, makes the yeoman farmer myth live again by moving it back into the distant past. Jefferson's independent and virtuous farmer becomes in Ford's hands the lowly horse soldier who, despite his occasional lapses, is truly virtuous. Like the early yeoman farmer, the horse soldier is bringing white man's civilization to the frontier against huge odds. While the yeoman farmer may have had his family to protect and support him, the horse soldier had his "family," the regiment, to do the same for him. Finally, the soldier goes about his job in the same unheroic way that the small farmer of the late eighteenth century made a modest living from the soil.

Significantly, however, Ford's yeoman soldier is removed from 1948 by almost a century; Ford refuses to create a hero out of contemporary American material. For example, if the soldier is the hero, Ford could just have easily depicted a modern day infantry grunt stationed on some faraway Pacific island bringing civilization to the natives, but he did not. Following the horrors of Auschwitz and Hiroshima, the individual heroism, decency, and virtuous independence of *Fort Apache* must have seemed impossible in the modern world. Some war movies did show the camaraderie of World War II troops, but they were made *during* the war, before the world learned of Hitler's concentration camps and before the bomb was dropped, and such movies ceased abruptly after Japan's surrender to be replaced by *film noir*. Disillusionment, fear, and uncertainty characterized the post-war period. The only way for Ford to portray the virtues he so admired, therefore, was to get out of the twentieth century altogether, and return to the past.

Heroes like John Wayne of *Fort Apache*, Randolph Scott, or Alan Ladd of *Shane* rode the ranges of the mythic West, not the subways of modern cities, or the expressways of the growing suburbias. When Hollywood addressed the concept of heroism in the modern world, the concept was changed to produce figures like James Dean in *Rebel Without a Cause* (1955), Robert De Niro in *Deer Hunter* (1978), or Paul Newman in *Fort Apache, the Bronx* (1981). These men embodied a more limited concept of heroism which nonetheless, shares with Ford's *Fort Apache* a belief in decency, sacrifice, and faith in the future.

Fort Apache - Instructor Guide

1. Discuss the American government's Indian policy in the latter half of the 19th century. How and why did this policy change from a policy of small reservations for Indians to the allotment plan of the Dawes act? Cite specific examples.

2. Discuss the careers of Cochise and Geronimo. Dee Brown, *Bury My Heart at Wounded Knee* (1971) is a useful source.

3. Write a brief historical sketch, assessing the significance of any or all of the following:

1. Geronimo
2. Sitting Bull
3. General George Custer

4. General Philip Sheridan
5. Wounded Knee

4. Describe the role of the Apache nation from its earliest appearance in the Southwest around 1700 to 1900. In your answer, you should consider the following:

1. role of the horse
2. Spanish policy on selling guns to Indians
3. arrival of Comanches
4. development of rancherias
5. reservations

5. Contrast the Indian and white settler's view of the land and the uses it was put to. Wilcomb Washburn's *Red Man's Land-White Man's Law* (1971) is a helpful source.

6. Write a book report, indicating the author's hypothesis and relating events in the film to events in the book, in any or all of the following:

1. R.K. Andrist, *The Long Death: The Last Days of the Plains Indians (1964)*
2. Dee Brown, *Bury My Heart at Wounded Knee* (1971)
3. R. David Edmunds, *American Indian Leaders: Studies in Diversity* (1980)
4. George E. Hyde, *Indians of the High Plains, From the Prehistoric Period to the Coming of the Europeans* (1959) reprinted 1981
5. Jules Loh, *Lords of the Earth, a History of the Navajo Indians* (1971)
6. Robert W. Mardock, *Reformers and the American Indian* (1971)
7. Edward Spicer, *Cycles of Conquest: The Impact of Spain, Mexico, and the United States on the Indians of the Southwest, 1553-1960* (1962)
8. R. M. Utley, *Frontier Regulars: The United States Army and the Indian, 1866-1891* (1973)
9. Wilcomb E. Washburn, *The Indian in America* (1975)
10. Wilcomb E. Washburn, *Red Man's Land-White Man's Law* (1971)

7. Choose oen of the books above and find the scholarly reviews of it in two or moe of the following journals:

1. *The American Historical Review* (published by The American Historical Association)
2. *Journal of American History* (published by The Organization of American Historians)

3. *History Teacher*
4. *History, Review of New Books*
5. *Choice*

Compare and contrast the reviews.   What did the reviewers like or dislike and why?

8. Compare and contrast the view of Indians, horse soldiers, the frontier, and the concept of honor in *Fort Apache* and *She Wore a Yellow Ribbon*, both directed by John Ford.

Ragtime - Pre-war America: Age of Innocence?

Released in 1981, *Ragtime* looks at life in America in the decade before World War I broke out in 1914. *Ragtime* uses film clips and newsreels to create an historical backdrop against which the film tells the fictional story of a typical turn of the century upper middle class family. This family is drawn into many of the social difficulties the rapid industrialization of the late nineteenth century produced. For example, to provide workers for new factories, the United States government encouraged immigration from overseas, but these "new immigrants" from southern and eastern Europe crowded into American cities where they remained unassimilated like Ashkenazy, the cinematographer in the film. The need for labor also encouraged wholesale migration of blacks from the south to the north as black workers fled the Jim Crow segregation of the south and sought higher paying jobs in northern industry. But blacks discovered that racism in the north was as strong as it had been in the south, and like Coalhouse Walker, Jr. in *Ragtime*, found their desire for racial justice stymied by white prejudice. As industrialization continued, whole new industries developed before the Great War, industries like moving pictures and the automobile. Such inventions encouraged a profound social and physical mobility that changed forever the sedate lives of the family in *Ragtime*.

Ragtime draws attention to its historical accuracy by using silent newsreels to frame various scenes in the film, but even a casual viewer notices that some of the newsreel footage actually dates from the pre-World War I period while most such "newsreel footage" is simply modern actors photographed in black and white. Thus, the scene of immigrants arriving at Ellis Island appears to be genuine while the "newsreel footage" of Booker T. Washington dining at the White House with Teddy Roosevelt or of Evelyn Nesbitt, Stanford White's mistress, clearly is not. Obviously, if either character is to be portrayed in the film, the director could not have the real Washington or Nesbitt in the newsreel footage. Such artistic license is normal when portraying real historical characters. However, a number of supposedly "real" events could not have taken place within the time frame of the film or in the order in which the events occur in the film. For example, Theodore Roosevelt ran for reelection in 1904 with Charles Fairbanks, but this event is supposedly contemporaneous in the film with the outbreak of war in 1914, 10 years later. The Model T Ford was invented in 1908 and the first ones came off the assembly line in 1909, but the "joke" played by the volunteer firemen on Walker's car had already occurred before Sarah sets off to see Vice President Fairbanks who was running for election in 1904, and who no longer held that office after March, 1909. The shooting of architect Stanford White occurred in 1906, but in the film this incident comes before the reelection campaign of Teddy Roosevelt which in fact occurred in 1904. Such historical inaccuracy detracts from the power of the fictional story being told, and furthermore is totally unnecessary. A simple subtitle identifying the year the action takes place would have been sufficient without bringing real historical events into the film and rearranging them at will.

For, indeed, the fictional story of *Ragtime* is based on real historical developments in America in the late nineteenth century, one of the most important of which was the vast flow of immigrants to this country. Between 1860 and 1920, over 28 million people immigrated to the United States. Of these immigrants, almost 70% came from southern and eastern Europe, unlike the pre-Civil War migrations from northern and western Europe, and these so-called "new immigrants" did not quickly assimilate into American culture, nor did they begin farming on the Great Plains. Instead, they usually crowded into urban ghettos like the one portrayed in *Ragtime*. Note that in the film signs are all in Hebrew characters. Because of immigration, cities mushroomed in size. The population of New York City, where *Ragtime* takes place, grew from 1.36 million in 1870 to 2.05 million in 1900. Some of the immigrants who came to this country came to escape persecution, but most came to earn money in the rapidly advancing industrial revolution. And they were remarkably well informed; when the American economy experienced hard times in the 1890's, many immigrants stayed home. Some people returned to Europe eventually. These "birds of passage" shuttled back and forth; in the early twentieth century, for example, almost as many people returned to Italy from the United States as left for America. Many immigrants later settled in the United States, of course, and like the immigrant cinematographer, Ashkenazy, in *Ragtime*, they braved the perils of overcrowded, dangerous American cities. Note how he keeps his young daughter on a rope to prevent her from being kidnapped. It is also true that many of the early film artists and entrepreneurs, like Louis Mayer, Darryl Zaunck, or even Charlie Chaplin, were recent immigrants who invested in this new industry.

However, once again, the viewer must be wary of the film's attempt to glamorize immigrant life or confuse dates. How is it, for example, when there are so many people outside in the ghetto streets that there is *no one* inside when Evelyn returns with a doll for the artist's little girl? The rooms she visits seem rather large for tenement immigrant quarters, and the naked lightbulb dangling on a wire assumes the tenement has electricity, certainly a dubious, if not impossible assumption, since many areas of New York City where this scene takes place were not electrified until the 1920's, long after the film's action supposedly takes place. After all, only 18% of American lived in dwellings with electricity in 1912.

Far more important for *Ragtime*, however, is the film's exploration of racial attitudes in the period before World War I. There had been in the 1890's and beyond a vast migration of southern blacks to the northern cities looking for jobs. At least 393,000 settled in New York, Pennsylvania, and Illinois, most in cities like New York, Philadelphia, and Chicago. The black population of New York City alone doubled between 1920 and 1930. These blacks discovered, however, that racism in the north was just as virulent as in the south, and that if special Jim Crow laws did not exist as in the south which legally segregated blacks, there was nonetheless segregation enforced by white group values and police indifference. Lynching, for example, remained a threat both north and south of the Mason-Dixon line. Between 1900 and 1914, more than 1000 blacks were murdered, mostly but not exclusively in the southern states. Blacks in the north were really in less danger of being lynched--at least until World War I--than of being humiliated like Coalhouse Walker, Jr. The "joke" the volunteer firemen play on Walker doesn't endanger his life, but it does, as Walker later explains, endanger his manhood. Walker's attempt to seek justice from the police and courts fails, and Sarah's attempt to intercede in his behalf results in her death. Note the difference between Walker's inability to get a police hearing and the ease with which Mother forces the police to honor her decision to keep Walker's baby at the seaside hotel. Significantly, however, in *Ragtime* it is only when Walker violently attacks other volunteer fire stations and ultimately commandeers the Morgan Library that he becomes sufficiently threatening to be gunned down in the end. Police Commissioner Rheinlander Waldo's order to shoot an unarmed civilian violates both legality and morality, and stands as a symbol of the no-win situation blacks found themselves in.

Walker's death is the most dramatic and violent example of *Ragtime's* portrayal of racism in the north before World War I, for the film dwells effectively on the more subtle forms of bigotry. When Walker visits Sarah, Father asks him to wait in the back, beside the kitchen door, and outside the house. Father is always polite to Walker, called him *Mr.* Walker and describing him as a "colored gentleman," but he is shocked when Mother brings the black baby *inside* the house. When the New Rochelle police chief explains to Mother that blacks are not really Christians and do not have the same sense of family as whites, Father quickly says, "Exactly!" The police chief had earlier proclaimed that blacks "breed like rabbits," and Father had offered no objection. Neither the police chief nor Father nor the doctor they call in to examine Sarah ever physically harms any black, nor do they engage in humiliating "jokes" and property attacks like the volunteer firemen. They even cordially despise Willy Conklin, the fire chief. But they are as racially prejudiced as Conklin ever was, and their assumption of black racial and social inferiority as unshakable. Or as Willy says when they threaten to turn him over to Walker, "Aren't we all in this together?"

Father, the police officer first called by Walker when his car is blocked, the city official to whom Walker turns for justice--all advise him to "forget about it." Father even offers to pay for repairing the damaged car if Walker will just marry Sarah and leave. They universally refuse to see this as a matter of pride and simple justice. Even the black lawyer Walker consults urges him to forget the matter and refuses to take the case, preferring himself to concentrate on "real problems," as he calls them, like starvation and eviction. The black lawyer, however, advises only a change of tactics, choosing to concentrate on more life threatening abuses rather than a petty dispute, but for Father and the other whites it is a question of being inconvenienced by demands from a man who really had no right to make these demands to begin with. Father explains to Walker that there are no legal means to redress the damage done to Walker's car by the volunteer firemen, but Brother quickly corrects him, protesting that there are legal steps which can be taken, but that they are time-consuming and expensive. It is not that the white-dominated justice system *cannot* help, but that it won't, and given this attitude, blacks would do well to forget the whole matter.

The foremost spokesman for blacks needing to prove themselves worthy of white respect and learning to turn the other cheek to examples of racial injustice was, of course, Booker T. Washington, who appears in *Ragtime* to urge Walker out of the Morgan library. Washington believed blacks had to "earn" their way into white society by working industriously and living righteously. His Tuskeegee Institute trained blacks predominantly for skilled manual labor jobs such as carpentry so that they would be able to earn a respectable living. Himself an ex-slave and a southerner, Washington designed his Tuskeegee program for the south in the heyday of segregation. Washington's program for black advancement was popular with liberal whites--Washington even dined with Teddy Roosevelt at the White House over howls of southern protest--because to a great degree the Tuskeegee program implied racial inferiority. At Tuskeegee, one learned carpentry, not Greek or Latin classics as in the major "white universities." Blacks had to earn the respect whites apparently were born with.

Naturally, when the white establishment had trouble with what Willy Conklin refers to as a "fancy nigger," they would call on Washington to make Walker see reason. Although Walker expresses great admiration for Washington, Washington accuses Walker of setting back the cause of black advancement for years by frightening whites with his killing of volunteer firemen and commandeering of the Morgan Library. Washington goes on to say that turning over the firechief to Walker and returning his repaired car will not bring back his pride, and that vengeance will only beget more vengeance. "I will turn the other cheek until people learn to respect me." Walker laughs in his face. "You speak like an angel. Too bad we're living on earth."

For, significantly, Walker is a northern black, active in the beginnings of the Harlem Renaissance, and would, had he known of them, agreed with the views of W. E. B. DuBois and Marcus Garvey. DuBois was born in Massachusetts, and while he describes with soul-wrenching clarity his first hand experience of racial injustice, he nonetheless held two doctorates, one from Harvard University and the other from the University of Berlin. Tuskeegee's emphasis on skilled manual labor and its acceptance of black racial inferiority were totally unacceptable to DuBois. He had formed the Niagara Movement in 1905 to end discriminatory laws in the United States, but after a tragic race riot in Springfield, Illinois, in 1908, he and white liberals helped to form the NAACP (the National Association for the Advancement of Colored People) between 1909 and 1910 which strove to eliminate racial injustice both north and south. As editor of the NAACP's magazine, the *Crisis*, he exposed prejudicial practices throughout the United

States. DuBois believed that the Talented Tenth of any racial population was equal to the Talented Tenth of any other, and could and should compete as equals. DuBois implied blacks were equal to whites now, and would not therefore have to "prove" anything or endure racial injustice. The best Booker T. Washington could offer Walker as they conferred in the Morgan Library was a swift and painless execution: DuBois could have offered the services of the NAACP's Legal Defense Fund.

Marcus Garvey, who was active in the1920's was a West Indian deeply influenced by his African heritage. He spoke directly to the issue of black pride, reawakening a sense of pride in American blacks' African heritage, and even established the Black Star line to transport blacks back to Africa. Garvey was able to survive, because he operated only in the northern black ghettos like Harlem in New York City in the relatively experimental twenties.

Harlem experienced such a cultural and artistic outpouring in the 1920's that the movement became known as the Harlem Renaissance. Black poets like Langston Hughes and writers like James Weldon Johnson created a sparkling intellectual life. DuBois lived in Harlem as did Claude McKay, the novelist. Harlem lies on the northern tip of the island of Manhattan in New York City. Originally settled by the Dutch in the seventeenth century, by the nineteenth century the area had become the abode of many upper class whites, some of whom even built large mansions there. Wide, tree shaded avenues and easy access to central Park gave Harlem an almost rural atmosphere. Blacks began moving into the area around the turn of the century, and most major black churches made the move uptown by 1910. By 1914, the area held 50,000 blacks, 73,000 by 1920 and nearly 165,000 by 1932. Many northern blacks who fled to Harlem were escaping the crime and violence of the Tenderloin district, an area in West Manhattan around 30th street. It got its name Tenderloin because a police chief, eagerly anticipating a huge personal profit from the graft of the area, is reported to have said that whereas before he had been eating chuck, he now looked forward to dining on the Tenderloin. Black preachers regularly preached against the violence and crime of the area, especially as it provided a bad model for children, and so, to provide a better life for their families, many church-going blacks fled the tenements of the Tenderloin for the relaxed, safe environment of Harlem. Whites in Harlem, fearing declining property values, sold to blacks and moved to the white suburbs. But while Harlem was a black ghetto, it was by no means a slum. Indeed, expensive nightclubs like the Savoy and Cotton Club catered to blacks and whites and were places of lively cultural exchange.

One of the most important examples of that exchange, of course, was increasing white acquaintance with black jazz. From 1880 to 1900, America generally had experienced a love affair with brass bands, but black brass bands developed a new sound by incorporating into their repertoire elements of ragtime and the blues, elements such as a syncopated beat, the duplication in instrumental form of the almost unlimited range of the human voice, and dance rhythms.

White musicians like George Gershwin trooped to Harlem in the 1920's to hear Louis Armstrong or Duke Ellington play, and many incorporated "jazz" elements into their own playing.   Because of unofficial color barriers, black musicians almost never played the downtown clubs.   White patrons, unable or unwilling to make the trek to Harlem, nonetheless enjoyed jazz music played by white bands downtown.   Some whites even played in blackface to recreate the aura of a Harlem club.   Black jazz rhythms and sounds likewise influenced serious, highbrow music.   George Gershwin created "Rhapsody in Blue" in 1924, and Aaron Copeland used jazz elements in his work as well.   The phonograph permitted black musicians to evade the color barrier as whites could listen to recordings of Louis Armstrong, say, without having to invite a black man into the house or make the trip to Harlem.

Ragtime explores this development of jazz and the Harlem Renaissance. Coalhouse Walker is a piano player who begins his career playing piano accompaniment for silent pictures, but eventually gets a job with the Clap Club orchestra which serves one of the many Harlem nightclubs.   An almost exclusively black operation, black men staff the orchestra and run the establishment.   Note that Walker is interviewed by blacks for his job as a piano player.   The Clap Club is so exclusively black that the appearance of Brother, who had come to warn Walker not to return to the house in New Rochelle, causes a stir. By contrast, many clubs in the real Harlem of the twenties were frequented by whites, especially the Cotton Club where Duke Ellington played background music to lavish, though silly, stage productions which featured lascivious sheiks or African locales.   Some of this fanciful silliness is preserved in Ellington's later titles like "Jungle Nights in Harlem."   Not only musicians but comedians and vaudevillians played these clubs too.   Redd Foxx, for example, got his start in Harlem by specializing in very sexually frank material.   Once again, however, vaudeville, like the production numbers at the Cotton Club, tended to ridicule blacks and non-whites.   Titles like "He's Just a Little Nigger, But He's All Mine" suggest the overt racism of such popular entertainment.

Ragtime music itself, however, was not invented in Harlem, but rather arose from St. Louis and ultimately may have its roots in New Orleans dixieland jazz. The music was associated with the low life, since it was frequently played by black musicians in bordellos to keep the customers amused while they waited.   Ragtime maintained its slightly disreputable image up through the Roaring Twenties, but in the decade of speakeasies and flappers such an image only guaranteed the music a greater audience.   Although Scott Joplin did not invent ragtime, he is responsible for some of the most enduring tunes like the "Pineapple Rag."   His tunes and rhythms were transposed to written sheet music and sold widely.   That may be the reason Brother appears familiar with ragtime music in the film scene where Walker plays the piano at the house in New Rochelle.

The decades around World War I which witnessed the popularity of Scott Joplin's ragtime also saw the rise of many new industries, especially the development of an inexpensive motor car and the movies themselves. Henry Ford did not invent the automobile, nor did he even develop the first low priced car which was in fact a "Merry Oldsmobile." Ford's significance was to increase "flow" by copying techniques used in the meat packing system where the carcass came to the worker who performed the same task on different carcasses rather than butchering the entire steer himself. Using this model, in 1908, Ford developed the Model T Ford, a simple durable car produced on a moving assembly line and available in any color, said Ford, "as long as it's black." The Model T began selling in 1909 when over 11,000 were sold in a year, and by 1925, Ford was producing 9000 cars a day at a price below $300. Nonetheless, at a time when manufacturing workers earned about $1300 per year, and clerical workers about $2300, Model T's must have been rare in the period when *Ragtime* supposedly takes place. Father, after all, still drives a horse and buggy.

The automobile dramatically changed the American lifestyle. New roadside businesses from motels to hamburger stands were made possible by the car, and by the 1920's, one tenth of the American GNP (Gross National Product) was the result of the automobile industry. The car encouraged the growth of suburbia by lessening commutation time, and by allowing suburbs to spread out perpendicularly to the trolley and train tracks which heretofore had been the only ways into the outskirts. The need for new road building culminated in the 1921 Federal Highway Act which provided federal aid for state roads and which in the process provided a major stimulus to the 1920's economy. Even the American death rate was affected as automobile related deaths soared 150% between 1920 and 1929.

As important as the development and widespread dissemination of the automobile was the rising popularity of the movies. Perfected by Thomas Edison in the late 1880's, by the early decades of the twentieth century, silent movies were being projected on a screen before audiences. The plot lines of early movies were primitive, as people paid a nickel to watch galloping horses or racing trains. By 1910, however, movies had learned to tell a story. D. W. Griffith pioneered new editing techniques which built suspense and likewise used varying camera angles to highlight certain actions and minimize the feeling of simply watching a filmed stage play. Significantly, his *Birth of a Nation* (1915), a true movie classic, was based on *The Clansman*, a book and later popular stage play which portrayed blacks as sexually threatening and morally inferior. President Woodrow Wilson, a southerner who reintroduced segregation into federal programs after his inauguration in 1913, proclaimed after seeing *Birth of a Nation* that it was like seeing "history written with lightning."

The effects of such inventions as the automobiles and movies impacted on everyone, including the sedate family of *Ragtime*. By the end of the film, Brother leaves driving a Model T, and Mother leaves with the by now self-styled "Baron" Ashkenazy, the film director, in a huge open car, taking with her her maid, the black baby, but not her son, as Father watches from a lace-curtained window. In fact, the divorce rate grew steadily in the decades before World War I. In 1880, 19,633 divorces were granted in the United States while by 1920, that number had mushroomed to 167,105. In the roaring twenties, the divorce rate skyrocketed, reaching a figure of 2 out of every 7 marriages in urban areas. The days when Mother would deferentially ask Father if she might ask the New Rochelle police commissioner a question were gone forever.

Ragtime reinforces this sense of an end of an era. The theme song of the opening and closing titles is "After the Ball is Over" and features a scantily clad Evelyn Nesbitt dancing. The very last scene portrays Houdini breaking out of a straight jacket to the cheers of the audience below. The pre-World War I period may perhaps have been an Age of Innocence with lace-curtained windows, deferential wives, and clearly enforced racial stereotypes, but as *Ragtime* suggests, it was also an age of change, symbolized by the use of cars and motion pictures. In a very real way, the twentieth century began after World War I was over in 1918, for then, the changes and strains in American society which *Ragtime* explores coalesced to produce the Roaring Twenties as Americans tried, unsuccessfully as it turned out, to deal with a new found consumer economy of abundance in a world where older moral values seemed less useful. In the post-war period, Americans may have broken out of their straight-jackets like Houdini, but such innocence as there was was irretrievably lost. The "ball" was definitely over; the rat race had begun.

Ragtime - Instructor's Guide

1. Write a book report, giving the author's hypothesis and relating events in the film to events in the book, in any or all of the following:

1. W. H. Chafe, *The American Woman : Her Changing Social, Economic and Political Roles*(1974)
2. Florette Henri, *Black Migration: Movement North, 1900-1920* (1975)
3. Nathan Huggins, *Harlem Renaissance* (1971)
4. James Weldon Johnson, *Autobiography of an Ex-Coloured Man* (1912)
5. August Meier, *Negro Thought in America, 1880-1915* (1963)
6. Gilbert Osofsky, *Harlem: The Making of a Ghetto* (1965)
7. J.B. Rae, *The Road and the Car in American Life* (1971)
8. E.M. Rudwick, *W.E. B. DuBois: Voice of the Black Protest Movement* (1982)

2. Choose one of the books above and find the scholarly reviews of it in two or more of the following journals:

1. *The American Historical Review* (published by The American Historical

Association)
2. *Journal of American History* (pulbished by The Organization of American Historians)
3. *Journal of Southern History*
4. *History Teacher*
5. *History, Review of New Books*
6. *Choice*

Compare and contrast the reviews. What did reviewers like or dislike and why?

3. Write a brief biographical sketch and assess the historical significance of any or all of the following:

1. Booker T. Washington
2. W.E.B. DuBois
3. Henry Ford
4. Scott Joplin
5. Marcus Garvey
6. Duke Ellington
7. Stanford White
8. D. W. Griffith

4. Compare and contrast the sound and organizational complexity in the music of Louis Armstrong and Duke Ellington in the 1920's and compare their careers generally.

5. Discuss the effects of the "new immigration" on the growing American cities at the turn of the century. The following sources may be helpful:

1. Stephan Thernstrom, *Poverty and Progress: Social Mobility in a Nineteenth Century City* (1964)
2. John Higham, *Send These to Me* (1975) revised edition 1984

6. Compare and contrast the views of Booker T. Washington and W.E.B. DuBois on racial equality and try to account for these differences.

7. Discuss the formation and early career of the National Association for the Advancement of Coloured People (NAACP).

8. Describe Stanford White's architectural style and show how it relates to architectural developments before and after.

9. Discuss the early career of the movies, from the 1880's to 1920, showing how movies learned to tell a story, how and why editing was used, and how and why Hollywood became the center of the new industry. The following sources may be useful:

1. D.J. Wenden, *The Birth of the Movies* (1975)
2. Jack Ellis, *The History of Film* (1979)

Birth of a Nation - Prejudice Triumphant

D. W. Griffith's *Birth of a Nation*, released in 1915, is one of the great American film classics. Utilizing new developments in filming and editing, Griffith elevated the sleazy new medium to a true art form. The story he chose to film, however, reeks of naked racism and enshrines many of the negative attitudes towards blacks which would dominate American movies until well into the 1950's. Arising from this racism is the film's wholesale endorsement of the Ku Klux Klan, whose members appear as true heroes. Complementing this view of the Klan is *Birth of A Nation*'s portrayal of Lincoln, whose untimely assassination, the film suggests, made the Klan necessary. Radical Reconstruction is presented as an unmitigated evil which led to black domination of the South and the destruction of a beautiful, civilized way of life. Born of nostalgia, *Birth of a Nation* was profoundly moving to Americans of 1915 who watched with alarm the trench warfare of World War I in Europe. The Great War's horrendous losses reminded many Americans of their own Civil War, and, like Griffith, most were determined not to embark on such a catastrophe again.

Birth of a Nation was both produced and directed by D. W. Griffith, who based the film on Reverend Thomas Dixon's *The Clansman*, a book which had already become a popular Broadway play. The film stands as a milestone in the development of movie-making and is rightly regarded as a film classic. To understand why, we must first appreciate how movies had been made before. Invented in 1880 by Thomas Edison, moving pictures had become a major growth industry by 1900. There were no major studios like Twentieth Century Fox in those days, and any enterprising cameraman could--and did--produce films. At first audiences were so delighted with the new medium that they willingly paid a nickle just to see the images move; one and two reelers were produced which simply showed galloping horses, rushing trains, and the like. By 1900, however, the movies had begun to tell stories, many of which were borrowed from the melodrama which dominated the New York stage. Partly because they used the same standards of stage acting and partly because silent films could not rely on dialogue to advance the plot or keep the audience's attention, these early films employed such extravagant gestures and overblown emotions that many of them are almost unwatchable today. Likewise, the camera, which was heavy and bulky, was kept stationary, with the action filmed always from approximately the same distance. The viewer had the best seat in the theater, but he was definitely inside a theater looking at filmed action. Only slowly did filmmakers begin to experiment with alternating closeups and long shots, indoor and outdoor scenes, etc.

Griffith had used many of these devices before he made *Birth of a Nation*, but the significance of that film is that he used techniques like rapid cutting, the dissolve, varying camera angles, and so forth, all in the same movie. Moreover, the scope of *Birth of a Nation* was immense. No one watching the battle sequence or thrilling horse rides of *Birth* could believe he was simply inside a theater watching a filmed stage play! By using closeups, Griffith was able to direct attention to significant details or emotions in a way which simply cannot be done in a theater where the viewer stays in one place. *Birth of a Nation*, then, is profoundly a true film; neither a moving picture nor a filmed stage play, Griffith's work created a new art form, the cinema.

Naturally, new art forms require new techniques. In *Birth of a Nation*, one sees the emergence of a new style of acting which abandons the extravagant gestures of the early twentieth century stage in favor of a naturalism which has become the hallmark of American film. While to our modern eyes, some of the action still appears stilted, only in comparison with previous work can the significance of the acting style of *Birth* be understood. Not only did the acting become more natural, but the makeup did so as well. In early films, actors had used traditional stage makeup , designed to make their facial features visible to audiences 50 feet or more from the stage. This technique is still used today in ballet, for example, where dancers' eye makeup especially is dramatically exaggerated. But in film, where images are blown up to larger than life size on a huge screen, such makeup makes the actor appear like a clown; its very artificiality distances the viewer from the action by reminding him that he is watching a play in which he is not really involved. By reducing the makeup. Griffith was able to create an immediacy and intimacy which has endured in film to the present time.

In a profound way, *Birth of a Nation* made film respectable by proving that it was an independent art form rather than a stepchild to what we are still pleased to call "legitimate theater." You can see how Griffith struggles to insure that respectability when he footnotes the sources for his historical tableaux such as the signing of the surrender at Appomattox. The film debuted in a huge theater in the Broadway area, rather than in the cheaper movie houses of lower Manhattan, to insist upon its legitimacy. Printed programs accompanied the film. Note there is no list of credits at the beginning or end. The film was hugely successful. Even then President Woodrow Wilson exclaimed after seeing the film that it was like seeing "history written with lightning." But what Wilson saw and applauded strikes most modern viewers with horror, for *Birth of a Nation* endorses racism, vigilante justice, and violence in a way which would be inconceivable today.

The film simply reeks of naked racism. Aside from a few "good" blacks, most of whom are elderly, blacks are portrayed as either happy-go-lucky dancers or as lascivious, violence-prone troublemakers. Griffith is obsessed with the fear of sexual intermingling of the races. Flora, Ben's little sister, jumps to her death to avoid marrying Gus, a black veteran of the Union army. Even though Gus says he does not want to hurt her, Flora hysterically kills herself anyway, and as the title informs us, learns "the stern lesson of honor." At the end of the film, the white men are prepared to bash in the heads of their women to avoid letting them fall into the hands of the evil black soldiers who surround their isolated cabin. Ex-Union veterans and southerners alike unite to preserve what the title tells us is their common "Aryan birthright." Significantly, those "good " blacks in the film are usually too old or physically unattractive to be sexual threats. Those who are young, however, like Lydia, Stoneman's housekeeper, or Gus, or Silas Lynch, the carpet bagger mulatto who becomes lieutenant governor of South Carolina, are sexually aggressive and depraved. More important, their sexual aggression is inevitably directed towards whites. Lydia is after Stoneman, Gus after Flora, and Lynch after Elsie. The film suggests that the secret desire of every black is to sexually possess a white.

Not only are blacks sexually aggressive, but they are also, according to the film, easily misled and just as easily frightened. Black votes are bought, black mobs gather at the drop of a hat, and blacks physically intimidate whites if given a chance. However, whites have a potent weapon at their disposal in that blacks are easily frightened. Ben gets the idea for the Klan outfit by watching two white children under a sheet terrify four black children into running away. The Klan plays on that fear when it denies the vote to freedmen simply by sitting quietly on horseback next to the voting boxes.

Of course, the Klansmen become the heroes of *Birth of a Nation*. Dressed in white, a color associated with purity--and also conveniently the color of most sheets--Klansmen were willing to die to defend their "Aryan birthright" and their women. The glorification of the Klan and the film's obvious racism ignited an explosion of protest in some quarters in the North--an explosion which took Griffith by surprise. A southerner himself, and one whose father had played a minor role in the Confederacy in Kentucky, Griffith explained he was only trying to show how things really were in the south after the Civil War. But were they that way?

The issue of black domination was then and still is one of the most emotional issues of Reconstruction. The fact is, however, that blacks did not dominate any southern legislature, except the lower House of South Carolina where the film takes place, and then only for one session. There were no black governors at all during Reconstruction. As a group, the few blacks who served the state and federal governments were at least as well educated as their white counterparts, and conducted themselves with integrity. Finally, blacks did not necessarily block vote on issues other than civil rights; instead, they frequently split their votes as black legislators tried to vote their consciences.

Another charge leveled at Reconstruction governments was their corruption. Without doubt, southern legislatures were corrupt and graft-ridden during Reconstruction. However, the corruption was bi-partisan and bi-sectional; the infamous Tweed ring operated contemporaneously in New York City, and the Credit Mobilier scandal occurred in Grant's first term as president. While this may not justify corruption in southern legislatures where blacks held seats, it does suggest that their being black or ex-slaves had nothing in particular to do with their being corrupt.   Moreover, what was sometimes regarded as wasteful extravagance was really just a case of bringing the south up to the same level enjoyed by the rest of the country. Reconstruction governments not only had the expense of reconstructing destroyed transportation lines and farms, but also of instituting free public education, for example. The expense was enormous, especially in an area not accustomed to high taxes and in a period of economic downturn following the bad harvests of 1867 and 1868.

Yet another emotional issue of Reconstruction was the imposition of federal troops in the south, which although galling, served a useful purpose. In *Birth of a Nation*, these soldiers are portrayed as being almost exclusively black, and they terrorize local whites. Note that the blacks surrounding the cabin at the end of the film are wearing Union uniforms. In fact, most federal soldiers in the south were white, and if at times, they turned rowdy and disagreeable, the sad fact is that large concentrations of soldiers frequently do so in periods of occupation. Federal troops were withdrawn rapidly from the south, and indeed, much of the violence, terrorization and intimidation the film decries occurred *after* their withdrawal, indicating that the presence of such federal troops did serve the purpose of creating peace and order. Even before their withdrawal, however, the number of federal troops was too low to deal effectively with southern violence against the freedmen, and after 1868, even this insufficient force was steadily reduced. The interesting question, then, is not whether troops acted honorably in the south, but why they were there in the first place.

The first federal troops to reach the south found themselves in occupation duty almost willy-nilly after having subdued New Orleans and portions of Tennessee. Lincoln developed a plan for Reconstruction which was designed to bring the seceded states back into the Union with all possible speed, thus freeing up those soldiers on occupation duty for further combat or demobilization. Lincoln's Plan for reconstruction required only that 10% of those who had voted in 1860 take the oath of allegiance to the constitution, and that they abolish slavery. Then the state convention could write a new constitution and elect representatives to the federal House and Senate. Both Louisiana and Arkansas were reconstructed in 1864 according to the President's plan. Note that Lincoln, however, showed little concern for the plight of the ex-slave, either financially or in terms of acquiring the franchise. Indeed, the net effect of Lincoln's 10% Plan was to turn power in the south back over to the ruling elite which had run the south before the Civil War broke out.

Lincoln's generosity was only partly inspired by his genuine compassion for his fellow man. Perenially short of troops, by 1863, Lincoln was driven to accept the draft which provoked fierce antagonism in the north, leading, for example to the July, 1863, draft riots in New York City. The fewer troops needed for occupation duty in the south, the more could be used for combat, and the draft accordingly reduced. And the combat was not going well for the North either. July, 1863, saw the victory at Gettysburg end forever southern hopes of bringing the war home to the north, but Lee had been allowed to retreat in good order and resistance in the south remained almost as high as ever. Since he did not seem able to win the war militarily, and certainly could not do so quickly, Lincoln was obliged to be generous in Reconstruction to encourage the other southern states to desert the Confederacy. Most important, Lincoln regarded the Civil War as an illegal rebellion which he alone would handle under his powers as Commander-in-Chief, for to declare war on the Confederacy would have been to lend it legitimacy as a sovereign foreign power. Only in 1862, when Lincoln issued the Emancipation Proclamation after the Union won at Antietam, did the war become one against slavery, but the Proclamation only freed slaves in areas still in open rebellion against the United States government, or in other words, in areas where it could not be enforced. Thus for Lincoln, the primary goal was to end this rebellion as quickly and humanely as possible, and his generous terms for reconstruction reflect his desire to encourage the south to lay down its arms voluntarily.

Nonetheless, Lincoln's generosity became the source of an enduring myth for the South which is captured in *Birth of a Nation*, namely that had Lincoln lived, the evils of Reconstruction could have been avoided. In terms of logic, that assertion is a contrary-to-fact conditional, and as a result impossible to prove or disprove. Likewise, we have already demonstrated that Reconstruction was not quite as bad as many believed it to be, and that Lincoln was motivated by very practical considerations when he proposed his generous Reconstruction plan. Nonetheless the myth remains and can be seen clearly in the film. Lincoln is called the "Great Heart" and magnanimously spares Ben's life. Northerners and southerners alike grieve over his death and southerners especially ponder "what will become of us?" Under Lincoln, Reconstruction proceeds well enough in the south; the Cameron family which had been reduced virtually to rags during the war now appear neatly if not lavishly dressed. This relative prosperity and harmony is totally destroyed after Lincoln's death by the institution of Radical Reconstruction which embodied the ideas of Austin Stoneman.

Stoneman is, of course, the fictional name for Thaddeus Stevens, the Congressman from Pennsylvania. Like Stevens, Stoneman envisions a future of racial equality in the south and encourages blacks to vote, hold public office, and generally to rise socially. He keeps a mulatto mistress, Lydia, his housekeeper, a fact which the film's title decries as a "blight to the nation." Stoneman's liberal views, however, are quickly discarded when his mulatto protegé, Silas Lynch, announces he wants to marry Stoneman's daughter, Elsie. Keeping white women "pure," Griffith suggests, is as vital to northern as to southern white men. However, Griffith here is deliberately confusing issues. The 14th and 15th amendments to the constitution did attempt to secure the right to vote for freedmen and to protect them from the black codes passed by southern legislatures which in effect robbed the freedmen of many of their civil rights, but with few exceptions, Radical Reconstruction never encouraged a social revolution in the south. Indeed, much of the motivation behind those amendments was political. A minority party, the Republicans needed southern black votes to keep the south from again voting solidly Democratic and so undoing much of the Republican program designed to protect small settlers in the west (Homestead Act), nascent manufacturing (Morrill Tariff), or the new national bank. All of these programs were passed during the war when southern Democrats were not around to stymie them, but with a reconstructed south once again sitting in Congress, many of the Republican achievements could be overturned. Finally, Stoneman's views in the film were not typical of most northerners or even most Republicans, and in fact the real Thaddeus Stevens was effectively restrained by Charles Sumner, Benjamin Wade, and other Republicans as well as by Lincoln.

Nonetheless, the myth remains that Lincoln's death plunged the south into the horrors of Stoneman's brand of Reconstruction from which the Ku Klux Klan saved it. Founded in Tennesee in 1866, the Klan was originally just a social club, but by 1868, it had been taken over by those who intended to use it as an instrument of intimidation of new black voters and carpetbagger whites. Using a combination of tricks and mumbo-jumbo language, the Klan quickly set about to restrict if not eliminate black voting. When intimidation failed, violence was employed. In Louisiana in 1868, 200 people were killed or wounded in two days, and a pile of 25 bodies was found half-buried in the woods. Republicans in Congress struck back with the Force Acts of 1870 and 1871 which made interference with voting a federal crime and allowed the president to call out troops and suspend the writ of habeas corpus to stop virtual insurrection in the south. By 1872, vigorous enforcement of these acts had crippled the Klan, but by then most of the damage had already been done. In the atmosphere of fear the Klan created, many freedmen simply stopped trying to vote, and those who continued to do so were usually either killed or physically harmed. Liberal whites either fled or were coerced into silence. More important, by the mid-1870's, northerners had also lost their taste for the social experiment Reconstruction had represented, and, caught up in the rapidly developing industrial revolution, simply shifted their attention elsewhere. Anti-black prejudice, after all, was almost as strong in the north as it was in the south. The draft riots of 1863 in New York City had been directed against blacks. Racism in the north received new impetus as the massive immigration from southern and eastern Europe which began in the 1880's produced a flood of unassimilated immigrants whose votes, many northerners were convinced, could be as easily bought and sold as those of the freedmen in the south.

Nevertheless, the KKK itself did not survive the Reconstruction period, partly because its work of intimidation had succeeded so well, and partly because cooler southern heads prevailed. Indeed, the Klan reappeared at about the same time as the release of *Birth of a Nation*, and many historians argue that the film lent legitimacy to the new Klan.

A former preacher, William J. Simmons, founded the new Klan in 1915. In the south, it began anew its efforts to harass blacks, especially returning war veterans, as World War I came to a close in 1918. Both north and south, the Klan broadened its attack to include not only blacks, but immigrants, Jews and Catholics. In 1920, two corrupt publicity agents, Edward Y. Clark and Elizabeth Tyler, took over the Klan organization, began a massive membership drive and claimed 5 million members by 1923. So powerful did this new Klan become that it even took control of the state legislatures of Texas, Oklahoma, Indiana, and Oregon. In 1920 alone, the Klan was directly or indirectly responsible for lynching 53 blacks. By 1925, that number had been reduced to 17, in part because the Klan was less powerful, and in part because intimidation had successfully silenced most "upstarts," making violence unnecessary.

The Klan's image of blacks was similar to that in *Birth of a Nation*: blacks were sexually aggressive, corrupt ,and power hungry. But the film is unusual in portraying blacks the way the Klan saw them. Indeed, in most American films until the 1950's, blacks were portrayed as childlike, trusting and usually incompetent. The thirties especially saw the emergence of Stepin Fetchitt, the black dancer and comedian who accompanied Shirley Temple. Blacks in film were almost inevitably servants, and like the mammy in *Birth*, usually devoted to their white employers. Other than in those few roles, blacks were virtually absent from American film. Even in crowd scenes set in large metropolitan centers, black faces were nowhere to be seen. The 1930's witnessed a spate of prison theme movies, but even here, the prison populations were almost exclusively white.

The absence of blacks in major studio films did not mean that blacks did not appear on film at all, however. In the 1920's, and more so in the 1930's, a thriving industry grew up to make films targeted at increasingly large black audiences in the new urban ghettos. Produced on a shoestring, these films were shown almost exclusively in movie houses which catered to blacks. Official and unofficial segregation rules meant that blacks could not attend the same "downtown" theaters whites did, so a separate but unequal black film industry developed to serve that particular market. Many of these black films have been lost, but those that survive suggest that they ran the gamut from B-grade comedy to melodrama. The lavish spectaculars or stories involving a large amount of on location shooting which characterized major studio films of the twenties and thirties were not to be found in these black films, mostly because of budget restraints, and this became even more noticeable in the thirties when the development of sound increased exponentially the cost of filming anything. Nonetheless, black films did present blacks in roles other than servant or jungle tribesman, and did provide a place for training black actors. The image of blacks projected by *Birth of a Nation*, then, was partially offset by the development of black films which unfortunately whites rarely saw.

Although black films rarely were seen, by the 1920's, urban, educated whites at least had become familiar with an outpouring of black creativity known as the Harlem Renaissance. Located in the northern part of Manhattan island in New York City, Harlem had originally been farmland until it was completely urbanized in the late nineteenth century. Starting in 1900, blacks began moving from the seedy black ghetto downtown known as the Tenderloin, to the spacious environs of Harlem to the north.   A thriving black culture developed by the 1920's which saw, for example, jazz musicians like Louis Armstrong and Duke Ellington courted by white audiences. Playing the famous Cotton Club with its lavish if silly floor shows, Ellington trained a generation of white musicians, and through his recordings, influenced American musical tastes nationwide. Not only musicians, but black artists of every kind, like Langston Hughes, the poet, thronged to Harlem which became the capital of black America. *Birth of a Nation*, released in 1915, may have condemned blacks as ignorant and lascivious, but the explosion of black creativity represented by the Harlem Renaissance of the 1920's argued otherwise.

The dominant concern of *Birth of a Nation*, however, is of course the Civil War, and this also makes the film unusual, for the Civil War has rarely been portrayed in movies. The other notable example of a Civil War movie is *Gone with the Wind*, but for the most part, the war is seen only as a backdrop to what amounts to a melodrama or a typical western like *The Undefeated*, a John Wayne vehicle. Even Griffith's *Birth* never discusses the causes of the war except to suggest vaguely it had something to do with importing African slaves. Our Civil War, like most civil wars, was so intensely divisive that it remains to this day an unpromising vehicle for a "hit" show. But significantly, both *Birth of a Nation*, released in 1915, and *Gone with the Wind*, released in 1939, appeared at times in which world war threatened the United States.   The success of these two films testifies to the deep ambivalence Americans felt about their own Civil War in particular, and war in general. A quick look at the statistics from the Civil War should indicate the appalling cost of the war.   600,000 Americans were killed or died of disease, and over one million in total were killed or wounded. Out of a population of a little over 31 million, this represents about 2% killed and 3% killed or wounded.   Only World War II approached this death rate, for then one out of every 450 people in the 1940 census died. The monetary losses of the Civil War were almost incalculable.   Direct monetary costs alone totaled $15 billion, but this figure does not include pensions or interest on the national debt.   There were still alive in 1915, when Griffith released *Birth of a Nation*, some Americans who had fought in the Civil War, and many American families had lost relatives in the great struggle. No wonder, then, Americans regarded World War I, which broke out in Europe in 1914, with such distaste. Not only were the issues of the Great War murky, and its possible effect on the United States difficult to gauge, but surely Americans, like Griffith, remembered the horrendous losses and upheavals of their own Civil War as they contemplated the slaughter in the trenches of France.

A further examination of *Gone with the Wind* and *Birth of a Nation*, moreover, illuminates some of the differences between the way American movies regarded war on the eve of World Wars I and II. Significantly, in *Gone with the*

Wind the hero is Rhett Butler, a blockade runner, not an infantry colonel like Ben Cameron in *Birth* who leads a hopeless charge into the teeth of Sherman's guns. Although willing to fight to save his and Scarlett's life, Rhett basically believes "The Cause" is tomfoolery and is almost a-political in his outlook. The true believer, the equivalent to Ben Cameron, is Ashley, an effete blonde who is obviously no match for Clark Gable. It is Rhett and Scarlett who survive both the Civil War and Reconstruction, and they do so by living by their wits. The noble heroism of Ben Cameron and *Birth of a Nation* died in the trenches of World War I, and by 1939, Americans would require a much more immediate, palpable threat to propel them into war. They got it at Pearl Harbor in 1941.

With the American entry into World War II, a new "cause" was born--one far more popular than the Lost Cause of the Civil War if for no other reason than World War II united Americans while the Civil War divided them. Compare the number of films dealing with the Civil War and those with World War II, and one sees how the latter war has become a quintessentially American experience, with the good guys against the bad guys--the ultimate American western. Whether this interpretation is valid is debatable, but that most Americans accept it is undeniable.

The Civil War of *Birth of a Nation* could never become the Great American experience the way World War II did. In spite of its subject, the film has nonetheless become an American classic. Hamstrung by its overt racism, its admiration for the Lost Cause, and its lauding of Klan violence, *Birth of a Nation* met with success when it appeared in 1915. And it has endured despite its faults because of Griffith's story-telling abilities and his pioneering use of film technique to create a powerful new art form.

Birth of a Nation - Instructor's Guide

1. Write a book report, giving the author's hypothesis and showing how events in the book relate to events in the film, on any of the following:

1. Fawn M. Brodie, *Thaddeus Stevens: Scourge of the South* (1959)
2. Jack Ellis, *A History of Film* (1985)
3. James Weldon Johnson, *Autobiography of an Ex-Colored Man* (1912)
4. Rayford W. Logan, *The Betrayal of the Negro: From Rutherford B. Hayes to Woodrow Wilson*, revised ed. (1965)
5. Daniel Novak, *The Wheel of Servitude: Black Forced Labor After Emancipation* (1978)
6. Kenneth Stampp, *The Era of Reconstruction, 1865-1877* (1965)
7. Allen W. Trelease, *White Terror: The Ku Klux Klan Conspiracy and Southern Reconstruction* (1972)
8. C. Vann Woodward, *Reunion and Reaction: The Compromise of 1877*

(1951)
9. C. Vann Woodward, *The Strange Career of Jim Crow* revised ed. (1974)

2. Write a brief biographical sketch and assess the historical significance of any or all of the following:

1. D.W. Griffith
2. Thaddeus Stevens
3. Jefferson Davis
4. Booker T. Washington
5. William Seward
6. Charles Sumner

3. Describe in detail how D.W. Griffith's *Birth of a Nation* utilized new cinema techniques and why the film is so signficant in the history of cinema. An excellent resource is Jack C. Ellis, *A History of Film* (1985)

4. Write an essay describing just how black voting power operated during Reconstruction and whether or not the period can be said to be "black dominated." You may wish to consider the following resources in your answer:

1. Thomas Holt, *Black over White: Negro Political Leadership in South Carolina* (1977)
2. Joel Williamson, *A Rage for Order: Black-White Relations in the American South Since Emancipation* (1986)

5. Discuss how and when segregation appeared in the South following Reconstruction.

6. Describe the military strategy of the South in the Civil War and why the North won.

7. Describe Abraham Lincoln's views on slavery and the black race. How were these views reflected in Lincoln's reconstruction plan?

Reds - The Disillusionment of American Radicals

Reds, released in 1981, tells the story of John Reed, a reporter who wrote *Ten Days That Shook the World*, and his wife, Louise Bryant Reed, who was active in the International Workers of the World (IWW), the militant labor union of Bill Haywood. At first, both Reed and Bryant adopted a relatively easy-going socialism, but like many leftists of the period, their socialism and pacifism were challenged and sorely tested by the outbreak of World War I in Europe in 1914 and the American entry into the war in 1917. For Reed and Bryant, neither one of whom was in the armed services, opposition to the war was a matter of philosophy and conscience, but to the Russian people, the war was an economic and demographic disaster; for them, opposition to the war became a matter of simple survival. Capitalizing on this war weariness and the obvious corruption of the tzarist government, Lenin came to power in November, 1917, in what came to be known as *the* Russian Revolution, but which was rather the last of a series of revolutions which had begun in March of that year. In Moscow at the time, Reed, as *Reds* makes clear, wrote glowingly about Lenin's revolution, but he did not stay to see the civil war the revolution produced. Instead, he returned home to form the Communist Party of America, and when he returned to the Soviet Union to seek recognition of his party, he became trapped in the police state Lenin had permitted the Russian revolutionary government to become. As *Reds* makes clear, Reed became disillusioned and his disillusionment was shared by many American radicals. As we shall see, Reed's loss of faith raises intriguing questions about the nature of communism and the American response to it.

The Communist Party of America which Reed formed was an offshoot of the former Socialist Party of America, formed between 1898 and 1901 by Eugene Debs. Debs had been converted to marxism while serving a prison term for violating an injunction of the Sherman Anti-Trust Act which had ordered him to stop the Pullman Strike of 1894. The formation of the Socialist Party in the United States was similar to developments in Europe at the turn of the century which saw the advent of Britain's Labour party (formed 1901) and Germany's Social Democrats (formed 1874). These socialist parties rejected the violence advocated by the more radical syndicalists and anarchists in favor of working within a democratic, parliamentary system to effect gradual change. For these socialists, "class warfare" was a metaphor, not an invitation to bloodshed in the streets; they believed in evolutionary rather than revolutionary change to improve the workers' condition.

Nonetheless, both in Europe and the United States, those who advocated violence to overthrow the capitalist system, the "direct action" believers, as they were known, remained an important part of left wing politics. In the United States, this group eventually took over the IWW, originally formed under Debs and Bill Haywood in 1905. Dedicated to the idea of "One Big Union" for everyone of all races and nationalities, the IWW was willing to use the general strike to achieve its radical goals.   While the other large labor union, the American Federation of Labor (AFL, formed in 1887) simply wanted a bigger slice of the pie for its predominantly skilled worker members, the IWW embraced socialism, and organized those unskilled workers the AFL would not even consider.   Perhaps because of its socialist views and because it was headquartered in the more violence-prone West, the IWW was the object of increasing attacks on the part of management, and so the union decided to fight fire with fire.   As time went on, the IWW urged deliberate sabotage and personal violence against capitalists.   As the union turned more radical, Debs left it to concentrate on the Socialist party which nominated him repeatedly for the presidency of the United States.   To disassociate himself further from the violent radicalism of the IWW, in 1913 Debs had Bill Haywood, the IWW's leader, expelled from the Socialist Party.

John Reed supported the IWW. *Reds* shows him with Haywood trying to recruit new members--until the police arrive and a fight ensues. His apartment is filled with IWW posters, and the unfinished poem he writes to Louise after her affair with Eugene O'Neill is, significantly, scratched on the back of an IWW leaflet. The movie never stresses the IWW's penchant for violence and sabotage, however; on the contrary, when its organizers appear, they are more "sinned against than sinning."   As viewers, we are led to believe Reed either does not know about IWW violence--or chooses to hear only what he wants.

Reed's socialism, like that of many liberals of the period, was a rather easy-going affair, more a matter of idealism than a plan of action upon which to base one's life. The sign on his door which reads "Property is Theft--Walk In" symbolizes the abstract nature of Reed's views, for while he may condemn property, he is nonetheless a property owner (he owns several houses in the film) and obviously is wealthy enough to pay for both his and Louise's trips to revolutionary Russia. Moreover, while Reed advocates free love in theory, he nonetheless marries Louise, and is heartbroken to learn of her affair with O'Neill. Reed and his friends, Emma Goldman, Max Eastman, Isadora Duncan, and Walter Lippman, to mention but a few, are what O'Neill sneeringly refers to as "village radicals." What causes these left-wingers to reassess their views and in some cases to become radical revolutionaries is the outbreak of war in Europe in 1914 and the Russian revolution the war helped produce.

Socialists worldwide regarded the war as a concerted British and French move, to which the United States later attached itself, to deny Germany her fair share of the world's profits. Indeed, in *Reds*, the first time we see Reed, he is at the Liberal Club in Portland, Oregon, and asked to discuss what the war is really about. "Profits," he says simply, and sits down. Reed gives what would later be known as the classic "Merchants of Death" theory for American entry into World War I when he allows Louise to interview him after his Portland speech. He claims that J. P. Morgan, the American financier, has lent $1 billion to Britain, and that if Britain loses, he won't get his money back--and that will plunge the

United States economy into a depression.   Thus, Americans are being urged toward war to save Morgan and protect his loans.   To socialists like Reed, such a war was immoral, and they consequently fought conscription and the selling of war bonds throughout the war, and even more so after the United States entered the conflict on the allied side in April, 1917.   Eugene Debs, for example, so criticized the war that he was indicted under a revised 1917 Sedition Act which made almost any criticism of the United States government a treasonable offense, and he was sent to jail for 10 years and robbed of American citizenship.   Many others were harrassed as well; Emma Goldman, for example, was arrested in 1917, served two years in jail, and was later deported to Russia in 1919.

For Reed, Louise Bryant, and Emma Goldman, opposition to the war was a matter of philosophy and conscience for which they were even willing to go to jail, but for the combatants overseas, the war was more immediately life-threatening.   This was especially true for the Russians, for whom the war proved to be a demographic and economic disaster.   In 1915 alone, for example, 2 1/2 million Russians were either killed, wounded or taken prisoner in the war. Many died from shrapnel wounds incurred because their government refused to issue helmets.   Of the 12 million men mobilized by the Russian government during the war, 1.7 million died, 5 million were wounded, and 2.5 million were missing when the war was over.   And the civilian population suffered as well.   At least 5 million Russians died of disease and famine.   *Reds* gives us a quick but graphic glimpse of the suffering: when the train Reed and Louise are riding on reaches the Russian border, they see scores of dead, dying, and wounded beside the railroad track.   Reed quickly interviews a Russian soldier whom he discovers to be only 14 years old.

The catastrophes of World War I exposed the corruption of the tzarist regime and helped to bring it down.   In March, 1917, after the tzar left for the front to lead the fight personally, an almost leaderless, amorphous revolution arose under the liberal aristocrat, Prince Lvov.   This group was interested in certain political reforms which would, in effect, have created a constitutional monarchy instead of the tzarist autocracy then in place, but these "revolutionaries" had no intention of changing the exploitive Russian economy which guaranteed them their wealth.   Mostly, they knew what they did not want--the status quo--but they were deeply divided on exactly what they did want.   In July, a second, more liberal "revolution" occurred under Alexander Kerenski, who likewise wanted political, not sweeping economic, change.   Kerenski decided to honor Russia's commitment to her allies and so continued to prosecute the war in spite of the suffering it visited upon the poorly equipped and abysmally led Russian soldiers. As a result, he could not risk major changes in land reform such as breaking up the big estates and giving the land to the peasants.   Although it would have been a popular move, land reform, Kerenski feared, might cause the peasant soldiers on the front to abandon the colors and return home to claim their land.   Yet another reason for avoiding major economic changes was that the Kerenski government was rent by factionalism, and the resulting squabbling made the government unwieldy and unresponsive.

On the other hand, the Bolsheviks, Lenin's communist followers, suffered from no such factionalism. Highly disciplined and devoted to their leader, they had a strength out of proportion to their numbers in the squabbling Assembly. What they did not have, however, was Lenin himself, who remained stranded in Switzerland. The German government, having extracted from Lenin a promise to end the war quickly after he seized power, put the communist leader in a sealed coach and conveyed him to a Baltic port from which he finally arrived in St. Petersburg, the governmental center of Russia, in April, 1917. In July, Lenin was forced into hiding, but by October, he had returned, outmaneuvered his opponents, and seized power in what the world came to know as *the* Russian revolution. Once in power, Lenin signed the Treaty of Brest-Litovsk, in March, 1918, which ended the war with Germany with humiliating terms for Russia: in the treaty, Russia lost 75% of her coal and iron deposits, 40% of her grain growing areas, 33% of her factories, and one million square miles of her territory. For Lenin, the main point was to end the war quickly and concentrate on furthering the communist revolution, but many Russians objected to the treaty after the sacrifices the country had already endured. Many also objected to Lenin's high-handed tactics: when he only got 25% of the popular vote in free elections for the new Assembly, Lenin simply disbanded the Assembly. Thus, the Russian civil war began.

Lenin's Bolsheviks, known as the Reds, battled a loose confederation of anti-communists, known as the White Russians, who ran the gamut from liberal aristocrats to anarchists. Leon Trotsky, Lenin's trusted aide, became Minister of War and whipped the Red army into fighting condition, even if it meant using former tzarist officers whose loyalty was questionable. Then, in June, 1918, Lenin grimly decided to eliminate all "counter-revolutionaries," that is, anyone who threatened the new Bolshevik regime. Thus, the Russian royal family was slaughtered in July, and Lenin unleashed the Cheka, or secret police, on his suspected enemies. Bolshevik fears reached new heights when in August, a young revolutionary woman shot and severely wounded Lenin. A true reign of terror ensued with thousands of hostages executed and the Cheka given extraordinary powers to arrest and summarily execute anyone suspected of opposing Lenin's government. These attacks are what Emma Goldman in *Reds* refers to in her talk with John Reed.

In late 1918, as Russia was convulsed in civil war, her former allies invaded Russia from the West at Archangel and Murmansk and from the East at Port Arthur and Vladivostok. The British eventually committed 9,000 troops, the Americans 15,000, and the Japanese 70,000. Theoretically, these invaders were there to "rescue" a Czechoslovakian contingent which had been fighting Germany but which had been trapped in Russia when she signed the Treaty of Brest-Litovsk. Unable to return to Czechoslovakia without crossing German lines, the Czechs were allowed to exit Russia from the Far East, but near the Ural mountains, they attacked the Trans-Siberian railroad and joined the White Russians. Lenin's Bolsheviks naturally counterattacked, and to save the Czechs, cut off by hundreds of miles from reinforcements, the allies invaded.

This was the theory. In fact, however, the allies supported the White Russian coalition because it promised to bring Russia back into the war. In September, when the invasion began, the war in Europe was not going well for the allies, in spite of the arrival of fresh American troops. Desperate to have a second front in Russia to relieve the German pressure on the Western front, Britain and France tried to topple Lenin's government and replace it with one which would repudiate the Treaty of Brest-Litovsk. The United States, to be fair, was less concerned with overthrowing Lenin than we were with bringing the Russians back into the war, but the Bolsheviks assumed we shared our allies' open hostility to the new Russian government. As it turned out, the war in Europe finally did drag to a close in November, 1918, and the allied troops in Russia suffered through a horrendous winter. Separated from one another by thousands of miles and from other White Russian armies by hundreds of miles, and without adequate lines of supply and communication, the invaders found concerted action impossible and soon lost interest in the entire enterprise. By May, 1919, most allied forces in the west had been withdrawn, although to the consternation of the Bolsheviks, the Japanese remained in place for years. Even without the invaders' support, however, the White Russians fought on until 1920. These are the "counter-revolutionaries" who, in *Reds*, attack the train Reed is riding on to deliver his speech in Baku. The existence of the White Russians was used by Lenin and the Bolsheviks to justify the continuation of the Cheka police state.

The brutally repressive tactics the Bolsheviks employed plus their uncanny ability to survive both the Whites and an allied invasion led to an hysterical fear of communism worldwide. Russia was treated as an infectious disease, and a "cordon sanitaire" or quarantine was placed on her by most nations, many of whom, like the United States, severed diplomatic relations. Russian ports were blockaded, and her borders sealed; needed supplies did not get in and foreigners like Reed, once in, did not get out. That is why in *Reds*, Reed has to undertake the perilous and lonely journey on a hand-pumped railroad car to flee Russia through Finland. He is captured by the Finns, and eventually exchanged by the Russian government for several Finnish professors.

Even had Reed made good his escape in 1919, he would have found his return to the United States deeply disappointing, for by 1919, the United States was in the midst of the Great Red Scare launched by Woodrow Wilson's Attorney General, A. Mitchell Palmer. As a scene in *Reds* makes clear, Reed had already tangled with the American government in early 1918: customs officials seized his notes for his new book on the Russian revolution when he and Louise returned after witnessing the November, 1917, Bolshevik takeover. Later, during his prolonged absence in Russia as he sought Comintern recognition for his newly formed Communist Party of America, FBI agents broke into Louise's house with a warrant for Reed's arrest on charges of conspiring to overthrow the American government, and proceeded to turn the house upside down searching for him.

What happened to Reed was symptomatic of the anti-communist, anti-foreigner prejudice which swept the country following World War I. Part of this prejudice was the result of bad economic times brought on when the country quickly demobilized its armed forces and so dumped thousands of ex-servicemen into a slumping economy. Workers hired during the war refused to make room for the veterans, nor did they wish to see their wages cut. A series of strikes like the Boston police strike and the violent steel strike in the spring of 1919 shocked many Americans as did the bombing in August of Attorney General Palmer's home. Claiming that the country was in imminent danger of being overthrown by left wing radicals and their worker "stooges," Palmer began a massive roundup of suspected radicals in November, and he deported many who either had never obtained American citizenship or who had lost it as a result of being imprisoned under the 1917 Sedition Act. Emma Goldman was among those deported in December, 1919, aboard the *Buford*, contemptuously called the *Red Ark* because it carried 249 radicals into exile.

Ironically, one of the events which convinced many Americans that Palmer's high-handed tactics were necessary was the creation by John Reed and others of the Communist Party in the United States, for now people feared Lenin's Bolsheviks had a base of operations from which to plot the overthrow of the American government. In fact, Reed's party never intended the violent overthrow of the government by a coup, although its members did hope to radicalize workers sufficiently to demand sweeping changes in the American government and economic system.

Reds presents the formation of this Communist Party in Chicago in 1919 as a clear case of those sincerely interested in reform and pacifism, the communists, breaking away from the now hopelessly bourgeois, chauvinistic socialist party. Indeed, as Reed and his friends are being physically removed from the podium, they defiantly sing the communist "Internationale" while the organist from the socialists begins playing "America the Beautiful" to restore order. Actually, the situation was not nearly as clear cut. To increase his voting strength in the Socialist Party, Reed and his friend, Louis Fraina, had flooded the Socialist Party with new immigrants who hailed from eastern Europe where parliamentary systems were virtually unknown. Thus, the socialist emphasis on working for gradual change within a democratic government did not impress them as either desirable or even possible. Instead, these eastern Europeans voted overwhelmingly for Reed and his radical cohorts who indeed were elected to the executive committee of the Socialist Party. Old line socialists, however, feared the radicals who, they felt, had simply "packed" the party with their followers in order to seize control. Thus the party voided the election as unfair and denied seats to Reed and the radicals. Frustrated in their attempt to take over the

Socialist Party, one group of radicals formed the Communist Party of America and another, the Communist Labour Party. Generally, Reed and his friends who founded the Communist Party were native born Americans who understood the historical realities of the American economic system, while Fraina and his friends who founded the Communist Labour Party tended to be recent immigrants who viewed the American economic system in terms of their European background. In the film, this difference is signified by the heavy accent Fraina uses and the fact his group will meet at the Russian house, a sort of home away from home for recent eastern European immigrants. In any case, both groups claimed to represent communism in the United States, and to resolve this dispute, both sent representatives to the Comintern, or International Communist Party, in Russia, to break the deadlock.

Reed returned to Russia in 1919, then, armed with an historical analysis which he hoped would prove his point that the American experience was different from that of Europe and would have to be approached differently as a result. Unimpressed, the Comintern ordered the two groups to merge and together to infiltrate the AFL. Reed was stunned by the ignorance of the Russian communists in regard to events outside Russia, and he was shocked and disillusioned when the Propaganda Minister would not make good on his promise to return Reed to the United States. When he tried to escape, he was captured by the Finns and eventually returned to Russia where he found himself a virtual prisoner in the Soviet Union.

In *Reds*, we see Reed seek consolation from Emma Goldman after his return from Finland. He has been trying to contact Louise for months without success, and unaware that she had begun the dangerous journey to Finland to save him from prison, he assumes from her silence in response to his cables that she has deserted him. Emma bluntly tells him it was his fight, not Louise's, and that by trying to contact her he is merely calling attention to her in the hysteria of Palmer's Great Red Scare. "Leave her alone," she advises. Throughout their talk, she complains about the lack of heat. "The system simply doesn't work," she grumbles. But Emma has an even more damning indictment of Lenin's revolution. "If Bolshevism means turning the land back to the peasants and the factories back to the workers, Russia is the one place on earth where there is no Bolshevism," she warns. Simply put, "Our dream is dying in Russia."

In the "Internationale," the stirring international communist anthem, there is one line which says, "The Internationale will unite the human race." Radicals like Emma and Reed believed that workers were the same worldwide, and that if once united in One Big Union, to quote from the IWW, together they would abolish war, achieve a fair redistribution of resources based on need, and in short, establish a socialist paradise. Thus, the Internationale would unite the human race in true brotherhood. As Emma has seen in Russia, however, the Cheka and Lenin's police state have turned Russian against Russian in a search for "counter-revolutionaries," and the "dictatorship of the proletariat" has succeeded in destroying the Russian economy.

In this conversation, Reed still defends communism, arguing that shortages are less the result of defects in the socialist system than the result of British and American blockades. He says that the workers will need to be led for the time being by a revolutionary elite because they don't know what is best for them. Finally, he seems strangely unmoved by the fact that Emma's mail from the United States is regularly opened and read by Russian censors.

Shortly thereafter, however, Reed is sent to deliver a speech to help radicalize the Middle Eastern population near Baku, and Reed's opinion of the entire Russian revolution changes. Like other speakers before him, Reed's speech is translated simultaneously into many different languages, creating a cacaphony resembling a miniature Tower of Babel. Reed is surprised to find his speech greeted with great enthusiasm: the crowd cheers madly and waves their swords defiantly. When Reed asks an official standing next to him why the people are cheering, he is amazed to learn they think he had called for a "holy war against the western infidels." In fact, he had only urged a "class war" against capitalism, with warfare being more of a metaphor than a clarion call to violence. On the train returning to St. Petersburg, Reed confronts the Propaganda Minister with this gross mistranslation of his words and meaning, but the Minister blithely explains that he regularly changes speeches around in order to give them more effect. Furious, Reed demands his artistic integrity be honored. Just at that moment, the counter-revolutionaries attack the train. A battle ensues, and the attackers retreat, but significantly, after scrambling down from the train, Reed desperately runs *towards* the counter-revolutionaries to escape his fellow communists. Like Emma before him, he is completely disillusioned with the revolution and wants out.

For radicals like Reed and Emma, who actually lived for a time in the Soviet Union, disillusionment came quickly. When she finally did get out of Russia, Emma wrote her famous book, *My Disillusionment in Russia*, and went on a lecture tour to denounce the Russian brand of communism. For the majority of idealistic radicals who never visited the Soviet Union, however, communist theory, with its emphasis on social consciousness and its pacifism, remained alluring, especially given the excesses of the Roaring Twenties. Even more did communism appeal to the idealistic young in the early 1930's when, during the Great Depression, the breakdown of the American economic system caused such widespread suffering. In Europe, the communists' pacifism and internationalism presented a welcome contrast to the jack-booted Nazis and Fascists with their chauvinistic war-mongering. Only after Stalin's brutal purges between 1935 and 1938 and the resulting, spectacular show trials did most young idealists in this country lose their enthusiasm for Russian communism. This is reflected in the fact that even though we were allied to the Soviet Union in World War II, the Communist Party in America did not significantly increase its membership during the war years in spite of propaganda which portrayed the Russians favorably.

One thing *Reds* does not explore in any depth is why there was such a fear of communism in 1917 and after, a fear repeated in the post-World War II period which saw the advent of McCarthyism and the execution of the Rosenbergs. The immediate causes may indeed have been the strikes and bombings we discussed earlier. Likewise, a certain sense of deceived expectations played an important role: Americans had thought the bloody war would be followed by international peace and goodwill once the evil Germans had been defeated, but now they had to face a new revolutionary threat from Russia.

But is it not just possible that Americans also feared communism, because, in their souls, they suspected it might just work after all, and what is worse, work better than American capitalism? Indeed, the Soviet communists from Lenin to Stalin did seem to have an uncanny knack of surviving the most devastating attacks. Moreover, the industrialization of the Soviet Union under Stalin had been spectacular; by 1932, for example, steel production was up 334% from 1929 levels while by contrast American steel production remained depressed throughout the 1930's and only achieved 1929 levels in the war years. As Lincoln Steffens, the American reformer who wrote *The Shame of Cities* (1904), enthused after his return from the Soviet Union, "I have seen the future, and it works!"

Ironically, that is exactly the fact that Emma Goldman disputes when she tells John Reed Bolshevism does *not* work. Lenin himself, it would seem, came to agree with her, for by 1921, in the face of widespread famine and with industrial output only 18% of what it had been before the war, Lenin instituted a measure of capitalism in the Soviet Union with the NEP, or New Economic Program. While major industries like banking and transportation remained state controlled, small factories were returned to private ownership. After farmers had produced their state allotted quotas, they were permitted to sell the excess for profit. Lenin intended these measures to be only temporary, arguing that Russia was not really an industrialized country before the revolution and was hence a special case. Nonetheless, under the NEP, the Soviet Union's agricultural output stabilized and the industrial sector improved. When Stalin reversed Lenin's NEP and collectivized agriculture in 1928, he produced starvation and riots which troops brutally put down; Stalin himself told Winston Churchill during World War II that 10 million Russians died as a result of farm collectivization. In short, history shows us that Lenin's measure of capitalism succeeded while Stalin's orthodox communism failed miserably. As Emma Goldman and John Reed had learned, Americans need not fear that communism works, let alone that it works better than capitalism.

The message of *Reds*, then, is very soothing to American sensibilities so jangled by Vietnam. Moreover, even though the film deals with political events of the World War I period, it is nonetheless primarily a love story. After all, the last scene in the film is of Louise sitting brokenhearted by the body of John Reed after his death in a Russian hospital. But it is also a love story in another sense.

The film is also about the love affair between American leftists like Reed and Goldman and the ideals of socialism. As the film makes clear, the Russian Revolution was at first greeted as the consumation of that love, but in the end it turned out to have betrayed all the trust and hope the leftists had so generously placed in it. It is a lesson liberals in this country have had to relearn periodically. As one American politician remarked after the Russians shot down a commercial Korean airliner in 1983, it is the Russians themselves who make being a liberal in the United States so hard.

Reds - **Instructor's Guide**

1. Write a brief history of the three 1917 Russian revolutions (March, July and November). Identify who led each, who supported each, and why Lenin's succeded while the other two did not. Consider in your answer:

　　1. the role of World War I
　　2. party discipline, terror
　　3. the role of Russia's allies

2. Write a brief history of the American Socialist Party from 1890 to 1920, highlighting the role of Eugene Debs, John Reed, Bill Haywood, and the split with the IWW (International Workers of the World).

3. Write a biographical sketch and assess the historical importance of any or all of the following:

　　1. Lenin
　　2. Attorney General E. Mitchell Palmer
　　3. Leon Trotsky
　　4. Emma Goldman
　　5. Eugene Debs
　　6. Alexander Kerenski
　　7. Eugene O'Neill

4. Compare and contrast the Great Red Scare of 1919-21 with the McCarthy period from 1950-54. In your answer, you should consider the breakdown of wartime alliances, desire for unanimity of opinion, the threat to civil liberties, the results of economic difficulties, especially labor strikes, the reaction to Soviet government, and why each ran its course.

5. Write a book report on any or all of the following, indicating the author's hypothesis and showing how events in the book relate to events in the film:

1. John Bradley, *Allied Intervention in Russia, 1917-20* (1984)
2. Stanley Coben, *A. Mitchell Palmer* (1963)
3. Robert Conquest, *The Harvest of Sorrow: Soviet Collectivization and the Terror Famine* (1986)
4. Isaac Deutscher, *The Prophet Armed* (1954) deals with Trotsky
5. George F. Kennan, *Decision to Intervene* (1958) deals with American intervention into Russia
6. Alexander Rabinowitch, *The Bolsheviks Come to Power* (1976)
7. John Reed, *Ten Days That Shook the World*, first published 1919
8. Leon Trotsky, *The History of the Russian Revolution* (1932)
9. Bertram Wolfe, *Three Who Made A Revolution* (1948) deals with Lenin, Stalin, and Trotsky

6. Choose a book from the list above and find the scholarly reviews of it in two or more of the following journals:

1. *The American Historical Review* (published by The American Historical Association.
2. *Journal of American History* (published by The Organization of American Historians)
3. *History Teacher*
4. *History, Review of New Books*
5. *Choice*

Compare and contrast the reveiws. What did reviewers like or dislike and why?

7. Show why the United States, Great Britain and Japan sent troops to the Soviet Union in October, 1918. What were the results in each country and in the Soviet Union? An excellent source is George Kennan's *Decision to Intervene* (1958).

Sergeant York - The Reluctant Great Crusader

Sergeant York, released in 1941, chronicles the story of a real, though reluctant, World War I hero named Alvin York. York's struggle to overcome his religiously motivated pacifism, however, was as real a concern in 1941 as it had been in 1917. By 1941, Europe had been at war against Hitler since 1939, and although the United States remained technically neutral, we were already opening a lifeline to a beleaguered Great Britain. As in the first Great War, Americans like Alvin York agonized over whether or not to go to war again. In a sense, York was similar to Woodrow Wilson, president in World War I, who struggled with his own moral and religious convictions before reluctantly committing the United States to war. The hell of trench warfare and the rabid racism of World War I confirmed many Americans in their pacifism which reached new heights by the 1930's. Many Americans in the depression years turned away from Europe and all it represented, and instead sought inspiration from our frontier past, much as York does from his association with the frontiersman Daniel Boone. *Sergeant York*, then, made in one period while telling the story of another, informs us of both eras, the prewar years before 1941 and 1917.

There was a real Sergeant York who did, in fact, distinguish himself at the Meuse-Argonne offensive in October, 1918, in the last weeks of World War I. He was a sharpshooter, who captured a large number of German prisoners, and received a hero's welcome upon his return. But it is significant that this hero's story is told in 1941, after the outbreak of World War II in September, 1939, but before American entry into the war in December, 1941, at a time when many Americans grappled with the decision whether or not to go to war again. Indeed, the cheerful and accommodating Cordell Hull, representative from Tennessee, who in the film greets York upon his return to New York City in 1919, became Franklin Roosevelt's Secretary of State in 1933, and would in fact be engaged in sensitive negotiations with the Japanese right up through Pearl Harbor. By the time *Sergeant York* was released, the United States government had already begun aiding Britain short of war, approving the destroyer deal in September, 1940, whereby the Americans agreed to swap 50 over-age destroyers to the British for convoy duty in exchange for 99 year leases on certain British bases in the New World.

In the spring of 1941, the United States Congress had approved the lend-lease program whereby the Americans agreed to lend or lease to Great Britain all that was necessary for her to win the war. Both lend-lease and the destroyer deal were highly unneutral acts, but more was to come. By the December attack on Pearl Harbor, the United States had begun convoying British ships halfway across the Atlantic, and had even signed joint war aims with Great Britain in the Atlantic Charter in August, 1941. Overwhelmingly, Americans wanted Britain and her allies to win in World War II, but most hoped she would do so with American material help alone, rather than risking American lives in another Great War.

The Great War, now called World War I, had also witnessed mass support for Britain and France, especially after the German invasion of neutral Belgium in 1914. Every member of Wilson's administration was pro-British except one, Secretary of State William Jennings Bryan, and he resigned over the *Lusitania* incident in 1915, to be replaced by the pro-British Robert Lansing. Yet most Americans hoped to avoid direct American participation in the war, mostly because in the eyes of many it was simply not our concern, not part of our corner of the world as York's neighbor Zeke explains to the salesman in the film. For some Americans, however, strong moral convictions about the uselessness of war or even its immorality convinced them not to fight. Alvin York, for example, is religiously motivated; believing every word in the Bible to be true, Alvin takes seriously the Biblical prohibition "Thou shalt not kill." When the young army captain at boot camp tries to debate York on the Bible's prohibition of killing, he discovers that York can find unimpeachable Biblical justification for his pacifism. Signficantly, what causes York to reassess his views is not the Good Book, but the book given him by the major, which recounts the history of the United States. York's realization that he must defend his freedom to worship as he chooses causes him to embrace the Biblical admonition to render unto Caesar what is Caesar's--and fight for his country.

In a sense, Alvin's struggle with his abhorrence of war closely parallels that of Woodrow Wilson, the president who on April 2, 1917, overcame his moral scruples and asked for a declaration of war. A stern moralist, Wilson was typical of the Progressives who felt sure they knew right from wrong, and who could speak confidently of making the trusts "behave." Wilson, for example, insisted on the provision in the Clayton Anti-Trust Act of 1914 which made officers of corporations personally responsible for the misdeeds of their companies, because he wanted to emphasize their "personal guilt." After all, Wilson had gotten the democratic nomination for president in 1912 when William Jennings Bryan, the titular head of the party but also a three time presidential loser, agreed not to challenge Wilson, in large part because he felt convinced by Wilson's evident religious sincerity and abhorrence of war. Like Bryan, Wilson believed America must serve as the world's "moral inspiration," not her arsenal. Wilson took great pride in the fact that he had not allowed the United States to be sucked into the war. Indeed, he permitted the democrats to use the slogan "He kept us out of the war" in his 1916 campaign for reelection.

Wilson, then, was a highly moral and religious man for whom war was a barbaric throwback to an earlier, uncivilized age. Because of his views, Wilson had tried, as he put it, to be neutral in spirit as well as fact, and he repeatedly attempted to mediate the disputes of World War I, only to be rebuffed by one side or the other. Some historians have argued that Wilson never understood the security issues at stake in World War I, namely that a united Germany was capable of dominating the European continent to the detriment of the United States' strategic and economic concerns.   In any case, the ever-enlarging definition of neutrality--he even went to the extent of declaring that unarmed merchantmen could not be attacked by submarines--guaranteed that eventually German submarines would attack American merchantmen as the Reich desperately tried to cut the American lifeline to the British and French which had allowed both to hold out longer than Germany had calculated.   After eight American ships were sunk in the spring of 1917, Wilson asked for a declaration of war on April 2, and received it four days. The less than unanimous vote and the length of debate before passage both indicate that others had not overcome their abhorrence of war as quickly or completely as Wilson and Alvin York had overcome theirs.

Like many a religious man, Wilson could only justify a war he hated to fight by making it a holy war, the Great Crusade to make the world safe for democracy. It was Wilson, after all, who had given the United States "missionary diplomacy" by which the American government had sought to bring the blessings of Anglo-Saxon democracy to the rest of the world whether they wanted it or not. What we now know as World War I, then, would be for Wilson the highest example of missionary diplomacy, truly the *great* crusade.   In a profound way, World War I did become a crusade both in the best and worst senses of the term. For example, the war period saw an outpouring of self-denial, as many troops "took the pledge" not to drink alcohol until the war was over, a Prohibition movement which climaxed in the passage of the 18th Amendment in 1920. It was unbecoming of those fighting the great crusade to be drunk while doing so, and moreover, grain was supposed to be made into bread to feed the gallant doughboys rather than into demon alcohol. People eagerly bought war bonds, and numerous leaders of industry agreed to work for the government for the token pay of $1 per year. The drive for women's rights accelerated. This high-minded idealism and self-denial were perhaps best exemplified by Wilson's 14 Points which promised a peace without victory to wartorn Europe.

As crusades will, however, World War I also awakened some of the worst aspects of the American character just as Wilson had foreseen. "Once lead this people into war," he had warned, "and they'll forget there ever was such a thing as tolerance." A wave of hysterical anti-German feeling swept the nation. In many areas, the teaching of the German language was outlawed; for the duration of the war, German shepherds became Dutch shepherds and rubella, the crippler of unborn children, became German measles. Note how in *Sergeant York*, the German adversaries are consistently referred to as "heinies" or "sauerkrauts." American newspapers regularly referred to the Germans as huns, baby-killers, Prussian curs, or worse. Especially following the successful Russian Revolution in November, 1917, a frenzied anti-communism coupled with anti-Germanism led many Americans to support the wholesale deportation of leftists, many of who were German, and the incarceration of many more, such as Eugene Debs, the head of the American Socialist party.   Known as the Great Red Scare, this hysteria lasted until 1920.

As World War I dragged to a close, anti-black prejudice replaced anti-German feelings. The wholesale migration of southern blacks to northern cities in search of work in the war industries created severe tensions in the already overcrowded cities. In East St. Louis in 1917, a bloody race riot left 40 blacks dead--clubbed, beaten, stabbed, and hanged. Twenty-five subsequent riots left hundreds more blacks dead. There were 70 lynchings in 1919 alone, 10 of which were of returning black war veterans; some black soldiers were lynched while still in uniform. The Ku Klux Klan was reorganized and, inspired by the movie *Birth of a Nation*, fed on the war's super-patriotism and intolerance. Wilson, a southerner, had permitted the reinstitution of segregation laws in federal buildings and projects, and it should not be surprising, then, that World War I was fought with segregated units. Note that in *Sergeant York* there are no black soldiers. Although the film makes much of the democratic effect of a draft which allowed a Tennessee backwoods boy like York and a voluble New Yorker like Pusher to become friends, the army's democracy did not extend to blacks.

Furthermore, the high-minded idealism and moralism of the Great Crusade and its tendency to glorify war could not survive its contacts with the disasters of trench warfare. The film vividly portrays the trenches, where men lived like animals below ground level. As in the film, an offensive was usually preceded by an artillery barrage--unless, as in the film, someone forgot and then sent the men on an almost suicidal race over a no-man's land that, with its bomb craters and lack of vegetation, looked like the moon. In several World War I battles, most notoriously the British disaster at Gallipoli, the failure to synchronize artillery barrage and infantry attack led to the slaughter of thousands. Even with good artillery cover, the losses of World War I were mind-boggling. In the 1916 offensives, for example, more than one million men died to gain a total of 125 square miles. In 1915, alone, 2.5 million Russians died, many from shrapnel wounds, because the Russian government had not believed helmets were necessary or becoming. Approximately 70% of all Germans mobilized in World War I were casualties, 33% of the British, 75% of the Russians, though only 8% of the Americans.

It is to stop this carnage that York abandons his pacifism and storms a series of German machine gun nests. Less motivated by any "great crusade" rhetoric than by a simple desire to stop the slaughter, York puts into practice all his backwoods Tennessee hunting skills, including tricking two Germans into raising their heads by imitating a turkey gobbling. But York is a hero and fights fair. Although he could certainly have shot more people more quickly with a machine gun, he continues to use his rifle and, secondarily,his pistol. This sense of fairness is outraged when a captured German prisoner throws a hand grenade which kills Pusher, and, like an avenging Old Testament Prophet, York shoots in cold blood a man who runs away, without benefit of due process and without even finding out if he is the guilty one. York kills, as he explains to his former major later, to save lives. Many Americans would have agreed with him. When the war had dragged on for three years of slaughter without either side winning, Americans saw themselves helping Europe stop the carnage by going to war in 1917 and getting it over with.

Significantly, however, many Americans had only the vaguest idea why they were fighting "over there." York's mother, for example, allows that she "can't rightly say" what the fighting is about, and even after reading the American history volume, York himself seems only vaguely aware of why the war is being fought. Certainly, no one, including Congressman Cordell Hull, even mentions United States security being at stake. It was the president's role to articulate the real reasons for fighting, and Wilson's obvious inability to do so led to great disillusionment when the war was over. Some of the disillusionment took the form of anger at the so-called merchants of death, the war profiteers who supposedly profited from the deaths of American soldiers. In fact, the group which profited most from the war buying spree was the American farmers for whom agricultural prices reached all time highs; by contrast, munitions represented less than 10% of total United States exports to Europe before American entry into the war in 1917, and even after that we produced so few munitions that American soldiers fought World War I with French guns. Nonetheless, many felt that we had been tricked into war by unscrupulous businessmen, and that feeling led eventually to the Nye Committee hearings of 1934-6 which produced two Neutrality Acts designed to keep the United States from getting economically involved in other people's wars.

Another symptom of the post-World War I disillusionment was the wave of pacifism which reached new heights during the 1930's. College students attempted to abolish ROTC on campuses, and many took the Oxford pledge of total pacifism. The Veterans of Future Wars or VFW was a young people's organization devoted to peace which contended noisily with the Veterans of Foreign Wars, the ex-servicemen's organization which still glorified war. Many intellectuals flirted with communism or socialism, both of which promised the brotherhood of all peoples in spite of national boundaries, and both of which were in theory opposed to war.

One major reason for the pacifism and leftist flirtations of the thirties, of course, was the great depression. With 15 million people out of work by 1932, and the threat of social and political upheaval, foreign problems paled into insignificance. American artists and writers of the twenties who had lived abroad and experimented with new, European art forms like Da Da were dismissed in the depression thirties as trivial and un-American. In literature, writers like William Faulkner, Sherwood Anderson, and Thomas Wolfe began exploring American themes set in American locales, while in art, men like Thomas Hart Benton developed a whole new school of painting, the regionalist school, which abandoned European abstraction and DaDa in favor of an art which portrayed Americans at work and play. This turning inward to America and the exploration of our American heritage can likewise be seen in *Sergeant York*.

Throughout the film, York is closely identified with Daniel Boone, that quintessential frontiersman, who discovered the Cumberland Gap linking what would become Kentucky to Virginia, and who, in open defiance of the British Royal Proclamation of 1763, began the settlement of land east of the Appalachian Mountains. Boone's virtues survive intact in Alvin York: both share a love of the land, a capacity for hard work, a fearlessness in the face of danger, a skillfulness with the rifle, and a certain innocence. Most of all, they are both fiercely independent. When Alvin's mother says grace, she asks the Lord to make the family beholden to no one. In a sense, York is a modern day frontiersman, trying to wrestle a living out of the rocky upland soil, or as his mother says, trying to get corn from rocks, while still dreaming of owning the rich bottom land.

But herein lies a major difference between Boone and York, a difference between the eighteenth and twentieth centuries, which the film does not stress but which a sensitive viewer can easily detect. For by York's day, there is a class system of the haves--who own bottom land-- and the have-nots--who live in the uplands. While movement between the classes is possible, it is rare; Alvin's father almost killed himself trying to earn enough to buy bottom land, and Alvin himself sees the land he wants sold to his rival, Jeb. Nor can Alvin just move farther west to farm, because the available land had already been snapped up long before 1917. Alvin only gets the land when the people of Tennessee buy it for him in grateful recognition of his heroism in World War I. Of course, a more rigid class system existed in Boone's time, but the frontier offered a way out, a place where a rough equality did in fact exist. In York's time, however, there is no unowned land, and hard work to buy land fails.

The film, however, chooses to ignore the class divisions which the lack of a real frontier created. *Sergeant York*, therefore, is no call to arms to overthrow a tyrannical aristocracy, or to adopt a program of land reform. Alvin's righteous anger after being cheated by Mr. Thompson and Jeb is completely dispelled after Alvin's religious experience on his way home from the saloon. His next neeting with Thompson and Jeb is actually played for laughs: we know Alvin has some to apologize for losing his temper, but Jeb cringes like a coward behind a well and Mr. Thompson dives behind his mule to escape what they are both sure is Alvin's wrath. To be fair, both Jeb and Mr.Thompson try to make up in a small way for their having cheated Alvin out of his land, but the fact remains that Alvin has been reduced to sharecropping, and without his help it is questionable whether his family can continue to farm the upland property they own. As viewers, our attention is diverted to Alvin's wholly admirable integrity and frontier virtues, but we know that Alvin is no longer living on the frontier. Instead, he and other farmers like him were plunging willy nilly into the twentith century.

The way of life in Alvin York's little hamlet was being threatened by the realities of new developments in technology, transportation, and agriculture. For example, by the end of the film, a telephone has been installed in Pastor Pile's store, and he is driving a car. Both the telephone and the automobile would end the isolation--and the resulting self-assured independence--of the American farmer. His very livelihood would now depend on events in countries as far away as Russia and Argentina where grain failures could send the price of American wheat soaring, but where bumper crops could spell disastrously low prices in the United States. In fact, farming worldwide remained depressed economically throughout the 1920's, precisely because of low grain prices brought on by catastrophic over-production. Farm income in the United States alone slid from 15 billion dollars in 1920 to 5 billion dollars in 1930, and the farmers who suffered most were the sharecroppers like Alvin York's family, many of whom were driven off their land.

Alvin's isolated hamlet was increasingly out of step with a country which was becoming more urban as the new century progressed. The massive immigration from overseas after 1880, coupled with a dramatic movement in the country from south to north, led to an increase in urban population. In the 1920 census, for example, more people lived in urban areas than on the farms. As the country became more urban, true frontier areas naturally began to disappear. According to the famous thesis of historian Frederick Jackson Turner, the frontier closed in 1893, and while many historians would dispute that date, all would agree that frontier areas were very rare, if not impossible, to find by the World War I period.

In fact, the frontier--and frontier virtues--were quickly passing from the American scene, even though the frontier maintained a strong hold on the American imagination. Most rugged yeoman farmers had already had to learn the virtues of combination: many of them had pooled their resources as early as the late nineteenth century and formed cooperative grain elevators and banks, for example. But York's mother's prayer that the Lord should make the family beholden to no one flew in the face of such cooperative efforts, let alone the dependence of farmers on the international grain exchange. For the twentieth century American farmer engaging in "agro-business," then, Daniel Boone was less of a model than J. P. Morgan. Nonetheless, in times of stress, Americans have traditionally sought inspiration from their past, especially from the frontier heritage Boone represented. Before Pearl Harbor, Americans generally, like Alvin York a generation earlier, agonized over whether to go to war again. York's struggle with his conscience could be understood by the vast majority of Americans watching the film in 1941, and the film's popularity today indicates that Americans still grapple with the moral decision of when and for what purpose this country should go to war.

Sergeant York - Instructor's Guide

1. Write a book report, indicating the author's hypothesis and relating events in the film to events in the book, in any or all of the following:

1. T.A. Bailey, *Woodrow Wilson and the Lost Peace* (1944)
2. Harvey A. De Weerd, *President Wilson Fights His War* (1968)
3. David M. Kennedy, *Over Here: the First World War and American Society* (1980)
4. Arthur Link, *Wilson the Diplomatist* (1957)
5. Paul L. Murphy, *World War I and the Origin of Civil Liberties in the United States* (1980)
6. Laurence Stallings, *The Doughboys; The Story of the A. E. F. 1917-1918* (1963)
7. Stephen L. Vaughn, *Holding Fast the Inner Line: Democracy Nationalism, and the Committee for Public Information* (1980)

2. Write a brief biographical sketch and assess the significance of any or all of the following:

1. Alvin York	4. John J. Pershing
2. Cordell Hull	5. Henry Cabot Lodge
3. Colonel House	6. Robert Lansing

3. Describe the conduct of black soliders in World War I. A useful resource is A.E. Barbeau and Florette Henri, *Unknown Soldiers: Black American Troops in World War I* (1976).

4. Compare and contrast the views of Woodrow Wilson and Henry Cabot Lodge on the best ways to preserve American national security. Consider in your answer especially the debate over Article X of the Treaty of Versailles which pledged everyone to preserve the territorial integrity of member nations.

5. Show how World War I helped to bring on the three Russian revolutions of 1917, especially that of Lenin in November.

6. Write a brief history of the temperance movement and show how World War I advanced the cause of Prohibition.

7. Show how Wilson's Fourteen Points, especially open covenants, openly arrived at, popular determination, freedom of the seas, and disarmament, were finally incorporated into the Treaty of Versailles. Why did the Europeans object to these points in the first place?

8. Using J. B. Rae, *The Road and The Car in American Life* (1971), show how the car affected American society in the World War I period. Consider in your answer the role of the truck and ambulance, as well as private cars.

City Lights - Urban Pressures and the Little Tramp

City Lights, released in 1931, stars one of the most well-loved and durable comedians of this century, Charlie Chaplin. Perhaps one of the reasons for his universal appeal is that he worked in silent films in which various national languages did not impede the viewers' appreciation. Another reason for his success may be that we can all empathize with the Little Tramp's unequal fight to survive in a hostile world. Certainly in 1931, when *City Lights* was made, the struggle to survive was even more difficult for everyone as the country slid further into the Great Depression. One thing which made the Depression more difficult and which had begun even before the stock market Crash of 1929, was the increasing urbanization of the United States. The 1920 census showed that more people lived in the cities than on the farm, while farm population actually declined. In crowded cities, a new urban culture flourished. Ethnically diverse, a-religious in orientation, this new urban population openly flouted Prohibition and as a result permitted the rise of gangsterism and, with it, a basic disrespect for the law. Traditional values were challenged as women, for example, increasingly became more emancipated, especially after gaining the right to vote in 1920. Against this background, *City Lights* appears at once both remarkably nostalgic and bitter. At film's end, Chaplin's Little Tramp has been reduced to rags because of an act of kindness, and even his romantic relationship with the blind flower girl appears to be at an end. The disillusionment of the depression thirties had begun in earnest.

City Lights not only starred Charlie Chaplin, it was also written and directed by him. Chaplin even composed the music for the soundtrack. Few American filmmakers before or since have had such complete control over their films. Only D. W. Griffith exercised such control, but after the enormous failure of *Intolerance*, he too had to compromise his standards in order to attract financial backing. Chaplin's films, on the other hand, were cheap to produce since they did not involve elaborate sets or huge numbers of extras, and because of his popularity, Chaplin's films were almost always financial successes. As a result, Chaplin early on organized his own production company, and with several other stars, such as Mary Pickford, formed United Artists to release and distribute his completed films. To a remarkable degree, then, Chaplin was free of big studio influence. Likewise, when we speak of Chaplin's films, we can legitimately speak of Chaplin's views revealed in them in a way we cannot with other directors whose story lines, casting, and editing were provided by others.

Surely one pertinent example of Chaplin's total control over his films is his insistence on shooting *City Lights* as a silent even though serviceable sound production had been available for several years and most other studios were racing to produce "talkies" which the public found so enticingly different from the silents. Of course, Chaplin's early successes had been in silent films, which may have prejudiced him in their favor, but Chaplin also understood the universal appeal of silents, for no matter what language a film was made in, a vast portion of its audience worldwide would be unable to understand it without benefit of dubbing or subtitles. Subtitles are annoying and moreover depend upon a literate audience which can read them quickly. Note how even in *City Lights*, the printed frames seem to run an agonizingly long time to allow the slowest readers in the audience to puzzle them out. On the other hand, dubbing distorts the inflection of the actor's voice and creates its own annoying problems of lip synchronization. Many a star of silent films could not make the transition to sound because his voice was inadequate or because he did not speak the language used in the film. By contrast, the world of silent film making was truly international with actors and directors of different nationalities working alongside one another to produce films with international appeal. With the introduction of sound, however, such an arrangement would have become a cacaphonous Tower of Babel.

Chaplin's insistence on filming in silence with only a musical soundtrack and a few special sound effects, like the whistle he mistakenly swallows at the Millionaire's party, preserved his universal appeal, but it also shows him turning his back on new developments in film making. In *City Lights*, for example, the sets are remarkably old-fashioned. They are obviously movie sets in a way in which, say, the sets of *Scarface*, produced only two years later, were not. Very few scenes are set outdoors, a remarkable fact when one considers that location filming was far easier with silent films than with talkies in which one had to worry about extraneous noises while at the same time recording serviceable speech. Moreover, the character of the Little Tramp had not developed much either since his invention by Chaplin in the early teens. The clothes, the mannerisms, and the situations remained almost identical with those in Chaplin's earlier films like *The Gold Rush* (1928). Chaplin's Tramp seems even more out of place in the bustling world of 1931 than he had in 1919, but it was precisely this inappropriateness which is at the bottom of Chaplin's appeal for most audiences.

Although we may all pity the Tramp, we can also all empathize with his heroic efforts to survive in a hostile universe while at the same time trying to maintain his dignity and traditional morals. Chaplin is almost always smaller in stature than any of his foes, and so our sympathy is immediately drawn to this perennial underdog. Early in *City Lights*, for example, Chaplin nearly falls through a hole in the sidewalk when a service elevator descends to below street level. He remonstrates with the worker who emerges as the elevator comes back to street level, especially when he is taller than the worker. But when the elevator reaches street level, he finds himself staring up at a giant of a man, and Chaplin rapidly beats a retreat. His adversaries are not only bigger, but more numerous. Even when he chides the newspaper boys who are smaller than he, he loses because there are two of them.

Nowhere is his struggle to survive more clearly seen than in the boxing sequence in *City Lights* which makes physical and obvious what had only been hinted at before. Needing money to help the blind flower girl pay the rent and regain her sight, Chaplin agrees to a boxing match with a man who promises not to hurt him and to split the prize money 50-50. But the man has to get out of town in a hurry, and is replaced by a big bruiser who will not agree to the bargain and who, of course, proceeds to knock the Little Tramp out. That Chaplin will lose is a foregone conclusion. It is his grace under pressure, to borrow a phrase from the novelist Ernest Hemingway, that makes his defeat noble. Chaplin does not run away, for example. He tries to live up to his obligations. Furthermore, he uses his wits in the fight, putting the referee between the other boxer and himself. And he does manage to get in a few good punches even though he cannot get his opponent to fall down and has to take a running jump to floor him. Perhaps most important, however, is the Little Tramp's sheer physical grace which ennobles him and makes him appear less pathetic, for the boxing match is as much an elaborately choreographed ballet as it is a fight. With his baggy pants and oversized shoes, the Tramp is no elegant Fred Astaire, but he is capable of a grace and split-second timing of which any dancer could be proud. Moreover, Chaplin survives the boxing match, somewhat battered to be sure, but nonetheless physically whole and willing to keep trying to find the money he needs.

As the Great Depression took hold, the ability to survive symbolized by Chaplin's boxing match became a very real virtue as unemployment rose and the desire to acquire more was replaced by the very real fight to keep what little one had. *City Lights* is not a ringing indictment of the Great Depression the way *The Grapes of Wrath* would be few years later, but the film does make us aware that times are not good. Chaplin, for example, races a hobo for a cigar butt. It is, however, the first scene in *City Lights* which frames the film's ironic vision of 1930's America. As the film opens, a politician who looks very much like Herbert Hoover delivers a speech before unveiling a monument to Peace and Prosperity. Because the film is silent, the politician's speech is made up only of whistles and honks, a set of nonsense sounds which mean nothing. We are reminded of Hoover's statement that "Prosperity is just around the corner" and also of Hoover's role as Food Administrator during World War I. When the covering is lifted from the monument we see the Little Tramp asleep in the lap of Columbia. When he tries to climb down, however, he gets stuck on the sword held aloft by the fallen warrior, a sword which ironically gets him in the seat of the pants. Hoover's inaction on the deepening depression had likewise caused many Americans to get it in their rear ends. Moreover, we are reminded that many Americans had by 1931 taken to the roads as hobos and were sleeping wherever they could find shelter. Without once depicting a Hooverville, Chaplin reminds the audience that the Depression exists and that an uncomfortably large number of Americans have come to resemble Chaplin's Little Tramp.

While Chaplin is aware of the Depression, then, he reserves his choicest barbs for the changes which had occurred in American society during the 1920's. Most of these changes arose from the signficant development in the 1920's of a new urban culture as the country's population increasingly chose to live in cities rather than on the farm. The 1920's census showed that more people lived in cities than in rural areas and that the farm population was actually declining. This was a fact much noted and widely feared in the twenties. For one thing, the bigger the cities got, the bigger the problems they had, and the more intractible these problems seemed. In *City Lights*, for example, Chaplin, as a street cleaner, scoops up the leavings of a dog with obvious distaste on his face, but he is aghast when a troop of mules immediately marches by, and when a circus man parades an elephant in front of him, Chaplin gives up and leaves.

Not only did Americans fear cities because they were physically huge and thus hard to control, but many Americans, especially rural dwellers, saw in cities an attack on traditional American values, and mounted a vigorous counterattack in response. Assuming that America's frontier heritage had shaped the values of American society, many Americans in the twenties feared that the alien cities, inhabited as they were by still unassimilated immigrants and non-Protestants, would destroy traditional American values. To stop cities from growing any further, a series of restrictive immigration laws were enacted such as the Johnson Act of 1924. To stop city ideas about religion from corrupting American youth, some states tried to outlaw the teaching of evolution: in Tennessee, which did outlaw it, the Scopes trial of 1925 pitted William J. Bryan and Clarence Darrow against one another in a classic confrontation between rural populist and urban liberal. The Ku Klux Klan likewise reared its ugly head in the 1920's as many dissatisfied rural dwellers sought to protect traditional American values by using force or intimidation. Significantly, the Klan's membership spread both north and south of the Mason-Dixon line, reaching a total of 5 million in 1923, and, with its anti-Catholic, anti-immigrant, anti-semitic platform, it represented as much a rural attack on the growing power of cities in America as it did anti-black prejudice.

But by far the most important example of the widespread rural attack on the new urban culture was the passage of the 18th Amendment--Prohibition. Prohibition was not invented in the World War I period, of course. It had begun in earnest as part of the religious upheaval from 1810 onward known as the Second Great Awakening. Some early temperance reformers later jumped to the anti-slavery movement as one can see in the career of William Lloyd Garrison. Many early temperance refomers were women who wanted alcohol outlawed so as to protect themselves from drunken husbands. Most important, a sincere religious conviction that alcoholic consumption was a sin prompted many to support the temperance movement, but while it frequently went under the name of temperance, meaning a temperate use of alcohol, in effect most temperance reformers meant prohibition, the foreswearing of any form of alcohol whatever. Such reformers assumed that one could not sin in degrees, and so, if drinking were indeed a sin, to consume any alcohol at all made one a sinner. Thus, an educational campaign to encourage the temperate use of alcohol was abandoned in favor of a total ban on alcoholic consumption.

The fortunes of the prohibition movement waxed and waned throughout the nineteenth century, but the movement really reached its zenith in the World War I period. Encouraged by President Wilson who saw America fighting the Great Crusade, prohibition reformers took advantage of the outpouring of moral fervor of World War I to press for a national law banning the sale or consumption of alcoholic beverages. It was considered unbecoming for nation fighting the Great Crusade, the war to end all wars, to be drunk while doing so. Likewise, many hoped to use scarce grain for bread to feed the Allies rather than turning it into liquor. Finally ratified in 1920, the 18th Amendment to the Constitution forbidding the sale or consumption of alcoholic beverages was supported by many who approved of temperance rather than prohibition, but the Volstead Act of 1919 which defined alcoholic beverages made clear that those interested in prohibition had triumphed. Not only was hard liquor outlawed, but so were beer and wine, both of which had for centuries been integral parts of immigrant culture from the cafés to the beer hall.

Immigrants saw in prohibition the same anti-urban, anti-immigrant, anti-Catholic bias they also discerned in restrictive immigration laws and the rise of the Klan. Determined to drink alcohol in spite of the law, they bought liquor illegally from gangsters who grew in prestige and influence as the twenties wore on. Another film in this series, *Scarface*, discusses this growth of a crime industry. For our purposes here, it is enough to note that prohibition represented part of the widespread rural attack on the city witnessed in the 1920's and that it had not been repealed, although it was widely ignored, in 1931 when *City Lights* was released.

In spite of Prohibition, then, in *City Lights*, people drink openly and frequently to excess. Indeed, part of the film's humor derives from the fact that when the Millionaire is drunk he loves Chaplin's Little Tramp, but does not even recognize him when sober. At the wild party given by the drunken Millionaire, his guests drink continuously, and most are quite obviously drunk. Yet Chaplin's film does not condemn them. Drunks may be silly, but not dangerous. Moreover, alcohol is associated with glamour and wealth; the blind flower girl who is poor does not drink, but the Millionaire, his glamorous guests, and all the patrons of the cabaret do. One thinks immediately of the running joke in the *Thin Man* movies involving Nick's ability to drink excessively. Urban filmmakers, most of whom like Louis Mayer of MGM came of immigrant background, made films for predominantly urban audiences, and so portrayed on celluloid this new urban culture of which alcohol consumption was so integral a part. As the thirties wore on, alcohol ceased to be quite as necessary to indicate one's maturity and glamour, especially after prohibition was repealed by the 21st Amendment in 1933, but the long term effects of prohibition were insidious and endured a long time.

One of the long range effects of prohibition was that it fostered a deep disrespect for the law. Many otherwise law-abiding citizens regularly disobeyed the law of the land by drinking and buying alcohol, much as nowadays such upstanding citizens regularly exceed the posted speed limit. Those alcoholic purchases poured money into the coffers of organized crime which then used its wealth to corrupt politicians and infiltrate labor unions. So powerful did gangsters become that the law seemed powerless against them. Police were seen in films, for example, as incompetent and sometimes even vicious. This disrespect for the law and those sworn to uphold it can be seen clearly in a film like *City Lights*.

In the beginning scene at the new monument to Peace and Prosperity, a policeman shakes his fist menacingly at Chaplin as the Tramp tries to climb down from Columbia's lap, but significantly, the policeman doesn't do anything to or for Chaplin. His threatening neither hastens Chaplin's departure nor helps him get unstuck from the sword. The law in *City Lights* is thus protrayed as incompetent, vaguely menacing, and clearly on the side of the rich and powerful; standing next to the policeman is the Hoover look-alike politician who just as menacingly shakes his fist and with an equal lack of results. Later we see Chaplin go out of his way to avoid a motorcycle cop, even though he is innocent of any wrongdoing. When the law does arrive, it is either too late or arrests the wrong man. For example, Chaplin falls afoul of the law through no fault of his own. The Millionaire, in a drunken stupor, gives Chaplin $1000 for the blind flower girl, but the police do not believe Chaplin's story, and when they check with the Millionaire, he is now sober and of course does not recognize Chaplin at all. Later, Chaplin is arrested and sent to jail for several months for this crime he did not commit. He emerges from prison in rags to be tormented by everyone including newspaper boys. How could anyone respect the majesty of the law or lawmen when such flagrant injustice is done?

The unreliability of the law underscores another theme in most Chaplin films, which was echoed by many other Hollywood productions, namely that pure chance played a large role in success. Rarely, if ever, does the audience see anyone work his way up the ladder to financial success. Chaplin is fired from the one real job he has in *City Lights* as a street cleaner, and so tries his luck in the boxing ring. But even here, the deal he had with a friendly boxer collapses through no fault of his own, and he must take his chances with a dangerous opponent who eventually floors him. Not only does Chaplin not go back to the gym for more training to improve his skills, neither does the victor. He is clearly not working his way up to become Heavyweight Champion of the World. The victor simply takes his prize money and disappears. For a brief period in the film, Chaplin enjoys the rewards of success--money, drink, a car, and luxurious surroundings--but not because he has earned them. The drunken Millionaire gives these luxuries to the Little Tramp, but he can as easily take them away again once he becomes sober. Chaplin has no skills he is trying to improve, no training he is trying to advance. When he succeeds, it is through pure luck as when he saves the drunken Millionaire from drowning himself one night and thus remains his buddy--as long as the Millionaire does not sober up. The only figure who does have a job is the blind flower girl who does improve her financial position by the film's end; from selling flowers on the street from a basket, she is able finally to open small flower shop, but only because Chaplin gave her $1000 he received from the Millionaire in one of his drunken stupors, and Chaplin pays dearly for her success when he has to go to jail for supposedly stealing the money.

The Horatio Alger myth by which one works steadily to achieve financial success and in which one's competence and skills are rewarded rarely found its way into American film. Either the wealthy who had already achieved financial success were portrayed on film, such as the Millionaire in *City Lights*, or someone made it to the big time through sheer luck. In this regard one can note those numerous films in which a chorus girl is "discovered" after replacing a star who is temporarily unable to perform. People who work hard at their jobs are rarely the heroes of Hollywood films; on the contrary, they are frequently ridiculed as drudges. The plot of *Topper* (1937), for example, depicts the ne'er-do-well Cary Grant attempting to get the workaholic Topper to relax. Perhaps in the topsy-turvy world of the Depression in which men who had worked diligently were fired as easily as those who had no job experience, the element of sheer luck in achieving success seemed more realistic than any call to work hard and postpone gratification for future rewards. Likewise, in the grueling years of the Depression, American audiences seemed to feel the need for escapism and so paid good money to watch the rich cavort on theater screens. In any case, it is clear from popular American films of the twenties and thirties that success was idolized and its rewards devotedly sought, but how one achieved success was rarely shown on screen except to suggest that blind luck played the most important role.

All through the twenties and into the thirties, Americans eagerly sought successful people and turned them into heroes. For example, movie stars were carefully cultivated as heroes and heroines by the Hollywood studios. Some popular heroes, like Charles Lindbergh, had indeed accomplished feats of daring and skill, but many had not. They were, on the contrary, victors in what we now call "trash sports," like marathon dancing, flagpole sitting, or goldfish eating. No particular skill was required for these "sports." In marathon dancing the expertise of Fred Astaire is less crucial than the simple ability to endure. Moreover, intellectual training and expertise rarely qualified one as a culture hero. Flash Gordon was a hero, but Dr. Zarkov was not. In the 1920's, sports heroes were widely popular as organized spectator sports developed in the growing urban areas. City dwellers lionized their home teams in part because of their need for heroes and at least in part because, in cheering their team on to victory, they could release their pent up aggression.

Human beings have always been aggressive animals, but in crowded cities where one is in constant contact with other equally aggressive people, open physical aggression could spark a riot and threaten the very basis of civilization. Note in *City Lights* the scene in the city cabaret which Chaplin and the Millionaire visit. It is one of the few scenes involving many people. Moreover, they are bunched up closely next to one another, so close in fact that the cigar Chaplin tosses away lands on the chair of a nearby female patron and burns her dress. Repeatedly, Chaplin and the Millionaire get into scrapes with various people and start to take off their coats for a fight. The other patrons and waiters respond in kind, and the entire sequence threatens to explode in violence. When it does, significantly, it involves Chaplin's defense of what he perceives to be a battered girl. Two dancers appear and begin a rather violent dance in which the male dancer hurls the girl at Chaplin's feet. Chaplin leaps to her defense, thus sparking a mini-riot which the orchestra tries to quiet by launching into a dance tune. The dance floor is immediately as jammed as any city boulevard during rush hour. Chaplin feels left out, and, grabbing someone else's partner, begins a wild dance sequence. He thus releases his frustration and aggression in an organized, socially acceptable way by dancing, just as many another city dweller released his frustration by urging the home team to "Kill da bums!"

Significant in the cabaret scene is Chaplin's instinctive defense of the otherwise defenseless girl, for it shows us a great deal about his troubled relations with women generally. Chaplin wants to be a hero, but, small in stature and practically defenseless himself, the only way he can be a creditable defender of women is to have his heroines either smaller in stature than himself or in some other way weaker and even more defenseless than he. Thus in *City Lights*, the woman he protects is blind and can therefore benefit from a protector as unheroic as the Little Tramp. But when her sight is restored by the end of the film, she is now his equal and, moreover, is a successful businesswoman while he is a ragged tramp. He can no longer be her protector, and since that protection was the basis of their relationship, that relationship is now dead. "You can see?" he asks. She responds,"Yes, I can see now." And the film abruptly ends.

Chaplin's heroines, like those of many directors of the early silent films, were patterned on the ingenue heroines of nineteenth century American novels of the Victorian period. Even in the nineteenth century when the image of the ingenue was being solidified by novelists, however, that image did not correspond to the reality of hardworking frontier housewives, let alone the ever-increasing number of women who worked outside the home in jobs which were boring, repetitive, and frequently dangerous. In 1838, 49% of the labor force in the 7 largest woolen mills was female, and in cotton mills, the percentage was even higher. By 1900, 20% of all American women worked outside the home. Far from being ingenues, these women were hardworking members of the Amerian labor force much as the blind flower girl is in *City Lights*. She is the sole support for herself and her grandmother, and she overworks herself so greatly she is taken ill. She obviously knows her business because with the investment she receives from Chaplin's Tramp, she is able to open her own shop and seems to be doing well by the end of the film. Her success dooms her relationship with the Little Tramp, however, in the same way that many women entering the labor force after

World War I found their relationships with Victorian-minded men deeply troubled.

In the 1920's, more and more women worked outside the home. By 1930, for example, 10.6 million women held jobs compared with only 8.4 million in 1920. These labor statistics show that the 1920's flapper was in many ways more emancipated than any of her forebears. She had earned the right to vote in 1920, divorce laws were relaxed, and Margaret Sanger's drive to distribute birth control information began to make some progress. Even in dress women enjoyed a new freedom, as the flapper's chemise weighed in at only a few ounces while the typical outfit of the late nineteenth century weighed beween 10 and 15 pounds. This new freedom for women, however, involved a great deal of emotional and sexual tension. There was always the possibility that the wispy Greek goddess might turn into the massive, powerful, and sexually unalluring Columbia.

The change in women's status in the 1920's reflected a profound revolution in post-World War I American life. It has been said that for America the twentieth century began not in 1900, but in 1920 following the Great War, and it is certainly true that traditional American values seemed to be under attack in the 1920's. Not only did the chain-smoking, bathtub-gin-drinking flapper seem a world away from the Victorian ingenue, but even patriotic faith in the constitution seemed undermined by radical socialists and communists, so much so that Wilson's Attorney General Palmer launched the Great Red Scare in 1919, with a series of raids on suspected radicals and later in the decade, the anarchists Sacco and Vanzetti were executed in 1927. Saving for a rainy day was a fine idea when one had no money; in the twenties' economy of abundance, however, consumers did not save, but rather spent their excess available income on the installment plan, thus blurring the distinction between the present and future markets and making it very difficult for businessmen to predict future sales. Mom and apple pie were praised, but the birthrate went down. We have already seen how the Horatio Alger myth of working oneself steadily to financial success was praised in theory, but rarely in popular art forms like the movies. In short, an enormous gulf opened up between what Americans traditionally preached and what Americans in fact practiced.

Nowhere can this gulf between theory and practice be seen more clearly than in the Stock Market Crash of 1929. In theory, stock prices were supposed to reflect the value of the company, but in fact, investors had wildly bid up the value of stocks in an attempt to make a quick profit. Trade associations during the twenties had kept prices artificially high. The resulting large profits had at first gone into investment in plant and equipment, but from 1927 onward, these profits had instead been plowed into the stock market, thus creating an inflationary push on stock prices. In 1925, the value of stocks on the New York Stock Exchange stood at $27 billion, but in June of 1929, this figure had risen to $67 billion. Three months later, however, the figure had skyrocketed to $87 billion. Some form of rectification of the market was inevitable, and when it occurred in

October, 1929, stocks quickly lost 40% of their value. The resulting credit contraction eventually plunged the United States into the Great Depression.

The Great Depression was not confined to this country, however; it was a worldwide economic downturn. A sickly world economy during the 1920's had been kept afloat to a large degree because American bankers lent money to Germany to pay its huge reparations debt acquired as a result of World War I. Germany used the money to pay off its foreign creditors, who in turn bought from the United States. When the severe credit contraction of the Stock Market Crash dried up foreign loan funds, the German economy collapsed and with it much of the rest of the world's.

The Great Depression strained the world's political system to the breaking point and in some places democratic processes fell apart. Thus, Adolph Hitler took advantage of Germany's economic collapse to rise to power in 1933, and then began a concerted program to undo the Treaty of Versailles. In France, governments came and went with a bewildering rapidity, and many in France came to support a fascistic or totalitarian system of government to correct the economic abuses. Even in Britain, the bastion of European democracy, those interested in strong man rule formed an increasing part of the electorate.

The United States was not free from demagogues from the political right like Huey Long or Father Coughlin, but this country did begin to address the problems of the depression within a democratic framework. Franklin Roosevelt, capturing both the urban and rural wings of the Democratic party as Al Smith had been unable to do in 1928, won the presidency in 1932 and once inaugurated in 1933, began the splendid First Hundred Days which sought to put a floor under the depression to keep it from getting any worse. In 1935, 15 million people were out of work, yet in spite of the New Deal, by 1940, 11 million people were still unemployed. In Europe, such staggering unemployment had resulted in enormous political upheavals which led to World War II. In this country, on the other hand, though the social and political fabric was stretched almost to the breaking point, a traditional faith in law and order and a deeply engrained democratic system combined to preserve the constitutional principles of the founding fathers.

As the country slid once again into an economy of scarcity, traditional moral values were reasserted. The thirties generation condemned the twenties as that frivolous decade between the two great eras of reform. The experimentation of Ernest Hemingway and F. Scott Fitzgerald was abandoned in favor of a more socially engaged literature of Sherwood Anderson and John Steinbeck. The hemline went down and ruffles were back in vogue. The theory of saving for a rainy day was hailed once again to a large degree because no one had much money to save anyway. The gulf beween theory and practice narrowed, but Americans were not much happier. Rather, deceived expectations created a certain bitterness and a fear of the future which was atypical of the American experience.

This inability to cope with the future can be seen clearly in *City Lights*. The blind flower girl, her sight now restored, searches for her benefactor. She expects, not surprisingly, to find him a rich, handsome, young man. Instead, she finds Chaplin's Little Tramp, hardly attractive and dressed in rags. Her profound disappointment shows in her face as she says, "Yes, I can see now." Chaplin had created a lighthearted comedy before these final frames, but even this great comedian could not face the future, stark as it was. Not only do the two of them not find a rosy future together, but it is even unlikely they will remain together at all. This sense of deceived expectations, bitterness, and fear characterized the Depression years. In the words of Franklin Roosevelt, "We have nothing to far but fear itself," but that fear nonetheless was truly something frightening.

City Lights - Instructor's Guide

1. According to Robert Sobol in *The Great Bull Market: Wall Street in the 1920's* (1968), what factors helped cause the stock market crash in 1929?

2. According to John Rae in *The Road and the Car in American Life* (1971), what effects did the car have on American social life and industry?

3. Investigate the cult of heroism in any or all of the following books, indicating why these men were so popular.

    1. Kenneth Davis, *The Hero, Charles A, Lindburgh* (1959)
    2. Robert Creamer, *Babe* (1974)
    3. Randy Roberts, *Jack Dempsey* (1980)

4. Discuss the movement in American intellectual history from individualism to concern for the society as a whole. A useful source is Robert Crunden's *From Self to Society: Transition in American Thought, 1919-1941* (1972). What role did the Great Depression play in this change?

5. Write a brief biographical sketch and assess the significance of any or all of the following:

    1. Charles A. Lindburgh
    2. Henry Ford
    3. Clarence Darrow
    4. Sacco and Vanzetti
    5. Charlie Chaplin

6. Discuss the changes which occurred for working women during the 1920's. A useful source is Leslie Woodcock Tentler's *Wage Earning Women: Industrial*

Work and Family Life in the United States, 1900-1930 (1979).

7. How did the movies affect Americans' image of themselves? A useful source is Robert Sklar, *Movie Made America* (1976). Also see Andrew Bergman, *We're in the Money: Depression America and its Films* (1971).

8. Write a book report, indicating the author's hypothesis and relating events in the book to events in the film, in any or all of the following:

1. Frederick Lewis Allen, *Only Yesterday* (1931)
2. Andrew Bergman, *We're in the Money: Depression America and Its Films* (1971)
3. Caroline Bird, *The Invisible Scar* (1965)
4. D.M. Chalmers, *Hooded Americanism: The First Century of the Ku Klux Klan, 1865-1965* (1965)
5. Milton Friedman and Anna Schwartz, *The Great Contraction, 1929-1933* (1965)
6. Charles Kindleberger, *The World in Depression, 1929-1939* (1973)
7. William Leuchtenburg, *The Perils of Prosperity* (1958)

9. Write a short biography of Charlie Chaplin, indicating why he was so popular and why he chose to leave the United States for Europe.

Inherit the Wind - Gimme that Ol' Time America

Inherit the Wind, released in 1960, portrays the famous 1925 Scopes trial in which a young biology teacher was tried for teaching Darwin's theory of evolution. In doing so, the film draws compelling portraits of the defense lawyer, Clarence Darrow, and the prosecutor, William Jennings Bryan, two men who had often supported one another only to find themselves on opposite sides in 1925. Clearly prejudiced in favor of Darrow, *Inherit the Wind* never really addresses the validity of Darwin's theories which have recently been modified and challenged by modern scientists. The film does suggest, however, why such passions could be unleashed by the Scopes trial, for indeed, evolution was associated with "city slicker" ideas produced by the growing urban culture of the 1920's. Faced with a new society they did not understand, Bryan and his followers clung not only to "that ol' time religion," but more significantly, to "that ol' time America," which was fast disappearing in the 1920's.

In 1925, John Scopes taught the theory of evolution as put forward by Charles Darwin, in spite of the fact that the Tennessee legislature a few weeks earlier had passed a law making it illegal to teach any theory of man's origins which contradicted the Bible's story of creation. That he had violated the law was clear. What was on trial was the law itself, and that is why two of the most important figures in America came to the sleepy town of Dayton, Tennessee to try young Scopes. The prosecutor was a man who had run three times for President of the United States, the Great Commoner as he was called, William Jennings Bryan. The defense was entrusted to one of the great legal minds of the century, Clarence Darrow, who had already made a name for himself in the Leopold and Loeb case, in which he argued for a new insanity law, and in the defense of John McNamara, a labor organizer, accused of bombing the *Los Angeles Times*. In *Inherit the Wind*, Bryan becomes Matthew Harrison Brady; Darrow, Henry Drummond; and Scopes, Bertram Cates. The film's E. K. Hornbeck was in reality, H. L. Mencken, the cynical newspaperman who reported the trial for the national press. Scopes is a minor character in the drama, but the film draws compelling portraits of Bryan, Darrow, and Mencken. Are they accurate?

Gorging himself on fried chicken, blustering on about religion, and betraying the confidence of Rachel, the preacher's daughter, Bryan in the film is made to look the fool. That is unfortunate, for Bryan had had a long and distinguished career before the Scopes trial. He had run for the presidency three times, and had served as Secretary of State under Wilson. He had so supported the rights of the little fellow that he had earned the name "The Great Commoner."

Bryan first came to public attention in 1896. After capturing the liberal wing of the Democratic party, Bryan won his party's presidential nomination for the first time. He demanded that silver as well as gold be used as backing for paper currency at a ratio of 16 to 1. The inflation thus created would, he hoped, have eased the debt burden of the American farmer. In fact, part of the farmer's debt problem was the result of monetary forces. Between 1865 and 1890, the population of the United States doubled, but the amount of money in circulation remained the same; the result was severe deflation, and debtors found it hard to repay loans with dollars that were worth more. As a result, farmers were losing their farms. Since the nation had very litle gold but a great deal of silver, using the latter as backing for paper currency would have allowed the government to print more money, and since currency would have been easier to obtain, theoretically debtors should have been better able to repay their loans. The "silver issue" as these ideas came to be known, was really only a panacea, however, for creating inflation was just as bad as creating deflation. Inflation would have endangered the security of middle class savings at home and the value of the dollar in trade abroad. Bryan's inability to persuade the American people to accept his silver notions helped cause his defeat.

But Bryan would have had trouble in 1896 anyway. His Bible-thumping rhetoric, which *Inherit the Wind* captures so well, antagonized immigrants living in cities who were not Protestant. Urban people generally had difficulty relating to a man who ran his campaign as a series of revival meetings, and who lacked sophistication and "polish." Bryan was also the victim of intimidation; some businessmen paid their workers off before election day and told them not to report for work if Bryan won. Finally, grain failures in Russia and Argentina meant less grain on the international market, and the price of American grain correspondingly went up; as a result, many previously debt-ridden farmers voted Republican, the party of prestige.

The 1896 campaign showed Bryan at both his best and worst. Deeply concerned about the fate of the small farmer and urban worker, he was willing to use untried economic measures to help, and he marshalled his considerable rhetorical skills for battle. "I come to speak to you in defense of a cause as holy as the cause of liberty--the cause of humanity." And later, "You shall not press down upon the brow of labor this crown of thorns, you shall not crucify mankind upon a cross of gold!" But Bryan was also a product of rural America exclusively, and he distrusted the city and urban values. His Biblical rhetoric stirred voters in Nebraska, but left them cold in New York. Without the large urban centers and the urban middle class vote, the Democrats could not hope to win a presidential election, and these Bryan never could deliver. Recognizing this, party leaders urged him to step aside in 1912 in favor of Woodrow Wilson from New Jersey, and Bryan agreed to do so in return for being made Secretary of State in Wilson's administration.

The negative portrayal of Bryan in *Inherit the Wind*, then, is unfortunate in that it ignores his earlier career as a staunch defender of the common man. By contrast, the portrayal of his adversary, Clarence Darrow, is essentially correct. A brilliant debater and skeptic about human nature, Darrow, too, was a devoted defender of the downtrodden and unfortunate. The violence of the 1894 Pullman strike, for example, led him to defend the strike's leader, Eugene Debs. He went on to defend John McNamara, the man accused of dynamiting the *Los Angeles Times* newspaper offices in 1910, and he argued for a new insanity ruling in 1924 when defending Richard Loeb and Nathan Leopold in the murder of a 14 year old boy. In none of these cases was Darrow on the "popular" side, and he lost all of them. Nonetheless, his willingness to argue the "other" side of any case made him a legend in his own time.

The third major character, the film's E. K. Hornbeck, was in reality H. L. Mencken, who was as ascerbic as the film makes him seem. A Baltimore newspaperman, he founded the *American Mercury* in 1923, and immediately declared war on "homo boobiens." Mencken may never have said what Hornbeck does in *Inherit the Wind*, but he would have enthusiastically embraced the sentiment: "the duty of a newspaper is to comfort the afflicted, and to afflict the comfortable." A total cynic, Mencken delighted in the display of savage wit and the well-turned phrase. But while he attacked everything, he, unlike Darrow, affirmed nothing. In the film, even Darrow has had enough of him at the end of the trial.

During the trial, Darrow delivers a thundering denunciation of ignorance. If Darwin's theories can be prohibited, he says, "soon you will turn Catholic against Protestant, and then Protestant against Protestant." Eventually you will "march backward until you reach the sixteenth century when people burned others who dared to bring enlightenment." This is significant, for Darrow does not defend John Scopes on the ground he never taught evolution, for he obviously did. Nor does Darrow defend the validity of Darwin's theories as preferable to the Biblical interpretation of creation. Instead, Darrow defends Scopes' right to *teach* Darwin, or, as he puts it, the right to think for himself. He does this by putting Bryan himself on the stand as an expert on religion, and getting him to admit men have a right to think. Darrow then disgraces Bryan when he gets the latter to state he speaks directly to God and knows what God wants. The people in the courtroom, heretofore Bryan's unswerving supporters, are shocked by this bald display of pride. Bryan only makes things worse the next day when he delivers a poorly thought out, emotionally overwrought speech while the crowd noisily files out.

Why would William Jennings Bryan have fought evolution so passionately in the first place? He had, of course, been a devout Christian all his life, and his regular Bible reading obviously influenced his rhetorical style. Note, for example, the Cross of Gold speech cited earlier. But many other devout Christians, known as Modernists, as opposed to Fundamentalists, had no difficulty in accepting Darwin's theories. Bryan, on the other hand, saw in the phrase "survival of the fittest" a green light for wealthy industrialists to crush laborers and farmers in the name of science. For him, accepting Darwin meant rejecting reform, a cause to which he had devoted his life. Moreover, Bryan believed evolution and other scientific theories had produced Friedrich Nietzsche's philosophy which he blamed for encouraging German brutality in World War I.

Finally, Bryan could not accept God as a First Cause only, as a Creator who merely set the world in motion for human beings to admire. For him, God was a continuing presence whose intervention, by miracles, reminded mankind that appeal to Him was always possible.

Obviously, Bryan had misunderstood Darwin's theories, in part because he had never actually read either *The Origin of Species* or *The Descent of Man*. The "survival of the fittest" never meant a vicious battle for Darwin. "Survivors" were not necessarily more powerful, only better adapted to a changing environment. More important, that which survived was the species, not individual members of it; nature contained many examples of cooperation among the members of one species, like bees working together in a hive. Moreover, Darwin could not be held responsible for the interpretations, usually faulty, that others, such as Nietzsche perhaps, could have developed from his theories. What Bryan is really objecting to is the Social Darwinism of Herbert Spencer, who applied Darwin's theories to society. This very ignorance is what Darrow so successfully and publicly exposed and exploited in the Scopes trial. Darrow "wins" by making Bryan and all he believes in look foolish.

But could Darwin himself survive Darrow? To put it another way, could Darwin's theories stand up in a court of law? No, say some modern scientists. When Darwin wrote in the mid-nineteenth century, the fossil record was as yet incomplete, and Darwin had to argue from fragmentary evidence as a result. He assumed that given the great age of the earth, a fact all scientists agreed upon, the evolution of new species must have progressed gradually over the millenia. Thus, a small mollusk would become slowly larger and larger until a new species developed. That is the point some modern scientists like Stephen Jay Gould dispute.

Called "punctuationalists," these men can demonstrate using a much more complete fossil record that new species develop very rapidly in specialized environments, and then spread elsewhere if possible. For example, Lake Nabugabo in Africa split from Lake Victoria about 4000 years ago, a brief instant in geological time, and it contains within it five species of fish clearly related to the ancestor in Lake Victoria, but which are found nowhere else. Because Lake Nabugabo has a different environment than Lake Victoria, Gould argues adaptation was necessary to allow fish to survive in the new lake. In the process of adaptation to the new environment, five new species evolved. Most fish species are millions of years old, but the ones in Lake Nabugabo can only be a few thousand years old, and they must therefore have developed quite "rapidly" in terms of geological time.

Some modern scientists have tried to find the exact mechanism whereby such speciation occurs. Noting the tendency for animals to recapitulate their evolution before birth--a six week old human fetus has gills, for example--they argue that immature versions of the adult are born, survive, and hand on to their descendents through their genes whatever characteristics they have. An example is the axolotl, a Mexican salamander. All salamanders begin life in the water, later develop external gills, eventually climb out on land, and breathe through lungs when their external gills fall off. The axolotl, however, maintains its external gills into adulthood and never lives on land, yet it manages to reproduce itself; its offspring, too, never drop their gills. In a sense, the axolotl gets "stuck" in its development, and cannot become like other salamanders. Apparently, the lack of a pituitary hormone is what causes the axolotl to retain its gills. Whatever makes this hormone activate in other salamanders does not function in the axolotl, and the result is a new species.

Note that punctuationalists like Gould do not dispute Darwin's theories that all creatures evolved from more primitive forms of life. They object, rather, to Darwin's assumption of gradualism and seek to explain precisely, sometimes through microbiology, how adaptation and speciation occurs. Most important, they believe that their inability to explain everything at present does not undermine Darwin's theories, but on the contrary suggests new avenues for investigation and research.

This is precisely the point Darrow and Bryan disagreed on, for while the cosmopolitan Darrow was willing to accept the possiblity of change and was therefore willing to follow new ideas wherever they led, the more provincial Bryan saw change itself as the enemy and fought new ideas he considered dangerous to his moral system. For Bryan, evolution was associated with "city slicker" ideas, characteristic of the new urban culture of the 1920's, which undermined his deeply cherished values inherited from the Jeffersonian, yeoman farmer America of the nineteenth century.

In *Inherit the Wind*, Bryan represents rural America, and Mencken, alias Hornbeck, represents the new cities. The differences between the two could not be clearer. Bryan's rhetoric with its Bibilical cadences is a world away from Mencken's rapid-fire delivery of *bon mots*. Bryan is a teetotaler, but in spite of Prohibition, Mencken drinks whiskey as we see when he offers a drink to Darrow as they relax in the hotel. They even dress differently: Bryan's suspenders and dowdy suits contrast with Mencken's straw boater hat worn at a rakish angle. Bryan's devoted wife, Mary, who is Sarah in the film, testifies to his concern for family life; Mencken remained single. Bryan's Christianity contrasts with Mencken's open atheism and cynicism. The urban lifestyle Mencken represents constituted for Bryan all he abhorred: hedonism as opposed to engaged reform, and godless cynicism as opposed to Christian charity.

Bryan indeed had much to fear, for in fact the number of Menckens was on the rise. For the first time in the census of 1920, more people lived in urban areas than lived on the farm. This was a fact much noted and widely feared at the time, for cities were regarded by many rural people as un-American. Populated with immigrants who stubbornly clung to their old ways, including their old religions like Catholicism and Judaism, cities were considered unhealthy to the body and the spirit. Families broke under the strain of industrialism, and young people fell under the evil spell of liquor, non-connubial sex, and "atheistic" socialism. Cities were re-creations of Sodom and Gomorrah, and as Bryan warns in *Inherit the Wind*, their ideas could spread to small town America if the forces of evil like Darwinism were not stopped.

Needless to say, cities weren't all that bad, but changes were occuring which would have upset the likes of Bryan. When the 18th Amendment to the Constitution was passed in 1918, the consumption and sale of alcoholic bevereges were made illegal, and the consumption of alcohol did indeed go down nationwide--but not in the cities where Prohibition was deeply resented by many ethnic groups, especially the Germans and Irish. The wealthy and well-educated drank openly in speakeasies, wrote about drinking in the novels of the period such as F. Scott Fitzgerald's *Tender Is the Night*, and flocked to see movies in which people drank, frequently to excess. Associated with a sophisticated world of city night clubs and freedom, alcohol was consumed in huge quantities in cities; bootleggers supplied at least 150 million quarts a year in the 1920's, doing $2 billion a year in profit, or about 2% of the GNP.

Attitudes towards sex also began to change. Historians have long debated whether there really was an increase in sexual activity during the 1920's, but it is undeniably true that people *talked* about sex more. Explicit sex scenes in novels, such as Ernest Hemingway's *A Farewell to Arms* (1929), proliferated, while tabloids, like the *New York Daily News*, breathlessly reported sexual misconduct in lurid detail. The movies especially exploited sex. Despite such provocative titles as *Up in Mabel's Room* or *Women and Lovers*, the twenties' silents are rather mild by present standards, but they did portray sexually active women who were not punished at the end for their sexuality. Theda Bara, the "vamp," and Clara Bow, the "it" girl, scandalized prim audiences with their open sensuality. Young couples discovered that automobiles freed them from ever-present chaperones, and advertisers wooed potential customers with the promise of "six cylinder love."

The sexual revolution benefited women, especially. Not only could they talk more freely about their physical needs, but they also began insisting on their physical comfort--and in the process shocked their elders. A woman's dress which in the 1890's had taken 19 and a half yards to make and which weighed in at 10 pounds, by the 1920's had become a flapper's chemise requiring only 4 and a half yards to make and weighing in at 7 ounces. Gone were the corsets and stays which had crammed the internal organs of their mothers up inside the chest cavity, making it difficult to breathe and endangering life in pregnancy. Just as clothing became simpler and less restrictive, so did hair styles; the elaborate hair styles of the pre-war period were impossible to achieve alone, and since many young working women lived alone or at any rate without maids, they "bobbed" their hair. Respectable women also began to drink achohol and smoke in public. Indeed, because so many women smoked cigarettes rather than cigars, the cigar industry languished in the twenties while cigarette manufacturers thrived.

The degree of freedom achieved by women in the 1920's should not be overexaggerated, however. Clothing definitely became less restrictive, but women still worked long hours, in spite of labor saving devices such as the washing machine and vacuum cleaner. A woman without children spent at least 43 hours a week on household chores alone, and with children, her average work week climbed to 56 hours. More women worked outside the home as new job opportunities opened up which did not require brute strength, such as being a typist, telephone operator, or secretary; however, in 1930 the number of women thus employed had grown only 1% over what it had been in 1920. While the divorce rate went up, from 81 per thousand in 1900 to 166 in 1928, most women were still married, and marriage was still regarded as the only proper, long term role for women to play.

Not only did the newly developing city culture encourage more freedom for women and the increasing consumption of alcohol, but urban populations also began experimenting with socialism and left-wing politics. In 1919, there were only 60,000 Communists in the United States out of a population of 105,700,000, but they were almost exclusively isolated in cities. Seattle and Boston, for example, saw socialists successfully call major strikes in 1919. Six socialists, all from New York City, managed to get elected to the New York legislature, but they were thrown out in 1920. Hysterical fear of socialism led to the Great Red Scare between 1919 and 1920, but the same prejudice, mixed with hostility to immigrants, colored the entire decade, and helped, for example, to convict Sacco and Vanzetti of a payroll robbery and murder. To the horror of liberal opinion, the two men were executed in the electric chair in 1927.

In a lighter vein, cities also produced a sports mania in the twenties. Legendary figures like Babe Ruth in baseball and Jack Dempsey in boxing were heroes to millions. Although the participants may have come from rural areas, the sports figures played before urban audiences. Cities developed their own teams. Friendly, and sometimes not so friendly, rivalries developed between cities, and in the case of New York, between various boroughs of the same city; the Bronx bombers, the Yankees, sometimes fought the Brooklyn bums, the Dodgers, for the pennant. In crowded cities, spectator sports allowed citizens to unleash their bottled up aggression in socially acceptable ways as they cheered their team on to victory. Remember that the language of football, especially, is sublimated warfare, with offense and defense and running "attacks." Sports events were immensely popular and profitable. The Philadelphia Municipal Stadium, for example, was built in 1926 with a seating capacity of almost 102,000. Moreover, in the twenties, spectators were not content with traditional sports alone. Marathon dancing, flagpole-sitting, goldfish eating, bicycle races--all became spectator sports in the roaring twenties.

From alcohol, to the sexual revolution, to the emancipated woman, to godless socialism, to a mania for sports, the city dwellers of the twenties enjoyed a lifestyle of which Bryan and his followers heartily disapproved. Bryan, however, should have been comforted that the very Christian values he sought so earnestly to defend were not dying out at all. The number of church members actually went up, from 41.9 million in 1916 to 54.5 million in 1928. Evangelical sects like the Churchs of Christ and the Jehovah's Witnesses saw enormous growth as a result of their aggressive proselytizing. Even in cities, where many formerly rural dwellers came looking for jobs, religion prospered. Aimee Simple McPherson built the Angelus temple in Los Angeles with a seating capacity of 5000. Moreover, because of overrepresentation of rural areas in state legislatures and in Congress, rural attacks on the city, from Prohibition to curtail its drinking to immigration restriction to keep it from growing, met with success. What laws could not achieve peacefully, the revived Ku Klux Klan sometimes achieved by force. Broadening its attack to include foreigners, Catholics, Jews, and socialists as well as blacks, the new Klan attacked everything the city represented, from the "loose" women who didn't know their place to the immigrants who clung to their old religions. Even in the cities themselves, the flapper usually got married in the end, and as we have seen the sexual revolution and emancipation of women were more apparent than real. Bryan and his rural followers really had nothing to fear from cities--or from Charles Darwin.

This fact helps explain the title of the film, *Inherit the Wind*. The Biblical quotation from which it is drawn says, "He who troubleth his own house shall inherit the wind, and the fool shall be made the servant of the wise of heart." Given the strength of Christianity and the widespread respect for the virtues he supported, Bryan in the Scopes trial was, indeed, "troubling his own house" unnecessarily, and he did "inherit the wind" in the sense that his distinguished career ended on a note of bitterness and disgrace. Bryan won the trial against Scopes, but he lost his reputation as a statesman and defender of the downtrodden. Darrow made him look the fool on the witness stand, displaying for all to see his ignorance not only of evolution but of scientific principles generally.

Inherit the Wind clearly makes Darrow look "wise of heart." Played by Spencer Tracy, who specialized in portraying rugged individualists, Darrow emerges as the defender of freedom who nonetheless displays a becoming modesty and lack of zealotry. As the film ends, Darrow is about to leave the courtroom. He takes up the Bible in one hand and Darwin's book in the other. With a smile on his face, he slaps the two together, and walks down the aisle as the voice of Leslie Uggams sings, "His truth goes marching on." Darrow indeed was the wave of the future. Cosmopolitan and open-minded, Darrow tried to blend the best of ol' time America with the best the new century had to offer. It was a difficult task, and one that would trouble Americans repeatedly in times to come.

Inherit the Wind - Instructor's Guide

1. Write a book report on any of the following, identifying the author's hypothesis

and relating material in the book to events in the film:

1. W. H. Chafe, *The American Woman: Her Changing Social, Economic and Political Roles* (1974)
2. Robert W. Cherny, *A Righteous Cause: The Life of William Jennings Bryan* (1985)
3. Norman Furniss, *The Fundamentalist Controversy, 1918-1931* (1954)
4. Ray Ginger, *Six Days or Forever?* (1956) account of Scopes trial
5. Stephen Jay Gould, *Hen's Teeth and Horse's Toes* (1983)
6. Lawrence Levine, *Defender of the Faith: William Jennings Bryan, the Last Decade, 1915-1925* (1965)
7. William Manchester, *Disturber of the Peace* (1951) biography of H.L. Mencken, second edition 1986
8. Geoffrey Perrett, *America in the Twenties* (1982)
9. Winifred D. Wandersee, *Women's Work and Family Values, 1920-1940* (1981)

2. Choose one of the books above and find scholarly reviews of it in two or more of the following journals:

1. *The American Historical Review* (published by The American Historical Association)
2. *Journal of American History* (published by The Organization of American Historians)
3. *History Teacher*
4. *History, Review of New Books*

Compare and contrast the reviews. What did reviewers like or dislike and why?

3. Write a brief biographical sketch and assess the historical significance of any or all of the following:

1. William Jennings Bryan
2. Clarence Darrow
3. H. L. Mencken
4. Charles Darwin
5. Aimee Simple McPhearson

4. Explain what legal precedent Clarence Darrow set in the Leopold and Loeb case. What were the facts of the case and how did Darrow argue it?

5. Describe briefly developments in religious thought in the early 20th century.

6. Describe modern refinements of Darwin's theories. Stephen Jay Gould's *Ever Since Darwin: Reflections in Natural History* (1979) in a useful beginning reference.

7. Show how social scientists used Darwin's ideas to justify the "survival of the fittest." Richard Hofstadter, *Social Darwinism in American Thought* (1944) is a useful beginning reference. Why would Bryan have objected to the views of Herbert Spencer or William Graham Sumner?

Scarface - The Bureaucratization of Crime

Scarface, released in 1932, was part of the vogue of gangster films popular in the early years of the Great Depression. Based on the reality of a massive crime wave outside the theater, *Scarface* depicts the growing bureaucratization of crime, as gangsters adopted methods first pioneered by the robber barons of the late nineteenth century to improve the efficiency and administration of giant financial empires. In doing so, however, *Scarface* turns the self-made man myth on its ear and exposes the moral bankruptcy of law enforcement officials. Worse, movie gangsters like Scarface were portrayed almost sympathetically, and they were glamorous because they inhabited the exotic world of the city where in the 1930's more and more Americans came to live. Nonetheless, these "glamorous" criminals unleashed a spasm of violence throughout the nation. In an attempt to depict accurately such violence, however, *Scarface* became by far the most brutal film of the gangster genre, and its very brutality called forth a reaction which dramatically changed what movies could portray and how.

Scarface, like most gangster heroes, is a robber baron run amuck. Like a modern John D. Rockefeller building an illegal Standard Oil Company, Scarface understands intuitively the value of an organizational set up which would make small competing gang operations into a giant gangster monopoly, just as Rockefeller swallowed up rival oil companies to create Standard Oil. Scarface ruthlessly eliminates any challenge to his power: he begins by treacherously killing his South Side boss, goes on to acquire the North Side liquor business and ultimately has his nominal boss, Johnny Lovo, murdered. Like the robber barons before him, Scarface draws a neat distinction between his professional and personal life; outgoing and loyal to his friends and family, he is amoral in his business dealings. Most important, for Scarface the issue is the efficient and streamlined adminstration of a crime business, and he rationally, cold-bloodedly sets out to create one.

The efficient, sophisticated organization which Scarface desires was pioneered by the large corporations of the late nineteenth century and the industrial tycoons who created them. For example, Rockefeller's Standard Oil became the best example of what economists call "vertical integration," a monopoly attempting to control the product from the time it left the ground until the time it was marketed. "[Consolidation] had to come, though all we saw at the time was the need to save ourselves from wasteful conditions," Rockefeller argued. Understanding that even small economies in mass production could produce considerable savings, Rockefeller relentlessly cut costs, at one point actually reducing the number of drops of solder on a kerosene can from 40 to 39. By reducing the cost of refining crude oil into kerosene by only .082 cents a gallon, Standard Oil increased its annual profit by $600,000. Moreover, much as Scarface eliminates the North Side gang, Rockefeller ruthlessly bought out or took over rival oil companies, so much so that he was nicknamed "Reckafeller" by his enemies. Using these cold-bloodedly rational business techniques, eventually he controlled 93% of the nation's oil refining capacity, much as the real Al Capone, upon which *Scarface* is based, eventually controlled over 90% of the midwest's illegal liquor traffic.

Nor was Rockefeller alone. Commodore Vanderbilt's railroad empire eliminated rivals and streamlined operations as well. In fact, the railroads pioneered new business administration techniques such as cost accounting and using salaried managers to run these new empires efficiently. Ruthlessly attempting to destroy their rivals, railroads dramatically slashed prices to ship farm goods in areas where competition existed, and subsidized this practice by charging outlandish fees to Great Plains farmers where rail competition was non-existent. Rebates were given to large shippers to reflect the lowered real cost of doing business. Moreover, railroads built grain elevators to store produce so as to avoid having to sell at harvest time when the inevitable glut on the market drove down prices; the result was to even out grain prices year round and make predicting profits easier.

By the 1890's, however, the drive for efficiency received added emphasis from the creation of finance capitalism, one of the most famous--or notorious--practitioners of which was J. P. Morgan. As the industrial revolution matured, Morgan was convinced that profits could be kept high, not so much by inventing new processes, as by administering the existing companies more professionally. This philosophy was behind Morgan's founding of United States Steel in 1901, capitalized at the astounding figure of $1.4 billion. U. S. Steel was formed when Morgan took control of 200 small steel companies by purchase or stock manipulation, thus creating a behemoth which controlled three-fifths of the country's steel production and employed 168,000 people. He proceeded to close inefficient plants, hired salaried, professional bureaucrats to administer the company, and cold-bloodedly applied sound business management practices to the previously rough and tumble steel industry.

Significantly, one of the companies thus absorbed was Carnegie Steel. A colorful character willing to take great risks in the early days of the steel revolution, Carnegie was a symbol of the old order which had produced Rockefeller and Vanderbilt. He was a steel man who knew his business from the ground up, just as Rockefeller knew the oil business. But Morgan knew nothing about steel manufacturing; instead, he was a financier who knew all about the stock market and banking, and whose emphasis was less on creativity than on the bottom line. Morgan intended to keep the profit margin high by streamlining production techniques and being efficient.

This drive to streamline production to lower the cost per unit while at the same time increasing standardization is best shown in the early meat packing industry where Philip Armour reconceived the process by which an animal was turned into meat. Before this time, the animal was slaughtered, and then one man butchered the entire steer by himself. Armour instead had the carcass move to the butchers who performed the same task on many different carcasses during the day. The men stayed still and the carcass came to them by virtue of a series of moving hooks upon which it hung: production on a moving assembly line had been born.

Henry Ford applied these same principles to the automobile industry in 1908 when his moving asembly line began creating Model T's. Ford did not invent the car, nor was he even the first to market an inexpensive one, which was, in fact, the Merry Oldsmobile. But he did adopt the same principles of organizational efficiency and the streamlined, simplified production techniques which men like Morgan and Rockefeller had used before. Like them, Ford sought to lower unit cost which in fact fell from $850 per Model T in 1908 to under $300 by 1925, but he did not achieve that dramatic reduction by slashing wages as Rockefeller would do later at his Ludlow, Colorado mine in 1914, or the Pullman company had done in 1894. Instead, Ford made his fortune by accepting a smaller profit margin on a larger volume of sales.

As industry became more efficient and the number of competing companies was whittled down through finance capitalism, state and federal governments had to fight fire with fire: to control industry, they had to become as sophisticated in their administration and organization as businessmen were in theirs. Thus, first on a local and state level, and then on the national level, government began using specialized bureaucrats to oversee industry just as industry had invented salaried managers to oversee the workers. So it was that the state railroad commissions were invented to regulate the likes of Vanderbilt, and when they were declared unconstitutional in 1886 in the *Wabash* case, the Interstate Commerce Commission was set up in 1887 on the federal level. The Meat Packing Regulatory Act of 1906 led to the hiring federal bureaucrats to inspect Armour's meat plants. Finally, as the number of such federal regulatory agencies expanded, Theodore Roosevelt helped create the Department of Commerce and Labor in 1903 to oversee and coordinate the increasing number of federal bureaucracies.

Not only did government adopt the business adminstration techniques pioneered by industry to regulate industry, but Washington strove to make itself less unwieldy. Wilson, for example, introduced the caucus system in 1913 to improve Congressional efficiency in passing the President's proposed legislation. But the greatest drive for efficiency came during World War I, when the federal government's great War Boards organized the American economy to produce goods for the allied war effort as quickly as possible. Significantly, Washington used business expertise to streamline government operations, from procurement to transportation, bringing to government the same efficiency already found in industry. Serving for the nominal salary of $1 a year, these captains of industry ignored anti-trust law to eliminate competition, guarantee a 6% profit, and set prices.

It is against this background that Scarface's drive for streamlined administration, more efficient allocation of resources, and improved profit margin must be read, for in a profound way he was doing for crime what had already been done in industry and government. In fact, the real Al Capone saw himself primarily as a businessman. "Everybody calls me a racketeer. I call myself a businessman," he once said. Conveniently forgetting the violence his "business" had unleashed on Chicago, which was the scene of over 500 gangland killings by 1929, Capone brought in salaried managers, especially accountants, to help him determine profits accurately--and invest them. He hired a phalanx of lawyers to outwit the police and law codes. No longer a Jesse James highwayman, Al Capone created a crime empire which, doing $60 million a year in business, was almost as big as Standard Oil. Moreover, much as businessmen tried to eliminate cut-throat competition through the trade association movement of the 1920's, so the crime world, under the influence of Meyer Lansky, met in upstate New York in 1933, to divide the country into spheres of influence to eliminate the suicidal gangland wars such as that produced when Scarface cuts into O'Hara's North Side territory, gang wars which were reducing profits and increasing public hostility.

To a depression audience watching helplessly as the American economic system crashed down around them, Scarface and other gangsters served as mirrors of what was wrong with American businessmen. Those businessmen who had been hailed as heros in the 1920's became objects of scorn in the early thirties. Always disliked as ruthless, selfish, they were ultimately condemned for not being all that smart, because they could not foresee or prevent the depression. In the film, Scarface, too, is ruthless, selfish, and cunning, and his cunning, like theirs, has limits. He mistakenly murders his associate, Rinaldo, who he believes has dishonored his sister, Cesca, when in fact Rinaldo had already married her; "I don't know," mumbles Scarface as he stumbles down the stairs, aware for the first time of his ability to err. Scarface's error leads directly to his own death when the police gun him down. As Scarface paid for his sins with his death, American businessmen paid for their own short-sightedness and economic ineptitude with the depression. However, while Scarface's penance was solitary and personal--he is gunned down alone--the penance of an overly proud business community involved the suffering of an entire nation. The sufferers--the audience--could see in Scarface's death the punishment many would have gladly handed out to their employers.

As a robber baron run amuck, Scarface turns the myth of the self-made man on its ear. According to that myth, if a man started from the bottom and worked hard, he was supposed to rise economically and socially. But the self-made man in *Scarface* is Tony Camonte, the gangster, a man who also is hard working, knows all the details of his business, and has worked his way up from the bottom. Note how *Scarface*, like earlier gangster films (*Little Caesar* [1930] and *Public Enemy* [1931], for example), stresses the lower-class origins of the gangster. As he makes more money, Tony buys new clothes, begins going to the theater, and, significantly, acquires a house of his own, the city's equivalent to the yeoman farmer's farm. In the twilight world of the gangster film, social mobility is still possible, but only for the outlaw. If only the gangster could make upward mobility believable in the depression years, we can see how much legitimate institutions had failed.

Finally, by making the gangster the self-made man, a film like *Scarface* turns the nineteenth century Jacksonian distinction between moral and immoral wealth upside down. Self-made, earned wealth--as opposed to inherited wealth--was supposed to be moral money according to the Jacksonians. This fundamental American princple is reflected in movies like *Top Hat* (1935), for example, in which the aristocrats who are born to wealth not only are not the heros or heroines of the story, but they are effete and somewhat disreputable as well. By contrast, Fred Astaire's character, who is nonetheless as wealthy as they are, is a successful dancer in theater revues, has earned his money, and is therefore the hero of the film. But in *Scarface*, the myth collapses; although Tony works hard for his money, because he is a gangster, it is still immoral wealth.

In addition to displaying the bankruptcy of the self-made man myth, *Scarface* also raises troubling questions about the moral values underlying American law enforcement. The brutality of Tony Camonte is matched by the brutality of the police force. The cop, Guarino, early in the film, offers to "work over" Tony to extort a confession and is only prevented from doing so by the arrival of a writ of *Habeas corpus*. Without checking to see if Tony is alone or even in at the film's end, the police begin spraying his home with machine gun fire, killing his sister Cesca. When a wounded Scarface tries to escape at the end, the police gun him down in spite of their overwhelming superiority of numbers. While the existence of such gangsters might have encouraged the police to fight fire with fire, the fact remains that the police show little regard for the law they are sworn to uphold or even the lives of the innocent they are supposed to protect. Indeed, the police captain excuses the sentimental glorifying of the bad men of the old West, because, unlike modern gangsters, they shot it out alone at high noon on a deserted street injuring no one but themselves: he is conveniently forgetting that a shoot out is still an illegal act.

A similar disregard for the law and an acceptance of vigilante justice find expression in the newspaper owner's speech as well. After arguing that guns should be put in the same category as drugs and white slavery, he goes on to argue that we have to make the laws and enforce them even if it means martial law. The army will help, he says, as will the American Legion. The American Legion, however, is not an arm of the law any more than the Ku Klux Klan is. His contemplating using a vigilante group, the American Legion, to fight a band of gangsters indicates that he finds governmental institutions as well as the law enforcement system are powerless. Remember, *Scarface* portrays concerned citizens going to a newspaperman for advice, after all, not a government official.

Because Tony and his ilk are criminals, they must die in the end. However, gangster films succeed not so much because justice is served, but because they make the gangster sympathetic or at least intriguing while he is alive. On the simplest level, Tony's body language makes him more appealing than the upholders of the law; his slouching walk and his gestures make him bend like a human being whereas almost everyone else either sits still or stands erect like a machine. Tony is also charmingly naive, especially in the theater scene, but the film makes clear Scarface is no Gary Cooper in *Mr. Deeds Goes to Town*. Tony is capable of extraordinary violence and his rise to the top begins when he doublecrosses his southside boss. While we are never allowed to forget his viciousness, however, we still feel a certain sympathy with Tony's naivité and earthiness. Like Jay Gatsby in F. Scott Fitzgerald's novel, *The Great Gatsby*, Tony's desire to rise socially and his willingness to work hard to do so earn him our grudging empathy, even if we are shocked at the methods he uses. Like Gatsby, Tony is flawed, but he is also the most sympathetic and intriguing character in the film.

Gangsters were also intriguing to the early depression audiences, in part, because they inhabited the new world of the city. In the 1920's, for the first time, the number of people living on farms actually declined. This was a fact much noted and much feared at the time. William Jennings Bryan, the great populist, called the city "the enemy's country." In spite of the contemporary rural attack on the city as exemplified by the rise of the Ku Klux Klan and prohibition, a new urban culture developed steadily during the twenties. For example, city dwellers built a spate of new museums to house collections of abstract and impressionist art which rural dwellers condemned as worthless. The Museum of Modern Art, which opened in New York City in 1929, was one of them. 1925 saw the appearance of *The New Yorker* magazine, the first magazine totally devoted to the cultural life of one city. This urban culture was still new enough in the early thirties to be interesting in and of itself, and films explored it eagerly, from *Scarface* to the aptly named *City Lights*. Note that *Scarface* is set exclusively in the city, that much of its action takes place at night to dwell on city night life, that many people drink openly in glamorous night clubs in spite of prohibition, and that its characters speak city slang with city accents. The traditional yeoman farmer virtues of Jefferson are inappropriate or even dangerous in this urban night world of the gangster: saloon keepers who remain loyal to their suppliers end up dead.

Gangsters may also have been intriguing because, being immigrants, their existence helped confirm some strong prejudices against immigrants who, in the racist twenties, were blamed for many of this country's problems. The same newspaperman who advocates martial law, for example, also points out that half of the gangsters are not even American citizens. That, however, was not strictly correct, for while many gangsters had emigrated from overseas, most had become naturalized citizens. Al Capone, for example, emigrated from Italy, although by the 1920's he had become an American. Since the late nineteenth century, when the so-called "new immigration" from southern and eastern Europe began, immigrants huddled increasingly in large urban ghettos where crime in fact did increase. Moreover, immigrants tended to depress wage scales of native American by agreeing to work for less. In the 1920's, therefore, the Immigration Act of 1921 and the Johnson Act of 1924 sought to limit immigration, partly to reduce crime and partly to raise wages, but also to preserve American "racial purity" from contamination.

While these restrictive acts did reduce the flow of immigrants to a trickle, those who had already passed through Ellis Island searched for work in newly developing industries, among which were bootlegging and the cinema. Interestingly, many of the men who made movies about gangsters were themselves of immigrant stock. In the early 1930's, while a Russian Jew from Grodno named Meyer Lansky created the biggest criminal syndicate in American history, a Polish Jew from Krasnashiltz, named Jack Warner, became a Hollywood producer of gangster films. Later immigrants like Lansky and Warner found they could not enter Irish-controlled politics or the construction/manufacturing businesses of previous immigrant groups. Many of these later immigrants, therefore, found niches in crime or show business.

Like the crime world portrayed in *Scarface*, the movie industry in the early 1930's was also undergoing the same process of improving its organization and efficiency we have already described. Franklin Roosevelt's National Recovery Administration (NRA), for example, allowed the Motion Picture Association to formulate certain codes which in effect gave the more powerful studios the right to drive off competition and combine further in spite of anti-trust legislation. In Roosevelt's First New Deal, federal programs like the NRA frequently continued former President Hoover's idea of planned scarcity as a method of ending the depression. NRA codes such as those for the Motion Picture Association were thus basically a governmental extension and benediction of the trade association movement of the 1920's. In the Second New Deal starting in 1935, however, Roosevelt deemphasized planned scarcity and turned toward increasing consumer purchasing power, but in the early thirties of the gangster movies, organization which drove off competition was still seen as desirable even in government circles.

As the great studios produced gangster films, they sought to attract the audience with violence. *Scarface,* for example, tries to display gangland brutality accurately, and as a result, there is more violence in *Scarface* than in any other thirties' gangster film. Note the film's depiction of the St. Valentine's Day Massacre. The real massacre took place in 1929 in Chicago when Al Capone's gang shot to death seven members of the rival "Bugs" Moran gang on St. Valentine's Day. The victims were lured to a garage, lined up against a wall, and mown down by submachine gun fire. The massacre caused a national uproar and in the film even the last surviving member of the O'Hara gang, played by Boris Karloff, is shocked at this form of mass execution. Although such violence helps explain part of the film's success, *Scarface's* brutality helped usher in a new era of motion picture censorship.

As early as 1926, the Motion Picture Production Code had already tried to clean up the sexually explicit and violent films of the roaring twenties, but producers had long violated both its letter and spirit. According to the code, good was supposed to triumph in the end and it usually did, but the good rewarded/evil punished endings were frequently tacked on to stories which for the bulk of the film rhapsodized over the pleasures the evil-doers enjoyed. The punishment of evil-doers, therefore, appeared capricious, more a stroke of bad luck than a case of their getting their just deserts. Moreover, as we have seen, in gangster films, the "evil" criminal often appeared more glamorous and sometimes more humane than the inept cop who was physically plain and frequently just as brutal. This lack of clear-cut morality in movies and the violence which accompanied it came under attack from many groups, the most famous of which was the Catholic Legion of Decency. In 1933, the Legion was set up by Catholic clergy and laymen to bring economic reprisals against those who disobeyed the production code. One of the first to feel the effects of the Legion's efforts was Mae West, whose good humored vulgarity led her to be labeled box office poison. Her career never fully recovered. Naturally, gangster films likewise came in for a great deal of criticism. The Legion's pressure on studios succeeded in getting the crude excesses of realism removed from such films, but, also, much of the honesty as well.

After the inauguration of Franklin Roosevelt in 1933, realistically brutal gangster films gave way to escapism; costume dramas, adaptations of the classics, and spectacular musicals replaced the grimy, violent world of the gangster. Whereas the gangster had lived in a twilight world, the new escapist films provided a brilliantly lit, dazzling world where even the polished dance floors sparkle. Some of the brightness may reflect the optimism of the New Deal itself; happy days are here again--at least on the screen. Some of these changes resulted from the threat posed by the Catholic Legion of Decency and other groups disturbed over the violence and sex of the gangster films. But some of the rage for big budget spectaculars which spelled the death of the gangster epics arose from major technical improvements in motion pictures techniques.

As everyone knows, the development of talking movies created problems for the motion picture industry from 1927 onward. Famous actors' careers were smashed when their voices were found to be inappropriate to the "talkies," and the indiscriminate use of non-English- speaking foreign talent practically vanished. More important, to achieve even the scratchy sound of Al Jolson's *Jazz Singer*, the camera had to be hidden away behind a glass screen so that the recording equipment would not pick up its whir. Since the movie set had to be kept absolutely quiet, large sound stages had to be built so that all action could be filmed indoors. The huge bankroll it took to build these sound stages helps explain the growth of the big studio system in Hollywood around 1930. With a capital investment of $2 billion and employing 325,000 people, movies had indeed become big business.

Not only did erecting the huge sound stages determine which studios would survive and which would not, but the sound stages also determined what kind of story could be filmed. Movies filmed outside the sound stages, such as westerns brilliantly lit by natural sunlight outdoors, became practically impossible to produce shortly after the arrival of sound, because such location sets were too noisy and there was no place to hide the microphone. Imagine filming a western on the plains of Texas with the limitations which then existed? By contrast, the twilight indoor world of the gangster recommended itself for the use of early sound. Microphones could be suspended from a non-existent ceiling of a stage set and further camouflaged by darkening the room. As we have already noted, gangster films usually took place at night, indoors, precisely the kind of setting most easy to film in during the early days of sound. Finally, the sounds we associate with the gangster film could be easily reproduced in the early days of the talkies. Indeed, the squealing of a car's brakes and the harsh bark of a Tommy gun defined the gangster film and helped confirm its reality.

What became of the gangster in film? Influenced by New Deal optimism that reform was possible and knuckling under to the threat of the Legion of Decency which wanted to see good rewarded, the creators of gangster films turned their Scarfaces into G-men. Sometimes the same actor played both roles. James Cagney as Tommy Powers helped invent the gangster role in *Public Enemy* (1931), but by 1935, in *G-Men* , Cagney was playing a federal law enforcement officer fighting on the side of right. This metamorphosis raises disturbing questions, however. Can the amoral toughness of Scarface be made to serve the public good merely by pinning a badge on it? Moreover, if the local cop on the beat remains corrupt or inept, as they generally are in G-men movies, how can a federal lawman alone solve the problem of gangsterism? Just how much can the private citizen rely exclusively on the powers of the federal government?

Although gangsters like *Scarface* stopped being film heroes by 1933, and turned into the vile prey the G-men tracked down and destroyed, actual gangsterism itself did not disappear. Instead, organized crime, like film gangsters, changed too. With the repeal of Prohibition by the 21st Amendment in 1933, liquor was no longer an illegal business, and the gigantic profits built up by gangs like Capone's could no longer be obtained. Rather than disperse, however, organized crime entered so-called legitimate businesses like gambling casinos, infiltrated labor unions, corrupted police forces, and turned huge profits from still illegal prostitution and later the drug trade. After World War II, mob activities were exposed and condemned in films like *On the Waterfront*, *The French Connection*, and *Serpico*, and on television by *The Untouchables* (about the FBI and Elliot Ness) and, more recently, by *Miami Vice*. In all these works, however, the existence of organized crime is taken for granted. Moreover, crime itself is rarely destroyed; in *The French Connection*, the big fish gets away, and Serpico is driven from the New York police force and lives in fear of his life.

Especially with television series, while a particular criminal may be eliminated one week, the mob will inevitably produce another one by next week. The inevitability of organized crime seems to be accepted in the movies and perhaps in real life in a way it was not in 1932 when *Scarface* was released. Tony Camonte may have been easy to destroy as he staggered, sniveling, from his fortress-like apartment, but in real life, rooting out crime has proved to be far more difficult.

Scarface - Instructor's Guide

1. Give a brief history of the Prohibition movement from 1900 to 1920 and explain why the 18th Amendment passed when it did. James H. Timberlake, *Prohibition and the Progressive Crusade* (1963) is a helpful source.

2. Did prohibition cause gangsterism in the 1920's, or had gangsters been there already and simply taken advantage to provide a service to many Americans? What role did the mafia and Sicilian immigration play in the rise of gangsers like Capone?

3. Analyze why cities grew in size and prestige during the 1920's and give examples of a new urban culture which developed during this period. In your answer, you should consider all the following;

   1. growth of spectator sports
   2. the growth of the nightclub
   3. changes in fashion for men and women
   4. jazz

4. Write a brief biographical sketch, assessing the significance of any or all of the following:

   1. Al Capone
   2. Lucky Luciano
   3. Meyer Lansky
   4. Bugsy Malone

5. Write a book report, indicating the author's hypothesis and relating events in the film to events in the book, for any or all of the following:

   1. Andrew Bergman, *We're in the Money: Depression America and its Films* (1971)
   2. John Braeman, *et. al.*, eds. *Change and Continuity in Twentieth Century*

America; the 1920's (1968)

3. A. D. Chandler, *The Visible Hand* (1977) about business management

4. N. H. Clark, *Deliver Us From Evil: An Interpretation of American Prohibition* (1976)

5. Robert Divine, *American Immigration Policy* (1957)

6. Samuel Haber, *Efficiency and Uplift: Scientific Management in the Progressive Era, 1890-1920* (1964)

7. Jenna Weissman Joselit, *Our Gang: Jewish Crime and the New York Jewish Community, 1900-1940* (1983)

8. Elting E. Morison, *From Know-How to Nowhere; The Development of American Technology* (1974)

9. Humbert S. Nelli, *The Business of Crime* (1976)

10. Allan Nevins and Frank E. Hill, *Ford* (in 3 vols. 1954-1963)

11. F. D. Pasley, *Al Capone: the Biography of a Self Made Man* (1930)

6. Choose one of the books above and find the scholarly reviews of it in two or more of the following journals:

1. *The American Historical Review* (published by The American Historical Association)

2. *Journal of American History* (published by The Organization of American Historians)

3. *History Teacher*

4. *History, Review of New Books*

Compare and contrast the reviews. What did the reviewers like or dislike and why?

7. Describe the growth of organized crime, especially the career of Meyer Lansky, discussing why he held his 1933 meeting of crime heads in New York. Evaluate its success. How did crime change during the thirties?

The Grapes of Wrath - Happy Days Are Not Yet Here Again

The Grapes of Wrath was made in 1939, but released in 1940. 1939 was the year World War II began in Europe. 1939 also saw the death of FDR's New Deal, when Franklin Roosevelt's domestic reform coalition was destroyed by the disasters of the 1937 Supreme Court-packing scheme, the recession of 1937-38, and the unsuccessful attempt to purge the Democratic party of disloyal southern Congressmen. The Depression was nine years old, and happy days were not yet here again. *The Grapes of Wrath*, reflects these grim facts of life. Although the film still praises the New Deal and suggests that things will be getting better soon, it nonetheless explores the enormous personal cost of the Depression and calls for justice on the behalf of the oppressed. In its depiction of the migrant workers' plight, *The Grapes of Wrath* sets a new standard of honest realism. However, the film has a hard time explaining the causes of the problems it portrays. Why, for example, were there migrant farm workers in the first place? The film works itself into a basic paradox: overly attached to a nostalgic version of the yeoman farmer myth, *The Grapes of Wrath* condemns the increasing tempo of capitalist farming and the development of agro-business while at the same time praising the New Deal which encouraged both developments.

In the film, modern capitalist farming becomes synonymous with machines which are opposed to everything which is natural, organic, and humane. The huge caterpillar tractors which bulldoze Muley's shack remind one of the German tanks which led the blitzkrieg into Poland in September, 1939. The tractors are instruments of war used by a vaguely defined corporation to drive people off the land. Moreover, it is an unequal war, because there is no particular villain to do away with. Muley wants to know whom he should shoot to keep his farm, but the representative of the Shawnee Land and Title company driving the tractor says he doesn't know who is to blame. Neither did most Americans in the 1930's know whom to blame for the loss of their jobs, the reduction in their standard of living, or the repossession of the consumer goods they had bought in the booming 1920's. As a result, they could strongly identify with Muley's hopeless attempts to battle twentieth century agro-business corporations with the weapons of nineteenth century frontier America.

The problem, of course, was that American agriculture was no longer in its frontier stage. Increasingly in the nineteenth century, American farmers had gone into cash crop farming. This meant their year's profits depended on the price one or maybe two crops would fetch at harvest time. With all his eggs in one basket, so to speak, the farmer was at the mercy of fluctuations in the international market price of his crop. Grain failures in Russia and Argentina in the mid-1890's, for example, caused a shortage on the international market and the price of American wheat temporarily improved.

In addition to foreign competition, farmers had to do battle with the railroads as well. The Iron Horse was for many farmers the only practicable way to get their goods to market over the vast expanses of the Great Plains. As railroads moved onto the plains, there were increased distances between lines, and farmers living near one railroad were usually obliged to ship their grain on that line only. Knowing this, railroads frequently charged more for short distances where they had a monopoly than they did for long distances where they had to compete with other lines. This long-haul/short haul problem was not the only abuse, as far as farmers were concerned. The railroads' secret rebates and their willingness to foreclose quickly on the farm mortgages they held also angered the mid-west.

Thus it was that farmers had organized into Granges, the Farmers' Alliances, and later the Populist party in an attempt to control what they regarded as railroad price gouging, and hence regulate their farms' profits. Grange-inspired railroad commissions began to set maximum rates and forbade rate discrimination. In Illinois, the railroads challenged these regulations, but in 1876, the Supreme Court upheld the commission's rules, declaring railroads to be public highways and hence under the jurisdiction of individual states. Ten years later, however, the mid-western farmers' attempt to control the railroads was severely limited by the *Wabash* case, in which the Court ruled that such state commissions could only regulate *intrastate* trade, but that *interstate* commerce, that is trade between the states, was clearly the responsibility of the federal government alone. Accordingly, the Interstate Commerce Commission was created in 1887, but it proved to be of almost no value to farmers beset by high railroad rates; of the first 16 cases brought before the Commission, 15 were decided in favor of the railroads.

These men who battled the railroads in Congress and the Courts were no longer the yeoman farmers of Jefferson's day who grew a little of everything and were therefore relatively independent. On the contrary, these were capitalist farmers selling a product for profit. The farmers were undergoing the same process of organization and specialization which characterized business in the industrial revolution.

Small farmers, moreover, were trying to become big farmers in spite of paying lip service to the Jeffersonian yeoman ideal. They mortgaged their farms to purchase more land and labor-saving machinery like the combine and thresher to farm the land efficiently. As a result, falling crop prices frequently meant banks foreclosed on farm mortages as farmers could no longer make their payments. Small farmers, therefore, organized together to create cooperative banks and grain elevators, sometimes under the auspices of the Grange, in order to take advantage of the benefits large farmers enjoyed. The myth of the yeoman farmer may have prescribed sturdy independence made possible by self-sufficiency, but most farmers in late nineteenth century America were trying to make the switch to large cash crop capitalist farming. Those who failed to do so lost their farms and became sharecroppers or tenants. And many did. By 1900, one fourth of all farms in Kansas were farmed as sharecropping ventures. In the

1920's, and especially in the 1930's, this process of consolidation, which had begun before the turn of the century, increased in tempo.

It is against this background that *The Grapes of Wrath* is set and against which it must be evaluated. The Joads, who are driven off the land, are sharecroppers farming land someone else owns. Muley, of course, disputes the bank's claim, saying the land is his by virtue of his having lived and worked on it. Basically, he is offering here the nineteenth century notion of squatter's rights to lay claim to ownership. This philosophy may have underlaid the Homestead Act of 1862, but it is no longer appropriate to twentieth century realities. Indeed, *The Grapes of Wrath* struggles to explain who is to blame for the Joads' eviction, and finally offers a vague and not very satisfactory answer to that question.

In *The Grapes of Wrath*, it is the times that are at fault, not people. The radical discontent of Steinbeck's novel, upon which the film is based, is rejected in favor of a watered down, almost religious populism. The Joads are evicted by the instruments of faceless institutions which they cannot understand or control. The bank's representative who bulldozes down Muley's house is wearing a mask which makes him look more like a machine than a human being. Although impersonal forces may be at fault, however, the film makes clear that the law itself is not to blame for the migrants' difficulties. The preacher Casey exonerates law enforcement officers, blaming the migrants' problems on the scab security men, "them tin-badge fellas they call guards." By contrast, the film makes much of the hostility of nature, presenting haunting images of the Oklahoma dustbowl's desolation. Even the Joads' trip out West takes them through the forbidding American desert. But the farmer could no more punish nature for its harshness than he could punish faceless, machine-like institutions. As Casey says, "Maybe there ain't no sin and there ain't no virtue. It's just what people do." In short, the message of *The Grapes of Wrath* is that no one is really to blame, and therefore no one should really be punished.

If the film cannot explain who caused the Joads' problems, it strongly endorses government relief efforts which mitigate their suffering. These relief programs were the great shining success of Franklin Roosevelt's New Deal and created an almost personal bond between Roosevelt and millions of Americans. This bond is clearly seen in *The Grapes of Wrath* where the manager of the government-run migrant camp looks exactly like Franklin Roosevelt and even uses a cigarette holder similar to the president's. This manager oversees a relief effort which renews a sense of human dignity in the by now emotionally battered Joad family. In a sense, it is the manager who is the hero of the film. Tom Joad, played by Henry Fonda, must flee in the night as an outlaw because he killed a man in anger, while by contrast, the camp manager in his spotlessly clean clothes works within the government system to provide some measure of comfort for the surviving Joads. The Joads look to him, not to Tom and certainly not to Tom's father, for help.

By placing the government camp episode at the end, the film endorses

Roosevelt and the New Deal in a way Steinbeck's novel never did. In the novel, the government camp episode occurs in the middle of the book. Though the Joads were delighted with the camp, they are forced to leave it to find work because "You can't eat toilets," as Ma remarks. According to Steinbeck, the government camp was a decent relief effort, but it failed to address the real problems of lack of jobs and pitiful wages. Steinbeck's scathing denunciation of the New Deal relief programs as well-intentioned though practically useless finds no place in the film made from his book. Like the novel, the film shows the Joad family proceeding from one degradation to another, becoming more animal-like as the story progresses, until they finally reach the government camp. As the film ends, the Joads leave the camp restored in body and spirit, with jobs, we are encouraged to believe, waiting for them a little farther up the road. In both novel and film, the government camp is associated with F. D. R.'s New Deal, but in the novel the New Deal fails, while in the film the New Deal triumphs--although at enormous personal cost. By the time the Joad family leaves the camp, the grandparents are dead, Connie has run off, Preacher Casey's head has been smashed in, and Tom is on the run as a fugitive from justice.

Steinbeck's criticisms of New Deal programs in his novel are justified to some extent, for it was the large farmer, not the sharecropper, who benefited most from New Deal programs. While relief programs like the Federal Emergency Relief Administration (FERA), the Public Works Administration (PWA), and the Works Progress Administration (WPA) did seek to put unemployed people like farmers to work, the farm programs of the first New Deal themselves continued the concept of planned scarcity begun in the Hoover administration. Even though many went hungry, farm products and animals were destroyed to create a scarcity which would increase the prices for all farm goods. As a result, after a decade of decline, farm income actually doubled by 1935, but much of that income was in the form of government paid subsidies not to cultivate all the land. Moreover, most of the subsidies went to large farmers. In order to reduce the acreage they farmed and so receive government subsidies, large land-owners forced tenants and sharecroppers like the Joads off their land, and let it lie fallow as the government prescribed. Although farm efficiency dramatically increased with larger, better run farms, at least three million people were driven off the land in the thirties.

Roosevelt abandoned the planned scarcity approach of the first Agricultural Adjustment Administration (AAA) when that program was declared unconstitutional in 1935, but again, the sharecropper and tenant did not benefit much. The Second AAA of 1936 introduced a soil conservation system of benefit payments, but by 1936 significant crop reduction had already been achieved, partly as a result of the first New Deal scarcity policies and partly as a result of the severe drought of 1933-1936. Only in 1935 and afterwards did Roosevelt really turn his attention to to plight of small farmers and sharecroppers like the Joads, and even then, such programs as the Resettlement Administration barely made a dent in the enormous number of landless farmers. The Farm Security Administration (FSA), for example, was supposed to lend money to sharecroppers to enable them to buy their own land, but it lent money to only 2% of the nation's tenant farmers.

Nor did conditions for sharecroppers improve as the New Deal got older. After 1937, Roosevelt no longer commanded the huge bipartisan reform coalition he had in 1933, and was therefore in no position to pass more legislation to benefit small farmers even had he wanted to. Moreover, as events in Europe and the Far East became more threatening, Roosevelt's attention, like that of many Americans, shifted to foreign affairs. Like most presidents, Roosevelt found his foreign affairs coalition different from and hostile to his domestic reform coalition. The more Roosevelt addressed the problem of Hitler in Europe, the less time he had for the Joads of Oklahoma.

By the time *The Grapes of Wrath* was released, World War II had broken out in Europe, and no one watching the film could mistake the political message of the government migrant camp into which the Joads' truck finally coasts. For the govenment camp is a miniature United States federal government. It is an elected, representative democracy, self-policing and isolated from the rest of the world just as the United States was isolated from Europe and Japan by huge oceans. When subversive agents infiltrate the camp to provoke a riot, the camp men hustle them out with virtually no violence, and as a result, forestall a threatened invasion by semi-legal thugs. In Europe unemployed ruffians had become the cadres of Hitler's Brown Shirts and Mussolini's Black Shirts, but in the United States groups of unemployed youths were dispersed in the Civilian Conservation Corps (CCC), employed by the WPA, or at any rate given new reason to hope in government-run migrant camps. *The Grapes of Wrath*'s message about fascism is "it can't happen here."

There were, of course, real threats to American democracy in the 1930's. Demagogues of the far right questioned the principles of American democracy just as Hitler had ridiculed the democracy of Germany's Weimar Republic. The two most famous of these American right-wingers were Huey Long, the "Kingfish" from Louisiana, and Father Coughlin, the radio priest.

As governor of Louisiana, Huey Long ruled the state in a completely autocratic manner with almost no regard for the principles of democracy. In 1930, Long moved his executive dictatorship to Washington when he was elected senator from Louisiana. He became very popular with his Share the Wealth program which was designed, in his words, to make "every man a king." To do so, he promised to tax large fortunes out of existence and distribute the proceeds to the poor, thus immediately ending the depression. Tempting as the program was to a depression age America, Long's ideas had less to do with economic realities and more to do with advancing his personal domination over American politics. In 1935, Long was assassinated by the son of a man he had ruined in Louisiana. Nonetheless, Long's mailing list of over seven million people testifies to his popularity.

Though never in elective office, Father Coughlin, the Detroit radio priest, also presented a sharp challenge to American democratic principles. A Roman Catholic priest, Father Coughlin in his radio broadcasts advocated a program suspiciously close to Hitler's Fascism. Coughlin urged the nationalization of banks, utilities, and natural resources, and in 1938, he founded the Christian Front which was openly anti-semitic and anti-democratic. By 1934, Coughlin was denouncing the New Deal as the "Pagan Deal," and in 1936 he supported North Dakota Congressman William Lemke against Roosevelt.

Although Roosevelt labeled such men the "lunatic fringe," there was no denying their popularity. Indeed, some historians argue that Roosevelt pushed forward with the second New Deal in 1935 in order to head off more radical and less realistic plans like Long's Share the Wealth program, and to undercut critics like Coughlin. Second New Deal programs like Social Security, therefore, addressed themselves to those still suffering from the depression. Once again, however, just as with the AAA, farmers were given little direct help even from these second New Deal programs. After all, farmers were not covered at all by the original Social Security System of 1935, and even if they had been eligible, the system rewarded only those currently employed who might lose their jobs later; if one was currently out of work like the Joads, you could receive no benefits from social security.

It is clear then that no one suffered more from the depression than the dispossessed farmers portrayed in *The Grapes of Wrath*, yet the film never suggests they might fall under the spell of demagogues from either political extreme or "lunatic fringe." Those who buck the system are accused of being "Red" agitators, of course. The film makes clear they are not really card-carrying communists, but rather just men who don't want to be cheated. Tom Joad goes off to become a labor organizer, but that occurs off screen, and moreover, the way Henry Fonda plays Tom there is nothing of the ideologue about him. The only time the migrants organize in the film is in the government camp, a New Deal surrogate; the ex-farmers organize a miniature republic, not a communist party, and certainly not a dictatorial regime. According to *The Grapes of Wrath*, then, those who might have the greatest reason to fall under the influence of an American Hitler or become communists are proof against such temptation.

Like the New Deal itself which was new without being revolutionary, *The Grapes of Wrath* was honest without being pessimistic. While earlier films of the thirties had been escapist, suggesting there were no real problems, and others had suggested all could be made well again if only a few mean-spirited villains were removed, *The Grapes of Wrath* squarely faces up to the personal disasters of the Great Depression and offers reason to hope without indulging in quick fixes or contrived happy endings. Instead, the film suggests that the inherent decency of the American people, combined with the strength of their democratic heritage, would somehow see the nation and its people through.

In 1940, when *The Grapes of Wrath* was released, no one could know that within a year's time, that decency and American faith in democracy would be challenged by foes abroad as deadly as the depression at home. For, if the United States did not succumb to fascism, most of Europe had. In 1941, the United States went to war on a global scale fighting the most costly war in terms of human life and resources the nation had ever been involved in. Ironically, it was the war which achieved economic recovery, not the New Deal; although 13 million people had been unemployed in 1933 when Roosevelt assumed office, in 1940, after seven years of New Deal,11 million people remained unemployed. By late 1942, however, a labor shortage had developed, and women increasingly took jobs in industry to free men for combat overseas. Migrant farmers like the Joads either joined the armed services or went to work in the burgeoning defense industries of southern California. The depression was finally over, but a gnawing sense of unease continued to grip America even in the halcyon days of the 1950's; could the *The Grapes of Wrath* occur again?

The Grapes of Wrath - Instructor's Guide

1. Write a book report on any or all of the following, giving the author's hypothesis and relating events in the book to events in the film:

   1. Bernard Bellush, *The Failure of the NRA* (1975)
   2. Alan Brinkley, *Voices of Protest Huey Long, Father Coughlin, and the Great Depression* (1982)
   3. David E. Conrad, *The Forgotten Farmers: The Story of Sharecroppers in the New Deal* (1965)
   4. Abraham Hoffman, *Unwanted Mexican-Americans in the Great Depression*, (1974)
   5. William E. Leuchtenburg, *Franklin Roosevelt and the New Deal* (1963)
   6. Richard H. Pells, *Radical Visions and American Dreams: Cultural and Social Thought in the Depression Years* (1973)
   7. Van L. Perkins, *Crisis in Agriculture: The Agricultural Adjustment Administration and the New Deal* (1969)
   8. T. Harry Williams, *Huey Long: A Biography* (1969)
   9. Raymond Wolters, *Negroes and the Great Depression: The Problem of Economic Recovery* (1970)
   10. Donald Worster, *Dust Bowl: The Southern Plains in the 1930's* (1979)

2. Write a brief biographical sketch and assess the significance of any or all of the following:

   1. John Steinbeck

2. Huey Long
3. Father Coughlin
4. Harry Hopkins
5. Henry Wallace
6. John L. Lewis

3. After reading John Steinbeck's novel, *The Grapes of Wrath*, examine the differences in outlook and tone between the novel and the fiim. Is anything left out? Is anything added? What effect is thus created? Cite specific examples.

4. How and why were the First and Second AAA's different?

5. Discuss the growth of left wing politics during the Depression thirties. D. R. McCoy, *Angry Voices: Left-of-Center Politics in the New Deal Era* (1958) is a useful source.

6. Discuss the growth of labor union organization in the 1930's.

7. Account for the fact that Roosevelt was unable to pass more reform legislation after 1937. In your answer, you should consider the Supreme Court fight of 1937, the recession of 1937, the purge of the democratic party (1938), and the coming of World War II.

Top Hat - Escapism and American Dance

Top Hat, released in 1935, is an example of the escapist films so popular in the early thirties' Depression years. However, while most of the other lavishly produced fantasies have faded into oblivion, *Top Hat* remains as popular today as it was when it was made. Certainly, the Irving Berlin music, the witty dialogue, and the lavish sets all work to please the audience, but it is the spectacular dancing of Fred Astaire and Ginger Rogers that makes the film special. Although Astaire and Rogers had teamed up before in *Flying Down to Rio*, never had their dancing, Berlin's music, the dialogue, and setting all blended together so perfectly. Moreover, *Top Hat* changed definitively the way musicals were made by allowing the dance itself to advance the story line. *Top Hat* was also significant in the history of dance, for in it Fred Astaire created a fleeting synthesis of the newest developments in *avant garde* ballet with the popularity and power of vaudeville dance. Finally, the murky moral background of Ginger Rogers' character was symptomatic of the problematical position of women in thirties' escapist films, when Hollywood tried to reconcile the image of independent women pioneered in the late twenties with a revived insistence on "femininity."

In 1935, when *Top Hat* was made, 15 million people were out of work, about 25% of the labor force. Even more people were underemployed, either working only part-time for less than a standard wage or working at a job far below their training. The memory of the Hoovervilles, those shanty towns thrown up by the unemployed along railroad sidings, was still alive. New Deal relief measures had begun to make a dent in the unemployment problem, but the first New Deal recovery programs had only stabilized the faltering American economy. Franklin Roosevelt's optimistic assertion that we had nothing to fear but fear itself had taken away some of the panic, but Americans still feared the breadlines and the disgrace unemployment might bring.

The movie industry responded to these disasters by turning out a flood of lavishly produced romantic comedies set in faraway places which portrayed the rich in ridiculously silly situations. Most of these comedies' plots depended on a simple, almost simple-minded misunderstanding which the audience confidently expected to be resolved easily by the last reel. Many of these early thirties films were filmed productions of successful Broadway plays, many of which dealt with cases of mistaken identity. The message of these early comedies, then, was that the rich were just like us, only sillier, and that some problems at least were capable of easy solutions.

Top Hat, obviously, fits this genre of escapist films. Dale Tremont, played by Ginger Rogers, mistakes Jerry Travers, played by Fred Astaire, for the husband of her best friend Madge, and accordingly repulses his early advances. She is torn between her love for Jerry and her honorable concern for Madge, but her moral dilemma is quickly resolved when she discovers at the end who Jerry really is. Most of the moral problems of the Depression, such as whether or not to leave your family in search of a job, could not be solved so easily, but it must have been comforting to see that some dilemmas could be.   Indeed, the ultimate problem in *Top Hat*, the supposed marriage between Dale and Bedini, her Italian dress designer, is likewise solved by a case of mistaken identity; the marriage is invalid because Bates, the English butler, was masquerading as a clergyman when he married the couple.

Top Hat is also escapist in its selection of a foreign locale.   Like its predecessor, *Flying Down to Rio*, this Astaire/Rogers vehicle uses a romantic, mysterious place, Venice, to create a never-never-land beyond the rainbow where dreams really do come true.   The dreamlike quality of Venice is reinforced by the fact that the Venice sets are as artificial as the case of mistaken identity is trivial. Gleaming bright and extremely spacious, the film's Venice is a far cry from the real Venice with its narrow streets and befouled canals.   The grinding poverty of Mussolini's real Italy finds no place in the film's sets in which "peasants" dressed in satin and silk dance the Picalino on a huge polished floor.

Like many black and white movies of the early thirties, *Top Hat* grapples with the problems of portraying luxury without benefit of color.   *Top Hat* solves this difficulty by draping the sets and people in shining fabrics associated with luxury.   Not only do the flawlessly polished floors gleam, but do so the actors! Even the top hat against which roll the film's opening credits shines back at the audience.   Another way of indicating luxury is to show huge rooms in which there is an extravagant waste of space.   Luxury suites in 1930's hotels were indeed bigger than they are today, but no rooms were 60 feet wide with 18 foot ceilings like the Bridal Suite in Venice!

Such extravagant use of space and luxury fabrics, however, masked a severe limitation with which thirties movies had to cope: in the early thirties, new sound techniques were not sufficiently improved to allow filming on location where extraneous noise could ruin a scene and where there was no place to hide the microphones.   Like gangster films, therefore, escapist films such as *Top Hat* utilized instead indoor sets made possible by the huge sound stages the new movie studios were building.   Indeed, the necessity for building such expensive sound stages drove many smaller studios out of business and concentrated movie making capabilities in the hands of a few giants.   This pattern of oligopoly followed a trend already well established in the business community during the 1920's when, for example, General Motors, Ford, and Chrysler became the Big Three of the American automobile industry.   Especially for musicals where sound had to be carefully controlled, movie soundstages were decorated to *suggest* a foreign locale such as Venice by adding a few canals and a bridge or two, but the decoration was carefully planned to permit open spaces for dance numbers and concealed overhead boom mikes.

Top Hat, then, was like many artificial soundstage comedies of the early thirties.   But unlike most, *Top Hat* boasted the talent of Fred Astaire, considered by many dancers to be the best American male dancer of the twentieth century.

Astaire's genius lies less in his skill or technique, which is of course considerable, but rather in his grace and ability to fit dance step to music the way George Balanchine would do with classical ballet. To understand the significance of Astaire's dancing, we must first learn a bit about the state of dance on the eve of the 1930's.

In the late nineteenth century, a split developed in ballet between the Parisian school of dance, on the one hand, which was production oriented and used poorly trained dancers, and, on the other hand, the Russian school of ballet associated with Marius Petipa, who used dancers rigorously trained in classical, almost rigid dance patterns. The Parisian school of dance slowly developed into the vaudeville and Broadway musical of the early twentieth century, both of which emphasized lavish sets and costumes, popular music, and large troupes of adequately, although by no means perfectly, trained dancers. The Russian school, on the other hand, went on to produce the great classical ballets like *Swan Lake* and *Sleeping Beauty*, and Petipa continued to train dancers from an early age, but these perfectly trained dancers were confined in static dancing formulas which emphasized leg and arm placement punctuated by dramatic turns and leaps.

This Russian philosophy was challenged at the turn of the century by the great American dancer, Isadora Duncan, who developed a far more fluid style in which the back itself bends and turns rather than remaining rigid while only the arms and legs move as in the Petipa Russian model, but Duncan's insistence on spontaneity prevented her from writing down the new steps, and so her influence was accordingly limited. More imortant, therefore, was Sergei Diaghilev, the great ballet empresario, who, in 1909, gathered around him in Paris many Russian dancers upset with the confining rules of the Bolshoi. Utilizing new choreography of Michel Fokine, Diaghilev's dramatic male dancer, Nijinski, began to bend and twist his body to express a greater range of emotion. These movements were later extended by Martha Graham to whom most modern dance troupes in the country, from Alvin Ailey to the Joffrey ballet, are indebted.

Fred Astaire came out of the tradition of vaudeville and Broadway dance and by no means can be considered a classical ballet dancer, but he benefited from the revived interest in male dancing Nijinski had created. Moreover, Astaire did adopt Duncan's ideas on the use of the fluid back which became the distinguishing feature of American ballet dancers of the twentieth century. The result, then, is a temporary fusion of the glamour and popularity of vaudeville with the emotional expressiveness of modern dance. Note how Astaire not only bends from the waist like a Barbie Doll, but he also moves in such a way as to suggest his entire torso is swaying like a rope. Of course, the rib cage prevents the chest from bending in half, but Astaire's fluid movements make us believe for a moment that it can. Moreover, Astaire not only dances *in front of* the spectacular sets characteristic of the Broadway revue, he dances *with* them. For example, in *Top Hat* when Astaire breaks into an exuberant dance in his friend's hotel suite, thus awakening Dale in the room below, he taps out the rhythm with his feet while at the same time drumming on pieces of furniture. As the number ends, he is dancing with a statue when Dale knocks on the door.

Astaire's dancing is characterized by a grace almost all dancers envy. Though expert in his movements, he does not try to impress us with his skill. Contrast his style with that of Gene Kelly, for example, and Astaire emerges as the Cary Grant of dance; light, quick, almost feline in his graceful movements, he differs markedly from Kelly who dazzles with his sheer energy and skill. Where Kelly is exhausted from his dance routine, one can't imagine Astaire gasping for breath even after the most grueling number.

Astaire pioneered the "one take" dance number in which the camera films the entire dance sequence in one piece rather than shooting a series of takes which are later joined together, such as one sees in *Flashdance*. This procedure implies, of course, that any mistake means the entire dance number must be shot again from the beginning, but Astaire guarded against this possibility by practicing extensively with his partner before the cameras ever rolled. The more he practiced, the more he tinkered. As a result, the final costumes and even the sets were sometimes not completed before the final dress rehearsals. In *Top Hat* this produced unexpected results. Ginger Rogers' feathered dress for the "Cheek to Cheek" number was unavailable before the final dress rehearsal. When she wore it during the dress rehearsal, the loosely glued feathers began to fly off in all directions. Everyone dreaded the final "take," but as luck would have it, the feathers stayed on for the sequence which became part of the movie we see today.

Astaire's insistence on shooting in one take creates a fluid camera movement which parallels the sweeping grace of his own dancing. The camera in Astaire's films moves side to side and in and out, but only once in the entire film *Top Hat* does the it move up and down. The Picalino number at the end is shot from all kinds of camera angles and the pieces are intercut in the finished film. Significantly, however, when Astaire and Rogers dance in this same dance sequence, the camera remains at eye level for the duration of their part of the dance. Astaire had begun his career in Broadway where the audience is stationary, and the camera work in his dance sequences on film reflects that heritage. By contrast, the Picalino number of the chorus developed from the dance camera work pioneered by Busby Berkeley.

Berkeley was responsible for this dramatic new use of the camera in a rash of musicals like *Gold Diggers of 1933* in the early thirties. Using huge troops of, at best, adequately trained dancers, Berkeley created mechanistic routines in which the dancers look more like cogs in a machine than people dancing. In Berkeley numbers, dancers sometimes lie on the stage, moving their bodies to create pleasing, kaleidoscopic, geometric dance patterns. The camera works above, below, and to the side of the developing dance patterns, but almost never at eye level. Berkeley tried to combat the idea that the movie musical was merely a filmed stage show by putting the camera in places a Broadway audience could never be. The results are sometimes spectacular, but by no means can a Busby

Berkeley film be considered dance in its highest form. Rather, a Berkeley musical has more in common with an army troop parade or a marching college band at halftime.

Astaire's camera work for his dance sequences is not the only difference between earlier Hollywood musicals and his own; more important, in Astaire's films the dance become central to the developing storyline rather than serving as an interlude after which the story continues again. In previous musicals, the dance was an adjunct to the storyline which usually involved show people and chorus girls who dashed onstage for big production numbers á la Berkeley and who then came backstage to talk the storyline along. By contrast, Astaire woos *in* the dance itself, not exclusively before or after it. In the "Lovely Day" sequence in a London park, for example, he woos Dale first in song and then in dance. She responds by at first ignoring him, then dancing alongside him, and finally dancing with him, ending the number sitting in the exact same pose as Jerry. The dance, then, becomes a way to win Dale and also reflects her feelings for Jerry. Indeed, the Astaire dance sequences become psychological commentary. In the "Top Hat" number from which the film gets its name, for example, Astaire uses his cane to mow down the advancing army of elegantly attired rivals, just as later in the film he will dispense with Bedini, his rival to Dale's hand. The only time in the film Dale begins singing first, thereby initiating a romantic interlude, is in the Picalino number at the end where, although technically married to Bedini for all she knows, she has accepted Jerry and agreed to marry him. As a willing partner in the love match for the first time in the film, she can begin the wooing process through song and dance.

Dale's moral position remains equivocal throughout the film as her seemingly nonchalant attitude toward her marriage to Bedini suggests, but some of this moral equivocation is symptomatic of a change in the movie industry's view of women generally. When silent movies first began to be made commercially in the World War I period, women were generally portrayed as passive and weak; things happened *to* such heroines, but they rarely *caused* things to happen. By contrast, in the 1920's, women's improved economic and social standing outside the movie theater was reflected inside the theater in the images on the silver screen; new female stars, from Clara Bow to Joan Crawford, initiated the action. The flappers of twenties silents frantically danced their way to the top, picking up and dropping male admirers at will. A vamp like Theda Bara used her wiles to entrap men and make them serve her. Such suggestive films as *Up in Mabel's Room*, for example, rarely showed on celluloid anything as titillating as the title would suggest, but such films did make clear that women were sexually active, in the work force, and independent.

In fact, movies were reflecting a social phenomenon going on in real life. More women in the 1920's worked outside the home than had ever done so before in American history; in 1920, 8.4 million women were in the labor force while in 1930 that figure had grown to 10.6 million. They worked primarily in the burgeoning service industries as waitresses, telephone operators, and secretaries. As both business and government discovered they needed more bureaucrats to guarantee smoothly functioning operations, these bureaucrats required secretaries to draft, type, and send the memos they sent to one another. Such service industry jobs did not require brute strength; rather, they stressed fine motor agility, such as the ability to hit the right typewriter keys or connect the right telephone wire on the switchboard. As a result, young women increasingly worked outside the home after school and before marriage.

In the busy work force, these young women no longer had the services of maids to dress their hair or help them put on complicated clothing. As a result, hair styles became simpler, moving away from very long hair piled elegantly on the top of the head, to shorter, "bobbed" hair worn close to the head, and dresses became shorter and less cumbersome, moving away from the ankle length, layered look, World War I period outfit which took 19 yards to make, to the classic flapper's chemise which took only 7 and one half yards of material to construct. Fabrics too began to change; easier to care for synthetics like rayon and nylon began replacing cotton, not only for dresses but for hosiery which in the era of shorter skirts became more important. Increasingly, first ice boxes and then refrigerators eliminated the need for daily shopping, and vacuum cleaners and washing machines reduced the drudgery associated with housekeeping tasks. Women both in and out of the work force benefited from more leisure than they had ever had before.

Moreover, these women began experimenting with styles and habits previously reserved only for men. For example, the most liberated women began wearing slacks as the twenties ended, and in the era of Prohibition women drank openly in defiance of the law of the land. Interestingly, whereas the earlier bar had been the sole province of men, sometimes forbidding women to enter at all or only through a "ladies' entrance" into a separate room, the twenties speakeasy mixed the sexes in a way which would have been unthinkable before World War I. Women began smoking too, but, unlike men who smoked cigars, they preferred cigarettes; the cigar industry collapsed in the twenties while cigarette sales skyrocketed. After the nineteenth amendment was passed in 1920, women were able to vote in federal elections, and although they did not improve the moral qualities of the elected officials as some had hoped--women did, after all, vote overwhelmingly for Warren Harding--they did at least have the power to vote the rascals out of office just as they had the right to throw a male admirer out of their bedroom.

By the 1930's, however, the position of women in films, as in real life, became more problematical. Ruffles reappeared, curls replaced the flapper's bobbed style, and the hemline went down, but women's aspirations did not. In the Depression years, many women, both young and old, married or single, had to work outside the home to supplement the family's income, and the example set by the activist Eleonor Roosevelt ,who thought nothing of visiting a coal mine, was not lost on women of the period. In Hollywood, women still had to right to woo and to refuse to be wooed, but somehow, they were still supposed to be feminine and acquiescent to male desires. In the *Thin Man* series, for example, Nora is beautiful, clever, and inventive, but it is obvious that Nick, literally and metaphorically, wears the pants in the family. It is against this background, then, that we can evaluate Dale Tremont in *Top Hat.*

Dale obviously lives well, but the source of her funds is somewhat murky. She seems to be the companion of the rich Bedini whose clothes she models in high society. Jerry's friend, Horace, indeed attempts to portray her as a "scarlet woman" with a morally corrupt past, and he has her tailed. Dale's moral concern over romancing her best friend's husband, however, convinces the audience she is not the schemer Horace thinks she is. But, on the other hand, is she really as pure as Jerry assumes? The whole matter is conveniently resolved when Dale marries Jerry at the end and dances away with him over a polished floor. The goal of women in thirties' movies is marriage and Dale wins the race, but we are a bit uncomfortable about where she began it.

While Dale's moral position is ambiguous, Jerry Travers' is not. In *Top Hat*, he is a democratic, self-made man, a popular dancer in theater revues. Although dressed formally throughout the film, sometimes in top hat and tails but at least in a suit, Jerry quickly shows us he is no snobbish aristocrat; in the first scene in a stuffy London club, he deliberately breaks its rule of total silence by noisily folding a newspaper. He lives in high society, but is not of that society. He even takes the side of the butler in a silly debate about the proper tie to wear with formal dress. He is impulsive and clever, a man with whom the audience can easily identify.

Top Hat, then, is a democratic musical even though it is set in the playgrounds of the rich, and this democratic spirit may explain its success and that of other escapist thirties films. In *The Wizard of Oz* (1939), for example, Dorothy visits a technicolor palace in Oz' Emerald City, but, good Jeffersonian yeoman that she is, she stills longs to return home to black and white Kansas. The Depression audience may have hoped to leave their troubles in the theater lobby, but they still wanted to see the movies extol the virtues of home and hearth; Dorothy wants to go back to Auntie Em's while Scarlett O'Hara is punished in the end for her failure to love her husband, Rhett Butler, properly. More important, depression audiences desperately wanted to see the Horatio Alger myth triumph on the screen. Good guys make money and win in the end. In *It Happened One Night*, Clark Gable as a newspaper reporter wins the fight with his editor, vindicates his "news sense," and marries an heiress.

As the Depression wore on, however, and "Happy Days" were not yet here again, the spunky democratic faith Jerry Travers represents in *Top Hat* was severely shaken, and the myth of the average American winning success and happiness in four reels became less tenable. On the eve of World War II, 11 million people were still unemployed in spite of New Deal recovery programs.

The New Deal's failure to cure the depression meant Roosevelt's optimism was increasingly challenged by demagogues from the political right; men like Huey Long with his Share the Wealth scheme and Father Coughlin, the Detroit radio priest, bore an uncomfortably close resemblance to the fascists who gripped large portions of Europe. When the war did break out in Europe in 1939 to contain this fascist threat, escapism in American movies tended to disappear, to be replaced by the moral earnestness of *Sergeant York* or *Casablanca*.

World War II changed forever the world in which a Jerry Travers would have to succeed. Increased income taxes lessened the buying power of the rich while post-World War II prosperity allowed the middle class to own homes in Levittown. From grimy students to middle class businessmen on a package tour, Americans visited Europe; Venice and the other playgrounds of the rich were no longer remote. Although the drive for movie escapism might continue in the Sputnik dominated 1950's, the escape was into the distant past, such as *The Land of the Pharaohs* (1954) or ever more exotic locales, such as in *The Black Knight* (1954). More important, however, Americans in film increasingly came to grips with the present society they lived in and examined its flaws. In films from *On the Waterfront*, to *Rebel Without a Cause*, to *Fort Apache, the Bronx*, to *Deer Hunter*, Hollywood turned to the here and now.

Top Hat - Instructor's Guide

1. Discuss the development of American dance under Isadora Duncan and Martha Graham, and relate these developments to the style of Fred Astaire.

2. Contrast the styles of Fred Astaire and Gene Kelly.

3. Give a brief historical sketch and assess the significance of any or all of the following:

   1. Fred Astaire
   2. Isadora Duncan
   3. Martha Graham
   4. MGM musicals
   5. Radio City Musical Hall
   6. Judy Garland

4. Show how movie theaters' architecture reflected the desire to escape the frightening reality of the Depression years.

5. Write a book review, indicating the author's hypothesis and relating events in the film to events in the book, in any or all of the following:

1. Frederick Lewis Allen, *Since Yesterday* (1940)
2. Andrew Bergman, *We're In the Money: Depression America and its Films* (1971)
3. Abraham Hoffman, *Unwanted Mexican-Americans in the Great Depression* (1974)
4. Tom Kromer, *Waiting for Nothing* (1935) new edition 1986
5. Robert S. and Helen M. Lynd, *Middle Town in Transition: A Study in Cultural Conflict* (1937)
6. Jane De Hart Mathews, *The Federal Theatre, 1935-1939: Plays, Relief, and Politics* (1967)
7. Lary May, *Screening Out the Past: The Birth of Mass Culture and the Motion Picture Industry* (1980)
8. Lois Sharf, *To Work and To Wed: Female Employment, Feminism and the Great Depression* (1980)
9. Robert Sklar, *Movie Made America* (1975)
10. John Steinbeck, *The Grapes of Wrath* (1939)
11. Studs Terkel, *Hard Times: An Oral History of the Great Depression* (1970)

6. Choose one of the books above and find the scholarly reveiws of it in two or more of the following journals:

1. *The American Historical Review* (published by The American Historical Association)
2. *Journal of American History* (published by The Organization of American Historians)
3. *History Teacher*
4. *Hitsory, Review of New Books*
5. *Choice*

Compare and contrast the reveiws. What did the reviewers like and dislike and why?

7. How did the position of women change in the 1930's. In your answer you should discuss employment statistics, clothing, marriage, and divorce statistics. An excellent source is Lois Scharf, *To Work and To Wed: Female Employment, Feminism and the Great Depression* (1980).

8. Show how the depression affected any or all of the following groups:

1. farmers
2. minorities
3. labor unions

4. the elderly
5. businesses

9. Compare and constrast the dancing of Fred Astaire in *Top Hat* and the dance sequences in Busby Berkeley's *The Gold Diggers of 1933*.

Casablanca - A Farewell to Isolationism

Released in 1941, *Casablanca* has become one of the best beloved American films. It describes the events which turned one man, Rick Blaine, from isolationism to involvement, and thus parallels the movement in American public opinion from 1920's style isolationism to eventual endorsement of United States involvement in World War II. With the Neutrality Act of 1935, which was based on the erroneous "Merchants of Death" theory, Congress clearly stated America's intention not to become involved in *any* foreign wars. But with the institution of cash/carry in late 1939, through the aid to Britain short of war, the United States moved ever closer to entering the war on the Allied side--until Pearl Harbor settled the matter definitively. Rick's odyssey, then, from isolationism to involvement reversed symbolically the previous generation's "Farewell to Arms."

Rick Blaine, played by Humphrey Bogart, owns the Café Américain in Casablanca, Morocco, where, according to the film, exit visas are bought and sold. To understand the significance of these activities, we must understand the historical situation in early 1941.

World War II began on September 1, 1939, when Hitler's troops marched into Poland. By September 4, Britain and France were at war. Poland was expected to hold out for several months, but, unable to withstand Blitzkrieg tactics, she surrendered in a month. To everyone's surprise, however, the fighting essentially ceased, and Europe entered the period known as the "phony" war. Any idea that Hitler might have been satisfied with Poland was destroyed when the Blitzkrieg began again in the spring of 1940. In April, Norway and Denmark fell to the Germans in spite of the intervention of the British fleet. In May, Holland and Belgium were overrun, and the attack on France began. Cut off from their French allies, British troops were evacuated from the continent at Dunkirk between May 26, and June 4,1940, and without them and British air cover, French morale sagged. The government fled Paris in June for Bordeaux where they surrendered June 22. The peace settlement provided for German occupation of northern and western France, along the coasts from which Hitler would launch his submarines, but southeastern France was left unoccupied and technically neutral. The Pétain government installed itself at Vichy, and so unoccupied France became known as Vichy France.

Although the Vichy government was neutral, it collaborated with the Germans, and this fact earned it the censure of many worldwide. Nonetheless, Vichy, as *Casablanca* makes clear, did serve as a conduit whereby refugees could flee war-torn Europe. By traveling to Marseilles, then across the Mediterranean to Oran in French-controlled Algeria, and finally trekking overland to Casblanca, refugees with luck could reach Lisbon by air and from there the "freedom of the Americas," as the film puts it. In fact, few refugees could flee Vichy France to begin with, and to avoid antagonizing Germany and so losing even their limited sovereignty, the Vichy government hesitated to grant exit visas for Lisbon. So it was, that guile and even murder were used to acquire these visas in Casablanca.

The film correctly suggests that French officials, such as the fictional prefect of police, Captain Rénaud, granted exit visas for bribes or sexual favors. But when important refugees, like Victor Laslo, the fictional resistance leader, attempted to escape, visas were not to be had for any price.

Most major powers, including the United States and Britain, recognized Vichy diplomatically. They did so to maintain listening posts in Europe, and also to encourage the French to resist German demands to hand over the large French fleet then locked up at the Toulon harbor in southern France. By 1940, German submarines were ravaging British shipping, and they could not afford to increase German naval might by letting the French fleet fall into German hands.

Some people, however, denounced Vichy as a moral abomination. Claiming that France should never have surrendered and instead should have continued the struggle from her North African colonies, General Charles de Gaulle began an organization known as the Free French, a resistance organization headquartered in London. Their symbol was the Croix de Lorraine, associated with Joan of Arc. Thus, in *Casablanca*, when Berger, the resistance representative, shows Laslo a ring with the Croix de Lorraine on it, Laslo recognizes him as a friend. According to the film, de Gaulle had signed two letters of transit which for some reason German couriers had and which Ugarti steals and gives to Rick for safekeeping. These are the letters Laslo and Ilsa use to escape. Why the Vichy French, who had no dealings whatever with de Gaulle and who had made him a criminal, would honor these letters is incomprehensible. For the letters to have had validity, they would have had to be signed by Pétain. We are looking, therefore, at a dramatic device, not an historical reality.

Casablanca is correct, however, in noting that French officials in North Africa scrupulously maintained their neutrality. When Rick asks Louis Rénaud if he is pro Vichy or Free French, Louis astutely declines to answer. The film suggests, however, that most Frenchmen chafed under Nazi rule. Thus, when Germans begin singing "Das Vaterland," their national anthem, the café denizens respond with a hearty rendition of the "Marseillaise," the stirring French national anthem which glorifies resistance. In fact, however, most French officials and especially the conservative French army supported Pétain; when the British and Americans invaded North Africa in 1942, expecting to be welcomed as liberators, French shore batteries opened fire on the troops as they slogged up the beaches, and the "liberators" suffered appalling losses as a result.

Rick's reaction to the highly charged political situation in North Africa is at first complete isolationism. "I stick my neck out for nobody," he declares. For example, he does not move to save Ugarti when he is arrested for the murder of the German couriers. As the film progresses, however, Rick's sentiments change. When Rénaud attempts to blackmail a pretty refugee into having sex with him to acquire an exit visa for herself and her husband, Rick lets the husband win at roulette to acquire enough money to pay for the visa in cash instead. By the end of the film, Rick has become a partisan, shooting the German major, Strasse, and permitting Laslo and Ilsa to escape. He and Rénaud wander off into the fog to sign up with the Free French at Brazzaville. As Rénaud remarks to Rick," You've become a patriot."

Rick's "farewell to isolationism" parallels a similar movement in the United States. Deeply disillusioned about World War I which proved to be much less than the great crusade Wilson had promised, Americans watched approvingly while the Senate refused to ratify the Treaty of Versailles, even with the amendments proposed by Lodge to safeguard American foreign policy intitiatives. Later, the United States reneged on a pledge made to the French to sign a mutual defense pact. When the French government pressed for the pact anyway, the United States offered the virtually worthless and unenforceable Kellogg-Briand Pact in 1928, the treaty which outlawed war by binding all signatories not to resort to force to achieve national objectives.

American isolationism became more intense in the 1930's, especially as the Great Depression turned attention inward to domestic economic problems. Artists, for example, abandoned international abstract art by creating "regionalism," a school of art which glorified the American past exclusively in realistic terms. Architecture too abandoned European motifs such as gargoyles and Greek columns in favor of stark Modernism; this type of architecture relied for ornamentation on geometry which, if not American, was at least not European. Pacifism prospered as well, as many young people joined the Veterans of Future Wars, an organization devoted to outlawing war. ROTC was abolished on many college campuses, and students in large numbers took the Oxford pledge in which they swore not to go to war in any circumstances.

Ironically, American isolationism and pacifism grew as the threat from overseas became more pressing. In 1930, the militarists took over the Japanese government, and by 1931, had pushed Japan into invading Manchuria. Hitler became Chancellor of the German Reich in January, 1933, and immediately launched a vicious purge of his stormtroopers on the Night of the Long Knives. In 1933, when the League of Nations finally sanctioned Japan for her attack on Manchuria, Japan simply left the League, and Germany joined her as an "outlaw" nation in 1935, when the League condemned her for violating the Treaty of Versailles' provision against rearmament and reintroducing conscription. That same year, the Italians invaded Ethiopia, and when the British chose not to interpose their fleet to stop the Italian transfer of men, young idealists ran guns to Ethiopia. Rick Blaine was one of them, *Casablanca* informs us. Nevertheless, in spite of their help, Ethiopia fell in May, 1936.

Later that year began the horrific Spanish Civil War, when General Francisco Franco invaded Spain from Morocco to overthrow the Spanish Republic. The Republic had been taken over by leftists in February when in national elections, conservatives and moderates had refused to vote. Once in power, the leftists had begun a vigorous program of land reform which so antagonized the Catholic Church and large landowners that they invited Franco to attack. A fascist, Franco was lavishly supported by Hitler and Mussolini, while the Republic received virtually no support except from the Soviet Union. Even Stalin knew the cause was hopeless, however, and in 1938, cut his losses. By 1939, Franco had won the civil war which claimed the lives of one out of every seven Spaniards. Although the United States government did not aid the Republic, a group of young Americans formed the Abraham Lincoln Brigade to support democracy over totalitarianism. *Casablanca* tells us Rick Blaine was one of them. He was, therefore, a rebel in his youth, enough so that Ilsa fears for his life when the Germans invade Paris in 1940. But a disillusioned Rick wants no more lost causes. "I'm not fighting for anything anymore, except myself. I'm the only cause I'm interested in," he tells Ilsa.

This philosophy was captured fully in the first Neutrality Act of 1935. Senator Russell Nye had held committee hearings for a year in order to determine how the United States had been tricked into World War I so as to write legislation to prevent American involvement in future wars. He concluded the "Merchants of Death" theory was substantially correct. According to that theory, for greedy profit motives, American businessmen had gotten the United States so economically involved with the allies that when they got in trouble the United States had no choice but to go to war to defend them. Nye's belief was incorrect, however; only 10% of the nation's export to the Allies was in arms, ammunition, and munitions of war. The other 90% was in agricultural products. If anyone had reason to push the United States to war, then, it was the "farmers of death." Businessmen vastly preferred neutrality, for that way we got all the benefits but none of the risks of belligerency. Finally, most of the loans were secured with collateral inside the United States; Britain could have lost the war without the United States government losing a penny.

Nonetheless, Nye insisted that economic involvement, especially of evil businessmen, had catapulted the country into war, and he wrote legislation which would sever economic ties with any country involved in any foreign war. Nye made no distinction between wars which safeguarded American security and those which affected us little if at all. Instead, the Neutrality Act said that when the president declared hostilities had begun, the United States would immediately embargo all arms, ammunition, and munitions of war to *both* belligerents and would warn Americans against traveling on belligerent vessels. Franklin Roosevelt, then president, signed the Neutrality Act into law in 1935, in spite of misgivings. He had wanted a discretionary embargo which would have distinguished between victim and aggressor, so the United States could aid the first with arms while punishing the latter with an embargo. However, Progressive Republicans like Nye were absolutely necessary for the second New Deal, then in Congress, to stand a chance of passage, and so Roosevelt acquiesced.

The Neutrality legislation remained in effect until after World War II broke out in September, 1939, and accordingly, the President embargoed both the allies and Germans.   Roosevelt had half-heartedly attempted to repeal the Neutrality Act in the spring of 1939, but his leadership was not strong.   However, once the war actually broke out, American public opnion so backed the allies that the Neutrality Act was decisively repealed in November, 1939, and Congress substituted the "cash/carry" proviso in its place.   Cash/carry declared the United States would sell to belligerents, but they had to pay cash and carry the goods themselves.   This was clearly an unneutral act, for only Britain had the cash reserves and the merchant marine to take advantage of the change in American policy, and Germany knew it.   Nonetheless, Germany chose not to make an issue of cash/carry for fear of bringing the United States into the war which would clearly tip the balance in favor of the allies.

The substitution of cash/carry resulted less from Roosevelt's leadership than from the growing awareness of Germany's threat.   The speed with which she had dispatched Poland frightened Americans into helping the allies.   The success of the Blitzkrieg in the spring of 1940, plus the fortitude of the English in the Battle of Britain that summer, reenforced Americans' hostility to Germany.   Thus when Britain proposed to swap 50 over-age destroyers to be used for convoy duty in exchange for 99-year leases on British bases in the New World, Congress agreed in September, 1940.   The destroyer deal and cash/carry were the beginnings of an American policy of aid to Britain short of war.   These measures were followed in March, 1941, with the passage of lend lease.   With Roosevelt safely reelected to the White House for four more years in November, 1940, Churchill felt free to tell him that Britain's cash reserves had been depleted.   The Roosevelt administration agreed to lend or lease to Britain--and to those other countries fighting Germany--whatever was necessary for them to prosecute the war.   Like the other American actions, this was a clearly unneutral position for the United States to take.   Lend lease was clearly popular; it passed both houses of Congress by substantial majorities.   The American government had agreed to underwrite and support the British war effort, to create, if you will, a giant umbilical cord, through which would pass whatever it took for her to win.   The United States had become, to use Roosevelt's phrase, the "Arsenal of Democracy."   Germany's attempts to strangle Britain into submission were doomed to failure.

In June, 1941, Hitler made the mistake which may ultimately have cost him the war; he attacked the Soviet Union, going after the Baku oil fields.   The Soviets suffered terribly; out of an army of 4.5 million, 2 million were dead, wounded, or captured by fall, 1941.   Of 5000 tanks the Soviets possessed when the war began, only 700 remained.   The United States extended lend lease aid to the Soviet Union in July, clearly indicating our resolve to support resistance to Germany.

By the summer of 1941, the American navy had begun patrolling one half of the Atlantic Ocean sea lanes.   American ships escorted British convoys about half way across the ocean where they would rendezvous with British escort vessels.   Frequently, German submarines tracked the convoys, although they usually held their fire if they were sure an American ship was doing escort duty;

they still wanted to avoid bringing the United States into the war until they had finished off Britain and the Soviet Union. The American ships, however, would radio the position of the these submarines to British bases in Newfoundland, in theory to warn them of obstacles in the sea lanes, but within minutes, British planes would be in the air headed for the submarines to bomb them to oblivion. Because the American ships were in effect calling in air strikes against German ships, some German U-boat commanders decided to shoot at what they rightfully regarded as hostile vessels. In November, 1941, the American navy, following the *Reuben James* incident when an American ship was sunk, received permission to shoot submarines on sight.

In August, 1941, the United States moved even closer to abandoning her isolationism when Roosevelt and Churchill met on a destroyer off the coast of Newfoundland and signed the Atlantic Charter. This document had both leaders agreeing to joint war aims, even though the United States was not technically in the war at that time. A more unneutral act could not be imagined, yet by August, American public opinion supported Roosevelt in this action as it had in all the previous aid to Britain.

Even though the United States was moving inexorably towards war, many Americans still only wanted to aid Britain *short* of war. "Send guns, not sons" was their slogan. The isolationists were overrepresented in Congress, to be sure, but the fact remains that for many, the United States still did not have sufficient provocation to fight ourselves. The Japanese attack on Pearl Harbor on December 7, 1941, changed that forever. Japan had allied herelf with Germany in 1936, and with Italy in 1937. Even though the United States had been attacked by Japan, this government declared war on Germany and Italy anyway, and also agreed with Britain that the first priority was the defeat of Germany.

What caused the American people to support the moves to aid Britain short of war and then ultimately to support World War II so overwhelmingly was the increasing perception of the threat Hitler and his allies posed to this country and our friends. But what motivates Rick Blaine to make his "Farewell to Isolationism"? *Casablanca* never suggests he comes to perceive or understand the threat Hitler presents to the rest of the world with any greater clarity as the film progresses. Although Major Strasse is overbearing, Rick does not seem to fear him. Likewise, Rick's motivation does not stem from any concern that harm will befall his friends; he doesn't help at all when Ugarti is arrested, and Laslo is a rival for Ilsa. If Laslo is killed, Ilsa will be his by default, and no harm will come to her. Rick's personal safety is assured, so he cannot be motivated by fear. Even when he puts Ilsa on the plane, Rick does not explain why he is doing so, except to say the problems "of three little people don't amount to a hill of beans."

Maybe Laslo got it right when, as he walks to the plane, he says to Rick, "Welcome back to the fight. This time I know our side will win." After all, after running guns to Ethiopia and fighting for the Republic in the Spanish Civil War, Rick had proved he was no coward, and willing to fight if provoked. He had been disillusioned when nobody else came to support his causes, but his love for Ilsa overcomes that disillusionment, just as Louis's friendship for Rick leads him not to arrest Rick for Strasse's murder. The idea of being part of a larger community struggling for the same thing obviously appeals to Rick. As he walks off with Louis, he notes, "This could be the beginning of a beautiful friendship."

That sense of being part of a community of good souls battling evil together may be one of the reasons World War II has remained so popular for Americans over the years. The anniversaries of major battles, such as the Battle of the Bulge or Victory in Europe, V-E day, are regularly celebrated in the United States. Books about World War II, from memoirs to military history, regularly appear.

In fact, perhaps because of the attack on Pearl Harbor which made the United States definitely the aggrieved party in the dispute, Americans were never more united. This makes World War II unique among American wars, for in most conflicts Americans have been deeply divided about whether the country should have been fighting at all, let alone on whose side. In the Revolutionary War, for example, Americans showed a remarkable lack of interest in the conflict; less than one eighth of the men of miltary age served in Washington's army, and most for very short periods. Large numbers supported the British crown, either openly or surreptitiously. In the War of 1812, the northern, Federalist states were so incensed at the war which had destroyed their commerce that they almost threatened secession at the Hartford convention in 1814, and did lay down rules by which the country would be governed--or else. In fact, the northern commercial interests showed their displeasure at what they called "Mr. Madison's War" by lending more money to Britain, the enemy, than they did to the federal government in Washington! Many northerners regarded the Mexican War of 1846 as a land grab on the part of the southern "slavocracy," and one, Henry David Thoreau, was sufficiently aroused that he wrote *Civil Disobedience* which instructed its readers how to oppose the war non-violently. The Civil War provoked such disagreement that Lincoln was obliged to institute severe censorship of the press. He was almost not reelected president in 1864, and when the deluge of volunteers slowed to a trickle as the war dragged on, Lincoln was obliged to call for a federal draft, a measure which led to five days of rioting in New York City. The War of 1898 was over so quickly and was such a success, that Americans had little time or reason to oppose it, but once it was over, William Jennings Bryan ran for president in 1900 on an anti-imperialist platform, claiming that a war to acquire colonies was immoral. In World War I, a small band of Americans vociferously objected to the war, so much so that a severe sedition law was enacted which deprived those convicted of criticizing the United States government of their citizenship.

Nor did Americans remained united in favor of war after World War II was over. In Korea, Americans were frustrated by the limited "police action" and the fact that negotiations for an armistice dragged on inconclusively for years. Even the Commander in the Pacific, Douglas MacArthur, publicly criticized President

Truman's war strategy and threatened to use nuclear weapons on China. And of course with Vietnam, the country saw such hostility to the war that demonstrations took place in the streets.

Many Americans of Rick Blaine's generation had been physically and emotionally scarred by World War I. They are sometimes called the "lost generation," and one of their voices was that of Ernest Hemingway who, in 1929, wrote *A Farewell to Arms* which he based on his experiences as an ambulance driver in the war. The image of war which emerges from this novel is harsh and vicious, where decency is destroyed in the name of order. War is ignoble, and truly moral men are corrupted by it. Later the Nye committee would echo the same sentiment that World War I had been a mistake, that American involvement was immoral. They went on to write legislation to keep the United States out of any future wars. In films like *Casablanca* and *Sergeant York*, Americans in 1940 and 1941 were reeducated about war, and told that some wars were indeed just and needed to be fought. Hollywood had finally responded to Hemingway with its own "farewell to isolationism."

Casablanca - Instructor's Guide

1. Write a book report on any of the following, stating the author's hypothesis, and relating events in the film to the book:

   1. Selig Adler, *The Isolationist Impulse* (1957)
   2. R. Albrecht-Carrié, *France, Europe, and Two World Wars* (1961)
   3. Raymond Carr, *The Spanish Tragedy: The Civil War in Perspective* (1977)
   4. Robert A. Divine, *The Illusion of Neutrality* (1962)
   5. Robert A. Divine, *Reluctant Belligerent*, 2cd ed. (1979)
   6. Lewis Ethan Ellis, *Frank B. Kellogg and American Foreign Relations, 1925-29* (1961)
   7. Herbert Feis, *The Road to Pearl Harbor* (1950)
   8. Warren F. Kimball, *The Most Unsordid Act: Lend Lease, 1939-1941* (1969)
   9. Robert Paxton, *Vichy France: Old Guard and New Order* (1972), reprinted 1982
   10. Gordon W. Prange, *At Dawn We Slept* (1981) about Pearl Harbor
   11. Michael S. Sherry, *The Rise of American Air Power: The Creation of Armageddon* (1987)

2. Choose one of the books above and find the scholarly reviews of it in two of the following journals:

1. *The American Historical Review* (published by The American Historical Association)
2. *Journal of American History* (published by the Organization of American Historians)
3. *History Teacher*
4. *History, Review of New Books*
5. *Journal of Southern History*
6. *Choice*

Compare and contrast the reviews. What did the reviewers like and dilsike and why?

3. Write a brief biographical sketch and assess the historical significance of any or all of the following:

1. Charles de Gaulle
2. Henri Pétain
3. Winston Churchill
4. Senator Robert Taft
5. Francisco Franco
6. Admiral Darlan
7. George Patton
8. Senator Russell Nye

4. Discuss the passage of lend-lease in March, 1941, explaining why some supported it and others did not, and showing how it affected the outcome of World War II.

5. Discuss the stages by which the American navy and merchant marine came to be involved in World War II before Pearl Harbor.

6. Explain why the Japanese attacked Pearl Harbor and why the United States had its fleet there to begin with. See Gordon W. Prange, *At Dawn We Slept* (1981).

7. Explain what the "Merchants of Death" theory is and what evidence was given to support it.

8. Discuss the onset and conduct on the Spanish Civil War from the overthrow of the monarchy in 1931 to Franco's victory in 1939. Raymond Carr, *The Spanish Tragedy: The Civil War in Perspective* (1977) is a useful source.

9. Explain why United States and British forces invaded French North Africa in

November, 1942 in the *Torch* landings. What problems were created by dealing with Admiral Darlan? What happened eventually to the French fleet in Toulon harbor?

Judgment at Nuremburg - Justice or Revenge?

Released in 1961, *Judgment at Nuremburg* recreates the trial of several German judges who were responsible for carrying out Hitler's laws. The film asks who was responsible for Nazi atrocities and what, if anything, they could have done about them. In trying to determine guilt, the defense counsel describes the events which made Hitler so appealing to the German people, while the prosecutor claims no extenuating circumstances could explain away participation in such horrors. To drive home his point, the prosecutor deliberately rearranges chronology, making the judges seem guilty for the extermination camps when they are only accused of violating civil liberties years before the extermination camps were even constructed. Moreover, the tribunal's judgment of 1949 is colored by contemporary events, especially the growing Cold War, which made assessing guilt more problematic. Finally, when the film endorses the presiding judge's moral condemnation of the accused, it chooses to ignore unpleasant events in our own history, and so raises troubling moral questions even today.

As World War II ended in 1945, the major Nazi figures had either committed suicide like Hitler or escaped like Adolph Eichmann, so the Allies rounded up second and third rank leaders. Many, like Rudolph Hess and Albert Speer, were later put on trial in military courts for their role in Nazi "crimes against humanity," the full disclosure of which came only with the liberation of the concentration camps. Some, like Speer and Hess, drew life imprisonment while a very few were executed. By 1948, when the trial of the German judges began, however, the flow of vindictiveness had ebbed, and what had been outrage at Nazi atrocities had metamorphosed into a feeling that Germany had been punished enough. The trial which *Judgment at Nuremburg* recreates, therefore, was not very popular either in Germany or in the United States where it quickly became "back page" news. Nonetheless, as Justice Haywood, played by Spencer Tracy asserts, these judges were profoundly involved in Nazi programs, although they never gassed or shot anyone, for they prostituted the German law system when they should have known better and when, theoretically, they were sworn to uphold justice. In order to assess responsibility, however, as the tribunal did between 1948 and 1949, we must understand first ,exactly what role these judges played in the German state, and second, how well they understood the state they served and its policies.

Judges under the Weimar Constitution of 1919 and later under Hitler's Reich were appointed by the Ministry of Justice, and served for life during the tenure of their good behavior, much as American Supreme Court justices do. Their duty was to carry out the law of the land. The problem for Ernst Janning and his co-defendants, however, was that that law was racist, degrading certain ethnic and religious groups on the basis of their heritage alone, and the penalties for violating the law were extraordinarily severe. Especially harsh were the Nuremburg laws of September 15, 1935, which stripped Jews of their German citizenship, forbade them to practice the professions like law and medicine, compelled them to adopt "Jewish" names, and forbade them to associate with "Aryans." The penalty for defying these laws was incarceration or death. When Feldenstein, an elderly Jew, was accused of having sexual relations with the Aryan, Irene Hoffmann, he was found guilty and ordered executed by Janning, as the law provided.

In the film the defense claims Janning was merely carrying out an admittedly imperfect law, while the prosecution claims the law was so heinous, the proceedings so pre-determined, and the punishment so severe that moral men should have resigned rather than carry out the law. The defense counters by saying that had moral men like Janning resigned, far less moral men would simply have replaced him and carried out the law, perhaps more viciously than Janning did. Moreover, had Janning refused to carry out the law, he would have been in violation of his oath to the state, and could have been removed from the bench.

Janning himself rejects the defense's argument and, instead, accepts his actions as immoral and a violation of the principles of civilized law to which he had devoted his life. Nonetheless, even Janning, at the very end of the film, as he speaks to Justice Haywood, while freely confessing his guilt, still maintains he had no idea that millions were being done away with.

This brings us to the vital question of how much men like Janning knew about Nazi atrocities, and when they knew it. That the Holocaust did occur is undeniable; at least 6 million Jews and other "undesirables" were exterminated as part of German state policy. The grisly footage shown by the prosecutor at the Nuremburg trials comes from real, vintage films now held in American archives. But did the German people know what was going on?

It is true, as defense counsel Rolf asserts, that the concentration camps were cloaked in secrecy and that the German state, though openly anti-semitic, never publicly acknowledged its extermination program to the world, let alone the German people. Using such phrases as the "final solution" for systematic extermination and "special treatment" for gassing, the German state carefully covered its tracks. It is also true, as Rolf argues, that the camps were located in remote areas. He could have added that the most notorious killing camps, as opposed to work camps or true concentration camps, were not even located inside Germany; Treblinka and Auschwitz, as well as the other four killing camps, were in Poland. Likewise, it is true that there was a breakdown of communication, especially in the last days of the war, as a result of allied bombing, and that news from such remote areas would have reached German population centers only with difficulty.

Rolf could also have mentioned that the vast majority of those exterminated were not German. Of the 6 million dead, 3 and a half million were Russian, 1 and a half million were Polish, 220,000 were French, and "only" 100,000 German. Jews constituted only 1.5% of Germany's population and most were clustered in ghettos; their disappearance, therefore, though noticeable, might not have been that striking.

Moreover, even if the German people had been aware that some of their neighbors were disappearing, and even if they had seen the trains of cattle cars rumbling across the country, they probably would have thought these prisoners were going to work camps as the government maintained. Nazi ideology demanded that women stay at home caring for children rather than join the work force as the fictitious Rosie the Riveter did in the United States, and so the Germans soon found themselves facing a major labor shortage. Jews and other "undesirables" from Germany and other occupied countries were therefore brought in for forced labor in work camps. Dachau, for example, located just outside Munich, Germany, and so one of the more "public" camps, was technically a work camp; over the gate was written, "Arbeit Macht Frei," work makes you free. Conditions in such camps, of course, were atrocious and many inmates died, as the grisly films shown at the trial in *Judgment at Nuremburg* prove. Nonetheless, the work camps accounted for less than 20% of Jewish deaths in the Holocaust. Of the 6 million Jews killed by the Nazis, over 3 million or 50% were killed in the 6 major extermination camps in Poland and 1.5 million in mobile actions (usually by shooting as in Russia): the vast majority of the remaining million died from the deadly conditions prevailing in the deportation trains, ghettos, and work camps like Dachau, Buchenwald, and Bergen-Belsen.

Moreover, it is important to note that the mass extermination only began in late 1941, when Chelmno in Poland, one of the 6 major killing camps, was constructed. The other five extermination centers did not begin full scale operation until very late in 1942. Indeed, one of the most frightening facts about the state extermination process is that it killed off so many in so little time.

Finally, even if stories had leaked out about the killing camps in Poland, sheer disbelief would have encouraged Germans to deny such reports any credence. Spending vast sums of money and precious manpower to kill off people whose labor the Reich desperately needed made no sense. Nor were the German people alone is discounting such rumors; in 1944, the American air force bombed Auschwitz' factories, but failed to bomb the gas chambers only a few hundred feet away, because this government refused to believe such chambers existed or were being used for systematic extermination.

Logically there was no way for Janning and other Germans to know about the entire extermination process in the thirties, for it in fact began very late in the war, no earlier than fall, 1941. Even after the mass killing started, German secrecy and outright disbelief would have made it unlikely that people like Janning would have known about it, or believed rumors had they heard them. *Judgment at Nuremburg*, however, implies that Feldenstein's execution in 1935 was part of the wholesale extermination practiced in the concentration camps, and that Janning and the other defendants knew it; indeed, the Feldenstein case is the prosecution's main evidence against Janning. To defense counsel Rolf, that is unfair. For one thing, that case occurred four years before the war broke out and seven years before the construction of Chelmno where the systematic extermination began. And for another, he shows that the German government went to great lengths to keep such information from its people once the process started.

In the film, Justice Haywood accepts the defense's argument that men like Janning could not be held responsible for the extermination camps like Treblinka or even the mass murder going on quietly far away in the Soviet Union. Instead, Haywood declares Janning guilty of something much less deadly but much more basic--the willingness to sacrifice, knowingly, the civil liberties and even the lives of people he knew to be innocent of any real crime. Janning explains he "never thought it would come to that, those millions of people." Haywood responds it had to come to that "the first minute you sentenced a man you knew to be innocent." In so doing, Haywood dismisses the German argument that offenders were merely "following orders" or, in the case of the judges, simply "carrying out the law," and he attacks head on the notion that affairs in Germany as early as 1935 were so grim that the rights of the few had to be sacrificed to insure the survival of the many.

Even Judge Haywood would have had to admit, however, that conditions in Germany in the early thirties were very bad indeed. For one thing there was a severe economic depression. This depression had begun as a result of the 1929 stock market crash in the United States, when stocks lost 40% of their value in a month, thus causing a severe credit contraction. Panicky American banks refused to roll over loans they had made to foreign governments like Germany, and refused to extend any new loans. Unfortunately, Germany had borrowed heavily to finance her $33 billion in reparations payments as a result of World War I, and when she could no longer borrow any more from the United States, she could not pay back her creditors in France and Britain, who in turn could not buy goods either from Germany or the United States. By 1931, therefore, the credit contraction had become a full depression.

In 1933, when Hitler became Chancellor of the Reich, 6 million Germans were unemployed, more than in the rest of Europe combined. This represented about 43% of the labor force, and if their families and those underemployed (those working part time) are counted in, as much as 60% of the German population were at or below the poverty line. Once in power, Hitler moved swiftly to address Germany's economic problems: he drafted unemployed young men into the army, cancelled all reparations payments, used high tariffs to keep out foreign competition, and from 1935 onward, began pumping money into the economy for rearmament, in clear violation of the Treaty of Versailles. The results were dramatic: by early 1936, unemployment was down to one million, and by late 1936, there was actually a shortage of German workers! But in 1935, when Janning condemned Feldenstein, the sense of economic crisis was still very strong, and gratitude to Hitler correspondingly great, as many Germans saw him rescuing their country from catastrophe.

Note that other industrialized countries never had the same success in curing the depression that Germany did. In the United States, for example, in 1933, when Franklin Roosevelt assumed the presidency, there were 13 million unemployed, or about 25% of the labor force. In 1940, however, after seven years of the New Deal, there were still 10 million people unemployed and "Happy Days Were Not Yet Here Again." In Britain, admittedly, the government was able to reachieve 1929 levels of production by 1934, but those levels had been so mediocre, that was hardly an accomplishment. Even in 1935, 1.5 million Englishmen were unemployed. In France, the depression came later, only reaching full force in 1931, but it lasted longer; not until 1939, the year World War II broke out, would France reachieve her 1929 levels of production, and even at that, at least one-half million people were out of work.

Hitler's popularity rested on more than gratitude for staving off economic disaster, however. Many Germans relished their new found sense of pride, especially following the wounds which defeat in World War I had inflicted on their country. When Germany had surrendered to the United States--and the United States alone--in 1918, she had expected to receive a generous peace treaty which would follow the principles of Wilson's 14 Points. Instead, she was obliged to sign a war guilt clause, by which she alone shouldered sole responsibility for the war, something which was manifestly untrue. The Treaty of Versailles hurt Germany badly: she was dismembered in favor of surrounding countries; she was separated in two by the Polish Corridor so that Poland could have access to the Baltic city of Gdansk, or Danzig, a city which had been German for 800 years; her army, which her people honored, was reduced to 100,000 men; her navy was to be handed over the the British, although the Germans scuttled it at Scapa Flow rather than do so; and she was saddled with $33 billion in reparations payments, an amount so outlandish that when Germany made a good-faith payment of $250,000,000 in 1921, her currency was shattered, and the mark which had been trading at four to one against the dollar in 1914 fell to 64 to one. German pride was deeply wounded, and her people felt betrayed by the constitutional government which had surrendered to the obviously vindictive allies.

But worse was still to come. In 1924, when Germany refused make any more reparations payments, France invaded the Ruhr valley, took over industries there, and sought to get the money out by force. The mark plunged in value, eventually in 1924 trading at 800 million to the dollar! German workers were paid twice a day so they could run to the stores to buy goods before the prices went up. Although the German government protested, it could do nothing; it had virtually no army of its own, and neither Britain nor the United States would even condemn verbally, let alone oppose by force, the French invasion.

It was in these dark days of 1924 that Hitler first came to national prominence when he led an attempted putsch in Munich to overthrow the German government. The so-called "Beer Hall Putsch" failed, but Hitler had touched a responsive chord in Germans everywhere when he denounced the French invasion of the Ruhr valley as illegal. More ominously, he began developing his idea that

Germany had not really lost World War I, but instead had been seduced into surrendering by communists, leftists, and those interested in democratic government, many of whom were Jewish. These ideas he incorporated into his book *Mein Kampf (My Fight)*, written while he was in prison following the attempted putsch. As the German economy got even worse following the Crash in the United States, Hitler's assurance that Germany's problems were caused by undesirable elements, like Jews, whom he claimed were not even German, soothed populace's sensibilities, calmed nerves, and increased German pride. Not only had Germany not lost the war after all, but if these alien peoples could be gotten rid of somehow, the "real" Fatherland could go back to being the great power she had been before the Great War broke out.

These are the realities which Janning in *Judgment at Nuremburg* tries to get Justice Haywood to understand. The German judge says there was great fear and national disgrace which Hitler promised would disappear when the devils among them, the Jews, gypsies, and communists, were gone. People who knew better went along because they were proud of their country. According to Janning, the trials arising from the Nuremburg laws of 1935, under which Feldenstein was convicted, were not really trials, but sacrificial rituals.

This is precisely the point that Haywood disputes, for he insists that while going along with Hitler might have been *understandable* given the conditions of the time, it remained *immoral*. In times of crisis, survival sometimes suggests that people adopt the means of the enemy, but to do so is wrong. People must "stand tall," because, according to Haywood, it is not enough to survive. One must survive as something decent and ethical. The judge then proceeds to give each of the defendants life imprisonment.

The film suggests that Haywood is being overly idealistic, because with the Cold War threatening to get hot in the Berlin crisis of the winter of 1948-1949, Americans would need the German people to stop Soviet advances in Europe, and they wouldn't get that help by sentencing their former leaders to stiff jail terms and raking up the past. As the general in charge of the Berlin air lift says about Haywood's court decision, "He just doesn't understand." How valid were these Cold War concerns, and how specifically did they affect the allied treatment of Germany?

Although the United States and the Soviet Union had been allies against Nazi Germany in World War II, it was only the threat of Hitler's domination of the European continent that glued this otherwise shaky alliance together. Once Germany had been defeated, the alliance began to break apart. One issue which helped drive a wedge between the former allies was what to do with defeated Germany. The Soviets preferred a very harsh peace that would strip Germany of all industry and "re-agriculturalize" her. By contrast, the American government vacillated between, on the one hand, following British advice and resuscitating German power as a bulwark against the Soviets, and on the other, following the Morgenthau plan which sought to destroy utterly Germany's industrial base.

Having finally learned the lessons of the Treaty of Versailles, the Americans were leaning towards the British position as the war ended, but then came the revelations of Nazi atrocities, and American outrage was so strong the desire for vengeance grew. As a result, the United States was prepared to let the matter of what to do with Germany drift; food was sent to alleviate widespread starvation and Allied forces kept order, but otherwise, the Allies in their occupation zones in what would become West Germany simply marked time. The Soviets did not, however. They stripped their occupation zone in what would become East Germany of all industry which they transported to Russia to aid in its recovery, and they established a friendly communist regime which utilized harsh measures to maintain order. The United States, Britain, and France made a few attempts to work with the Soviets on a concerted, unified German policy, but they failed.

By 1947, the United States had come to see Soviet power in eastern Europe as dangerous and growing. Already the Americans had moved to make things more difficult for the Soviets by cancelling lend lease. Then, in March, Truman put forward the Truman Doctrine which promised American aid to any free people anywhere attempting to resist subjugation by armed minorities, i.e., communist revolutionaries. The Doctrine was, in essence, a declaration of Cold War on the Soviet Union. To soften its effect, in June, Secretary of State Marshall put forward what became known as the Marshall Plan; this program was designed to resuscitate the European economy with American aid. These funds were offered to all European countries, including Germany, but the Soviets obliged their client states in eastern Europe not to accept. Congress was slow to approve the plan because of its cost, an estimated $17 billion over 4 years, but negotiations to revive the German economy began with her government anyway while Congress debated.

As *Judgment at Nuremburg* so aptly shows, the Germans had a long way to go to recover from the war. Many of their cities lay in ruins, and food was hard to get. In the winter of 1947, the harshest in 50 years, many Germans existed on less than 1500 calories a day. Note how in the film Justice Haywood allows his German servants to stay on, even though he does not like their fussing over him, because at least in his service they will eat. Note also how the bombed out buildings look as the judge is driven in from the airport.

Probably the most important issue to be resolved to get Germany back on her feet again concerned her monetary system. Before money could be lent through the Marshall Plan, the German mark would have to be tied into the rest of the European currencies at a realistic rate so it could easily be exchanged. The western allied occupation zones agreed to an exchange rate, but the Russians refused. With an absolutely irrational exchange rate for their own ruble, they could not afford to accept a realistic one for the mark without advertising the severe weaknesses of their own economy to the world. More important, the Russians were afraid that the integration of western Germany into Europe's economy might lead to its integration into Europe's political life as well. That, in turn, might lead to the re-militarization of Germany, a possibility the Soviets dreaded after having lost one tenth of their 1940 population in the recent war. The re-industrialization of Germany, the beginning of what is now sometimes called the "German economic miracle," terrified the Soviets, and in an effort to frighten the other allies into stopping it in June, 1948, the Soviets closed off land access to West Berlin. The Berlin crisis mentioned in the film was on.

The United States and her allies did not retreat from their announced position of re-industrializing Germany, nor did they retreat from Berlin. With land access cut off, they flew in supplies by air. The Soviets upped the ante by eliminating all multi-party governments in eastern Europe. Before they had permitted all non-fascist political parties to participate in these governments (although the communist party tended to dominate). Now, feeling threatened Russia insisted on purely communist governments in eastern Europe to serve as a bulwark between herself and what she considered a hostile western Europe. By early 1949, the allied airlift was flying over 7000 tons of supplies a day into Berlin. The city could thus hold out indefinitely, and Moscow dared not shoot down the planes for fear of being bombed with atomic weapons. As a result, the Soviets gave in and reopened land access to Berlin. At a meeting of Foreign Ministers called in the spring of 1949, the Soviets and the allies agreed to disagree; the Soviets continued with their plans to strip Germany of all movable industry while the allies went forward to re-industrialize their western occupation zones.

These are the Cold War concerns which the film shows bore heavily on Justice Haywood as he was obliged to determine the guilt or innocence of German judges like Janning. To stop Soviet encroachments on Germany, to give Germans a will to fight, certain Americans urged him to be lenient. Even one of the allied judges on the three man tribunal which Haywood heads dissented from his ruling. Yet, Haywood chose to ignore such political rationalizations, sticking instead to an almost Wilsonian insistence on morality above all. He condemned Janning, castigating him for having sentenced even one man he knew to be innocent.

Although *Judgment at Nuremburg* calls Haywood's idealism into question, it ultimately supports his views. After all, Tracy is the hero of the film--he gets top billing--and his castigation of Janning is quite literally the last word we hear. As viewers, we are left feeling that Germany was unique in succumbing to the political right as represented by Hitler, and that only the evil Nazis would have considered, let alone created, such things as concentration camps. But this film was made by Americans, for Americans, and so it downplays the very real threat from the political right which even this country experienced both in the depression thirties and during the war, and it ignores the creation in this country of concentration camps for those of Japanese descent.

To put Tracy's moralism into prespective, it might be helpful to remember that the United States too violated the civil rights of minorities, much as Germany violated the rights of Jews. Jews in this country, for example, suffered from organized anti-semitism from the revived Ku Klux Klan in the 1920's. In the thirties, Father Coughlin, the popular Detroit radio priest, formed the openly anti-semitic Social Justice movement which approved of the very 1935 Nuremburg laws which Janning in the film is accused of having carried out. Nor were Jews alone. Blacks, too, suffered at the hands of the Ku Klux Klan, and the depression hurt them even more than it hurt whites. In deference to conservative white southerners, before whose congressional committees his vital legislation had to pass, Roosevelt ignored civil rights, and the New Deal permitted separate and unequal pay scales in various relief programs. Moreover, in World War II, blacks fought in segregated units; the armed services would not be desegregated until 1949, and then only by Truman's executive order.

But the most striking example of violating civil rights was the treatment of people of Japanese ancestry during the war. Terrified that Japan would use these people to help her prepare an invasion of the west coast, the American government herded all those of Japanese descent, many of whom were American citizens, into concentration camps during the war. This was done without evidence of intended subversion, in clear violation of the Bill of Rights. These concentration camps did not engage in extermination like the six killing camps in Poland, of course, nor were conditions so bad that thousands died, but hundreds did die, probably sooner than they would have had they been left to go about their normal lives. Moreover, if we accept Haywood's argument that one is guilty when one sentences even one person known to be innocent, then the American judicial system which incarcerated these people and the American people who permitted it to continue are as guilty as Ernst Janning. The holier-than-thou morality of Haywood looks far less convincing than it did before.

To say that Americans also violated civil liberties and fell prey to anti-semitism is simply to state a fact, but it is important to make clear distinctions on such emotional subjects. The American and German concentration camps were fundamentally different from one another: German camps were designed either to exterminate or, by reducing rations to starvation levels while requiring strenuous work, to extort labor until the victim collapsed; American camps for the Japanese were simply holding operations. Anti-semitism was the state policy of Germany, and the 1935 Nuremburg laws stripped Jews of their citizenship and right to protect themselves; anti-semitism was never the official policy of the United States government, and Jews not only did not lose their citizenship, but actively participated in running the government.

Nevertheless, the fact that widespread violations of civil liberties could occur even here makes the assessment of responsiblity and guilt of those German judges far more problematical. Although it never got as bad, and although few people died, "it could happen here"--and in a limited way, it did. Perhaps, therefore, instead of Haywood's moralism, a more modest, self-reflexive judgment at Nuremburg is required: there but for the grace of God go we.

Judgment at Nuremburg - Instructor's Guide

1. Describe the legal precedents, if any, for the victors putting the vanquished on trial after World War II. Had there ever been a charge of "crimes against humanity" before?

2. Write a brief biographical sketch and assess the significance of any or all of the following:

      1. Adolf Eichmann   2. Mengele   3. Heinrich Himmler

3. Describe the American reaction to reports of Nazi atrocities against Jews before the liberation of Europe in 1945. Why did our government do what it did? In your answer, you should consider: anti-semitism, reliability of information, immigration restrictions, military concerns, and squabbling among Jewish groups in the United States. A good source is David S. Wyman, *The Abandonment of the Jews* (1984).

4. Describe the development of the six major Nazi death camps. Which were they and why were they located where they were, what were they designed to do, and why and when did they function?

5. Write a book report on any or all of the following, indicating the author's hypothesis, and relating events in the book to the film if possible:

      1. Alan Brinkley, *Voices of Protest: Huey Long, Father Coughlin, and the Great Depression* (1982)
      2. Lucy S. Dawidowicz, *The War Against the Jews, 1933-1945* (1976)
      3. Martin Gilbert, *Auschwitz and the Allies* (1982)
      4. A. Grosser, *The Colosssus Again; Western Germany from Defeat to Rearmament* (1955)
      5. Adolph Hitler, *Mein Kampf*
      6. G. Mosse, *Towards the Final Solution* (1978) history of European racism
      7. J. L. Snell, *Wartime Origins of the East-West Dilemma over Germany* (1956)
      8. Fritz Stern, *The Politics of Cultural Despair* (1961) on the origins of Nazism
      9. David S. Wyman, *The Abandonment of the Jews; America and the Holocaust* (1984)

6. After reading Hitler's *Mein Kampf,* explain his antagonism to Jews and other "undesirables." What did he promise to do about this problem in the 1920's when his book appeared. Is his antagonism based on religious ideas or something else?

Adam's Rib - The Working Woman Learns Her Place

Adam's Rib, released in 1949, portrays a loving relationship between almost equal partners which is threatened by the wife's defense of women's rights. The film raises disturbing questions about why the husband is upset with his wife's legal defense and what can be done to reestablish the couple's relationship at the film's end. Such a marriage of independent partners, both of whom have careers, is unusual in the history of American films, and almost unique in the Hollywood productions of the post-World War II period. In the late 1940's, the movie industry was reacting to the fact that returning veterans demanded their jobs back from the women who had filled them during the war. As Rosie the Riveter was either demoted or joined the unemployment lines, and women struggled to retain their wartime gains in salary and prestige, Hollywood films stressed that marriage and motherhood were the only suitable careers for women. Indeed, it was Hollywood's arch enemy, television, that first portrayed working women, and more important, working mothers, realistically and favorably. Although *Adam's Rib* might have become a blueprint for the movie industry's portrayal of working, married women, it was a blueprint the industry refused to adopt.

Adam's Rib shows a loving relationship between two individuals almost equal in terms of education and power. Amanda, played by Katherine Hepburn, is a lawyer who obviously is doing well financially, and Adam, played by Spencer Tracy, is a public prosecutor who, at the film's end, has been asked to run for a judgeship. In their playful banter and friendly clowning, they display a real affection for one another and a mutual respect. Neither is a perfect person--Adam sulks and Amanda flirts--but neither seems unduly wounded by the other one's imperfections--at least until Amanda embraces the cause of women's rights when she defends a woman charged with the attempted murder of her faithless husband. When Adam learns that she has taken the case, he literally drops all the cocktail glasses and spends the evening sulking. His distress causes him to become more concerned over Amanda' flirtation with Kip, the song writer, a flirtation which before he had regarded as innocent and even silly. Likewise, Amanda becomes more concerned with Adam's sulkiness. When she eventually implores him to explain his silence, however, he storms out of the house after a violent argument. Their imperfections are not caused by Amanda's case, but the issues the case involves magnifies their small flaws into real threats to their marriage.

What Adam *says* is annoying him is that Amanda is perverting the law by defending someone who has taken the law into her own hands. His proposition is that the law is equal for everyone and that, if the law is unjust, it should be changed, not "busted wide open." He eloquently defends this proposition when he later finds Amanda with Kip and pretends to shoot them both with a gun we later learn is made of licorice. His "attack" provokes Amanda to blurt out that he has no right to take the law into his own hands. However, although Adam's argument may be legally correct and defensible, the film makes clear that Adam is motivated by considerations other than the majesty of the law.

Just before the scene in which he storms out of the house, Adam was humiliated in court when Amanda's witness, a female acrobat, hoisted him up with one hand before a packed courthouse which roared with laughter. Although he had reason to be annoyed before, it was this blow to his manly pride which provoked his later outburst. Likewise, what annoys Adam in another scene when he is giving Amanda a rub down and provokes another argument, is the fact Amanda is singing a song Kip wrote for her. But again, he justifies his anger by accusing her of "shaking the law by the tail" in court. In short, it is Adam's ego which is damaged, not the law.

Ironically, Amanda's defense of her client rests on the fact that the women accused of shooting her husband has had her own ego badly bruised. Her husband is a shallow cad who physically abused and then deserted her, supposedly because she was too fat--although she looks not one pound overweight. When the wife says she tried to frighten her husband's mistress in order to save her home and family, the court is deeply moved. Thus, in spite of Adam's attempt to make her appear mentally unbalanced, the jury acquits her of the charge of attempted murder, obviously swayed by Amanda's defense. Amanda's defense, simply put, is that the crime was justifiable and would be justified by law if a man had shot an unfaithful wife, while Adam's argument is that no assault is justified, no matter what the provocation.

Once Adam has stormed out, the conventions of comedy require some sort of resolution and the reestablishment of domestic harmony, but as is the case with many comedies, this solution seems somewhat forced and contradicts much of what the film has already shown. In order to defeat Amanda, rub salve on his wounded ego, and yet ultimately win her back, Adam tricks Amanda twice, once when he pretends to shoot Kip and her, thus prompting Amanda to admit the justice of his legal position, and the second time when he cries at the tax accountant's office, thus convincing her he is deeply distraught by their separation. Amanda sees through the artifice of the first trick quickly, but she is taken in by the other--at least until Adam shows her he can cry on cue. They have by this point retired to the Connecticut farm they have only recently paid off. This farm had always been associated in the film with domestic harmony, and it is here their loving relationship is reestablished to a large degree because they both revert to traditional male/female sex roles. Amanda dons the flowery hat Adam had earlier given her as a present, and she literally tends the hearth when she builds up the fire in the bedroom. While their New York apartment had separate twin beds located on opposite walls, the farm's bedroom has a traditional four-poster double bed on the corner of which Amanda sits demurely. When she claims there is only a small, unimportant biological difference between men and women, Adam cries "Vive la différence!" and thus has the last word as the film ends and the credits roll. By reasserting his sexual dominance, Adam reestablishes the "traditional" form of marriage in which Amanda plays a secondary role, as Eve fashioned from Adam's Rib, not Adam himself.

The message of the last few minutes of *Adam's Rib*, then, is that women should adopt a secondary place if a marriage is to survive, but that proposition has been undercut throughout the film as we saw just how much freedom and respect each partner accorded the other. Although the relationship may not have been one of true equals, they were the most equal duo Hollywood has ever produced. The portrayal of any married couple in which both spouses work at jobs of equal status and remain loving and supportive anyway was very rare in the history of American film and almost unique in the period following World War II. Some Hollywood movies made before the forties showed career women being pursued by men with careers either higher or lower in status and pay than theirs, but to a woman they gave up their careers when they married at the end of the film, or they never married at all and usually were miserable as a result. A great number of movies showed women with low paying jobs such as secretary or waitress from which these women were eager to escape into marriage. But by far the vast majority of films portrayed women without any job outside the home, either young enough to be still supported by parents or married and tending house. In short, rarely did a wife have a career, or if she had a career she gave it up upon marriage. Marriage and a career for a woman were incompatible according to Hollywood.

Hollywood's hostility to working women who competed with their husbands may be a continuation from the earliest days of the industry when it adopted Victorian or Gothic novel plotlines. The heroines of such novels were ingenues, sweet virgins whose innocence was both their attraction for and defense from would-be seducers. When movies were first made in the teens, they simply borrowed Broadway plays. Since the plays were frequently based on Victorian/Gothic novels, and the movies based on the plays, the ingenue was imported directly into the early movie plots.

From D. W. Griffith's early masterworks in the teens, thus, through the 1920's, the most popular Hollywood female stars were ingenues, delicate, fluttering creatures like Lillian Gish, who would have been at a loss in a boardroom, let alone a courtroom. There were occasional vamps in the twenties like Theda Bara, but her vamping was so outrageous and unthreatening that few took her seriously. Moreover, such vamps no more had careers that did the ingenues like Gish. By the late twenties, as more women entered the labor force, movies responded by portraying young working girls on film, but they were never married, although many wanted to be, and they were rarely if ever shown at their jobs, none of which required much education. These flappers were portrayed as being more concerned with what clothes and pastimes their salaries would buy than with what they did to earn their salaries. Morover, these flappers only seemed uninhibited: although their language and dress may have been provocative, they were as innocent at heart and unthreatening to men as ever a Victorian heroine or Lillian Gish had been.

Under the impact of the 1930's Depression, the flapper disappeared and the popularity of the ingenue began to wane, but this did not mean at all that Hollywood was ready to portray working wives equal to their husbands on the screens of America. The flappers' nonchalance could not be condoned when getting *any* job was so important in the thirties, and the fluttering, adolescent ingenue could not survive in the brutal reality of the Depression years. If the ingenue appeared at all, she was a true child in years as well as emotional development. She became Shirley Temple or the youthful Judy Garland in *The Wizard of Oz* (1939). Adult movie heroines of the thirties were usually as innocent and sensitive as their earlier counterparts, but they also usually worked if they were unmarried and they always had a certain toughness which earlier ingenue types and even the flappers never had. Ginger Rogers as a showgirl waiting to break into the big time or Rosalind Russell as a reporter were verbally quick and at ease in any situation, and Jean Harlow made famous the wisecracking secretary as sidekick. Significantly, however, none of these Hollywood heroines were shown married on film, and none of those other stars whe *were* shown married ever held down a job at the same time.

Indeed, when married women appeared in films, they were rarely cast as the heroine. On the contrary, married women were usually matronly types, busomy, bejeweled, and well over 40. When young married women were portrayed, which was not at all often, they never had jobs and furthermore almost always played a secondary role to their husbands; they spoke fewer lines than their husbands did, they were seen in fewer scenes, and fewer scenes in which they did appear were set outside the home. Not only did such married women not have careers, they were frequently heiresses. Myrna Loy, for instance, dubbed the "perfect wife" by the fan magazines, was an heiress in the famous *Thin Man* series; not only did she not work herself, but her wealth permitted her husband, Nick, to give up his career as a detective as well.

In fact, almost all portrayals of married life involved spouses who usually lived in luxurious surroundings. Just like Amanda in *Adam's Rib*, they almost always had maids who performed the tasks like cleaning and cooking which most married women usually did themselves. While it is true that domestic help was easier to obtain in the depression thirties, very few women of even moderate means could afford full-time servants. Nevertheless, *Adam's Rib* for example, opens with Amanda and Adam being served breakfast in bed, and they return from work to find a catered dinner for 12 arranged by their maid already set out. To be sure, depression era audiences showed a great fondness for seeing how the rich lived, and such luxury fed the dreams which kept many Americans going through the hard times, but Hollywood's insistence that marriage was easy and work-free for young wives must have created some disillusionment for the real women who went home from the movies to finish cleaning the floors.

Not only did young wives in Hollywood rarely work either in or out of the home, but they also rarely had children. Married life involved only two adults.

While the pitter-patter of little feet may have been anticipated as the film ended, as the wife announced the impending "blessed event," the product of that event was rarely if ever shown on film. Note that Amanda and Adam in *Adam's Rib* have no children. Even when children were present, they were cared for by a nanny, not their mother, and were treated more as playthings than as an ongoing responsibility, such as Myrna Loy's child in the *Thin Man* series. When children from poorer families were shown in films in circumstances which made nannies economically impossible, they were shown interrelating with one another, and parents were rarely if ever present, as in the Little Rascals series. Judy Garland in *The Wizard of Oz*, for example, spends most of the film away from her family. Hollywood produced images of heroism, usually male, and self-sacrifice, usually female, but it could not produce images of happy family life which included young children.

Perhaps part of this inability to portray realistic family life was due to the fact that the movie industry was so completely dominated by men for whom the family was not that important. All studio heads and almost all directors and screenwriters were male, just as they are today. But while the people who wrote and produced films were male, the stars who acted in them were frequently female, and many of these heroines were married and had children. Real women outside the movie theater found out how these "working mothers" raised their children from fan magazines which described in sentimental tones how female stars reacted to their husbands and offspring. This fan magazine information, however, was as unrealistic as was the information in the movies themselves, for most stars were wealthy and had nannies raising their children. Indeed, the recent spate of nasty exposés written by stars' children, such as *Mommie Dearest*, suggest that actresses like Joan Crawford were better off letting their nannies raise the kids.

This unrealistic view of family life was the more unfortunate because in fact more and more women, married and single, worked outside the home during the depression thirties and even more so in the World War II years of the early forties. These women worked not because of some commitment to a vague idea of sexual liberation, but because they had to, either to supplement their families' incomes during the depression or to keep American industry going when men went to fight overseas. In the depression years, many men abandoned their families, either to search for work or because they couldn't take it anymore. The women they left behind usually moved in with relatives, and while the older generation cared for the children, the younger women went out to find jobs. Few day care facilities were available for working women, and such women, then as now, had to settle for "warehousing" their offspring as best they could. This problem became more severe when the war began, for married, working women with children frequently left their families to be near the defense factories or their husbands' military base, and so could no longer get help from the older generation. For example, in the San Fernando valley, where several war plants were located, a social worker once counted 45 infants locked in cars in one parking lot, and many older children were simply locked out of their homes until the mother returned from work. Juvenile delinquency rose sharply as a result. In San Diego, for example, 55% more boys were charged with crimes in 1945 than in the previous year, and for girls the crime rate soared 355%.

When Hollywood portrayed family life during the war years, it could not ignore the absence of men or the fact of working wives and mothers. As a result, the movie industry moved slowly to correct its unrealistic view of family life and the role of working women. Although most films produced still portrayed only unmarried working women, such as *The Maltese Falcon* (1941) or *His Girl Friday* (1940) or dealt exclusively with male wartime relations as in *So Proudly We Hail* (1943) or *Watch on the Rhine* (1943), some progress was made in portraying both working women and married women. Working women now had jobs that required more education. Ingrid Bergman in *Spellbound* (1945), for example, was a psychiatrist. Married women were shown coping with absent husbands and growing families in *Since You Went Away* (1944). But rarely did women both work and have a family, and when they did, they were usually portrayed unsympathetically as in *Mildred Pierce* (1945). This is why *Adam's Rib* with its portrayal of a happily married working couple of relatively equal spouses is so unusual.

Women made excellent employees during the war years. They worked faster with less supervision, did less damage to tools and machines, had fewer accidents, and were generally considered more cheerful than the male workers they replaced. And this was in spite of the fact that women almost always were paid less for the same job as men. For example, women in manufacturing earned only 65% of what men did. Much of women's adaptability to employment was explained away by claiming that since they had less initiative than men and were more creatures of habit, they consequently made more compliant and dutiful workers. Whatever the male establishment might have said to denigrate women's labor, in fact as well as on film, women entered areas of the work force previously closed to them   Compared to earlier epochs in American history, there was an enormous upsurge in the number of women in the professions such as law, medicine, and education, although in all fields women still remained a small minority. Two and a half million women also took over factory jobs which had once been considered too strenuous for them, and Rosie the Riveter became a famous if fictitious character. Women even entered the armed forced when the WACS were formed in 1942, followed shortly by the WAVES. Women became managers and foremen. The female witness Amanda called in *Adam's Rib* who was a shop foreman was not unique or even unusual as World War II manpower demands eventually required mobilizing 12 million men. As impressive as the number of working women was the fact that increasingly they were married (75%), and 2.7 million were both married and mothers. Women played a vital role in the war and made remarkable advances, but their role in the work force was only partially appreciated, and their advances would soon be severely curtailed.

The war was over in Europe in May, 1945, and the war in the Pacific several months later in August. As is normal in American history, the United States quickly demobilized its armies and thus released a huge number of returning veterans into an economy geared for war, not peace, in which jobs were hard to find. Many draftees and enlisted men had been promised their old jobs back upon their return, but once they came home, they found women occupying their places and in many cases doing as good a job as they had done themselves. Nor could returning vets find new jobs to replace the ones now held by women. It would take several years for the economy to readjust to a peacetime economy, and in 1945 and 1946, factories were actually closing as the demand for tanks and war machinery disappeared almost overnight. Within a few days of the surrender of the Japanese, 1.8 million people were fired and by 1946, 2.7 million people were out of work. The United States plunged into a recession similar to that it had experienced after all wars, but this recession after World War II was made worse by the fact that wartime wage and price controls, which had kept price rises to 4.2%, were abruptly removed when President Truman vetoed a bill to continue them. With no control on prices and yet with huge demand and available money built up through wartime savings and severance pay from the armed forces, a classic inflationary spiral resulted which saw the inflation rate in 1946 reach 18.2% in one year. Returning vets were buffeted by inflation and by their inability to find jobs in a shrinking economy, and as a result, they demanded that the women be fired and they rehired. Most employers obliged.

Most women did not want to give up their jobs, but since they usually, but not always, had less seniority than the returning vets, and since veterans could claim they had risked their lives overseas while women had not, most women found themselves either demoted or unemployed. A poll taken in 1945 showed that 80% of all women wanted to keep their jobs, but between 1945 and 1946, many women lost their jobs and the percentage of women in the labor force shrunk from 36% to 29%. Moreover, these figures do not show the fact that many women who did continue to work worked in jobs that paid less and had less job security. The wholesale firing or demoting of women was not opposed by labor unions because many women did not have seniority and because labor unions had more pressing concerns in other areas such as a series of strikes which prompted Congress to crack down on unions with the Taft Hartley Act of 1947. And while it is true that many returning veterans had seen combat overseas, most had not. With a ratio of 10 support troops to every combat soldier, the vast majority of "fighting men" returning from World War II had never fought anything mroe dangerous that a pencil or steering wheel. Nonetheless, ex-servicemen could lay claim to patriotism in a way women remaining stateside could not, and so Rosie the Riveter went back to the secretarial pool where she worked for less money or she joined the unemployment lines.

Hollywood, which had never been comfortable with the new role of working women in the war years, now returned with a vengeance to making films which stressed marriage and childrearing as the most important goals in a woman's life, such as *I Remember Mama* (1948). The movie industry was not alone, of course. Dr. Benjamin Spock first published his *Baby and Child Care* in 1946, in which he claimed that mothers were important as the guardians of future geniuses, provided of course that the child got the mother's full attention. In movies, if women worked at all, they once again gave up their jobs upon marriage. In short, Hollywood made films in which boy met girl and usually married her, but what happened after the "I do's" was considered unfit for the movie screen.

For Hollywood did not deal realistically with family life either. As we have seen, the movies were never very good at portraying a happy family life or children. Nevertheless, at least there had been *some* child stars in the thirties such as Shirley Temple. But child stars disappeared from the movie screen in the late 1940's. When children were shown, they were usually adolescents, and these adolescents were frequently emotionally disturbed such as the sociopaths in *Asphalt Jungle* (1950). Such debauched teenagers were a constant reminder of what could go wrong in family life if children were not given the mother's unswerving attention. Even as late as 1955, with the release of *Rebel Without a Cause*, no very young children are portrayed, and juvenile delinquncy is blamed on women who have become too "masculine."

Against this background, we see that the loving relationship of Amanda and Adam in *Adam's Rib* was highly unusual insofar as they were shown happily married, relatively equal in power in the relationship, and both employed in important jobs. *Adam's Rib*, along with several other comedies Tracy and Hepburn made during this period, might have become a blueprint for how two relatively independent people could stay happily married to one another. That it did not was largely due to television.

By the early 1950's, television had begun doing what Hollywood never had: it portrayed happy family life to those young couples with small children who stayed home rather than going out to the movies. From *Leave it to Beaver* to *Ozzie and Harriet* to *Lassie*, the "tube" showed children and young, middle class parents living together. In fact, television was the first to follow a pregnancy through from beginning to end when Lucy became "in the family way" (the sponsors would not allow her to be "pregnant") on the prime time *I Love Lucy*.

But while young, happy children reappeared for the first time since the 1930's, a working wife, with or without children, was much slower to emerge either on television or in Hollywood. Although television abandoned the glamour and wealth associated with the movie image of young married life in favor of a more middle class lifestyle, television comedies still portrayed wives who never worked outside the home, whether they had children, like June in *Leave It to Beaver*, or not, like Mary in *The Dick Van Dyke Show*. Nor did it matter what social class these families belonged to; lower class wives, like Alice or Trixie in *The Honeymooners* did not work outside the home either, even though the couples had no children and their husbands, a bus driver and sewer worker respectively, were not well off. In the fifties, it was an article of faith that a career and marriage, either with or without children, no matter what social class, were mutually incompatible.

However, long before movies came to grips with the phenomenon of the working wife and mother, television in the sixties began regularly portraying both single working women in such shows as *The Mary Tyler Moore Show* and married working women such as Emily in *The Bob Newhart Show*. Even Lucy herself had her own show in the 1960's, in which she was widowed, working for a living, and accompanied by her real life daughter, Luci. By the seventies, in such shows as *Alice* and *One Day at a Time*, women were shown raising children by themselves. By contrast, the movie image of women degenerated. From *Cleopatra* to *Straw Dogs*, women in or out of marriage were regarded as dangerous. Ironically, the so-called "boob tube" was the first to begin exploring with care and humor the changing role of women in modern America.

Adam's Rib - Instructor's Guide

1. How did World War II affect the employment of women? Why? Cite specific examples.

2. In the 1920's, women made enormous gains in their drive for equality with men, but their relative position in American society remained about the same. Discuss. In your answer you should consider all the following:

    1. 19th Amendment
    2. employment opportunities
    3. Margaret Sanger and birth control
    4. social advances

3. Discuss the passage of the 19th Amendment to the Constitution relating it to the activities of Susan B. Anthony in this country and the Pankhursts in England.

4. How is the 1960's women's rights movement similar to and different from other civil rights movements of the period such as black civil rights or the movment led by Caesar Chavez.

5. Write a biographical sketch and assess the signficance of any or all of the following:

1. Eleanor Roosevelt
2. Susan B. Anthony
3. Margaret Sanger
4. Germaine Greer
5. Coretta King
6. Barbara Jordan
7. Katherine Hepburn

6. Write a book report, indicating the author's hypothesis and relating events in the film to events in the book, for any or all of the following:

1. Karen Anderson, *Wartime Women: Sex Roles, Family Relations and the Status of Women During World War II* (1981).
2. W.H. Chafe, *The American Woman* (1974)
3. John Costello, *Virtue Under Fire: How World War II Changed Out Social and Sexual Attitudes* (1985)
4. Betty Friedan, *The Feminine Mystique* (1963) new edition 1983
5. Juanita Kreps, *Sex in the Marketplace: American Women At Work* (1971)
6. Leslie Woodcock Tentier, *Wage Earning Women: Industrial Work and Family Life in the United States, 1900-1930* (1982)

7. Discuss the way women have been depicted in Hollywood movies from the early twentieth century to the 1950's. A useful source in Molly Haskell, *From Reverence to Rape: The Treatment of Women in the Movies* (1973).

Rebel Without a Cause - 1950's: American Dream or American Nightmare?

Rebel Without a Cause, released in 1955, produced a new kind of hero for America in the person of James Dean. His heroism arises from his struggle to separate himself from his parents' bankrupt moral values and to make up for his parents' inability to provide adequate role models. Dean is an adolescent who by learning to take care of a real child becomes the man his real father is not. Dean's rebellion in the film reflected and justified a real social movement taking place outside the movie theater, namely the rise and spread of 1950's juvenile delinquency. Such delinquency was blamed on the material prosperity of the decade as symbolized by the growth of suburbia, and on the insecurity bred of the Cold War, but *Rebel Without a Cause* specifically blames the delinquency it portrays on the breakdown of traditional male/female roles arising from World War II. As the film makes clear, such juvenile delinquency frequently involved some violence, but the violence portrayed in *Rebel Without a Cause* actually encouraged and ritualized real teenage violence like the chickee run. Moreover, the violence of the film makes it characteristic of Hollywood in the post-McCarthy period as movies came to grips with the advent of television by portraying what the tube could not. Finally, *Rebel Without a Cause*, with its concern for an "important theme" like teenage delinquency, is similar to many serious American films of the 1950's which were still reeling from the long term effects of the House Un-American Activities' investigation of the movie industry.

Hollywood had always given America and the world images of true heroism, but not until the 1950's was a character like James Dean offered as a hero-type. Dean is not in the mold of those tall, muscular, taciturn men like John Wayne or even the shorter, hard-boiled cynics like Humphrey Bogart who came before him. The problems facing America in the fifties could not be solved with the virtues which had conquered the frontier; the raw strength of Wayne, for example, was not useful or necesarry for climbing the social ladder of a large corporation. Nor was Bogart's loner cynicism an appropriate response in a post-industrial society more and more reliant on service industries where the ability to ingratiate oneself was critical to the success of the business. Dean is neither tall nor strong like Wayne, and, unlike Wayne, who said very little--although what he said was always to the point--Dean talks constantly, mumbling his way through in a drive for self-expression. And surely the likes of John Wayne never struggled through a James Dean adolescent identity crisis--at least not on film. Not only is Dean different from the earlier heroes who preceded him, he is also different from the blond teenage stars Hollywood produced during the 1950's. While other teenage heart-throbs, like Troy Donahue, specialized in being sweet and bland, and usually wore the uniform of the fifties college preppie, Dean was brooding and dissheveled, and adopted what would become the uniform of the alienated--tight-fitting jeans which bepoke an open sexuality.

In how he looked, spoke, and acted, then, Dean was a rebel against the traditions of Hollywood heroism, and he was recognized as a replacement hero in the film itself. Plato, who deeply admires Jim, Dean's character in *Rebel*, and who comes to regard him as his hero, originally had a pin-up of Alan Ladd, a blond John Wayne type, on the inside of his locker door at school. In a marvelous scene, Plato sees Jim's reflection in a mirror tacked up just above Ladd's picture. In Jim, Plato had a real, accessible hero as opposed to a glossy photograph of the inaccessible and largely irrelevant typical Hollywood hero Ladd represents. Indeed, Plato's respect for Jim is based on his caring concern for Plato, a true father-son relationship which contrast sharply with Jim's unsatisfactory relationship with his own father.

Dean's rebellion against the morals of his society is symbolized in *Rebel* by his dissatisfaction with his parents. His cowardly father is henpecked consistently by his shrewish mother and grandmother, both of whom are more concerned with keeping "up" appearances than with living "up" to the moral values they profess to believe. Indeed, the film stresses this notion of "up"-ward movement. Dean is first seen collapsed in a fetal position while the credits roll, but at the end, he walks off under his own power, standing upright. Repeatedly in the film, he urges his father to "stand up" to his mother and thus provide him with a role-model, and at the end of the film, father and son do literally stand up together beside Plato's body. Jim wanted higher ethical and social standards than those of his parents, and nowhere can his parents' bankrupt morality be seen more clearly than in Jim's confrontation with his parents following Buzz's death in the chickee run.

When Buzz dies as a result of the chickee run, Jim tells his parents he must inform the police. His parents are appalled at this decision, and try to stop him from ruining his future life in suburban America through an excess of morality. When Jim tries to explain that they are all involved in Buzz's death, his parents refuse to listen. Indeed, they seem concerned only with themselves; all Jim's mother can think of at such a time is that she nearly died giving birth to Jim. The parents want Jim to wait, to compromise his values for material success, but Jim will have none of it. His parents' refusal to live up to their own moral values or to let Jim live up to his sparks an open rebellion in him: he tries to strangle his father and then storms out the door after putting his foot through his grandmother's portrait.

Of course, Jim's violent rebellion against his parents and their lack of real moral values found a ready response in many young people in the 1950's whose anti-social behavior was lumped together under the name of juvenile delinquency. Rebellious kids at war with their parents' society were nothing new, and from the Little Rascals to the Dead End Kids, Hollywood had portrayed them on film before. But there was a vast difference between the funny rascality of the earlier lot and the vicious meanness of the kids in *Rebel*. Playful pranks had become the calculated destructiveness of tire slashing and running stolen cars off cliffs.

Moreover, unlike the Little Rascals or the Dead End Kids who were usually poor and immigrants, the kids in *Rebel* came from nice, middle class homes. The phenomenon of middle class kids engaged in willful destructiveness we see in the film reflected a real social movement of the 1950's, when supposedly "nice" kids ran away from home like Judy or landed in the police station for intoxication like Jim. Moreover, in spite of a flood of ink spilled by writers in all sorts of publications from sociological journals to *The Reader's Digest*, no one was exactly sure why so many kids rebelled or what parents ought to have done about it.

The usual explanations of juvenile delinquency centered around the uneasiness most Americans felt with the 1950's economy of abundance and the insecurity bred of the Cold War. In the depression thirties, middle class Americans had had no money to spend on consumer goods, and in the war years of the forties, few consumer goods were produced, but after a short, post-war recession, the American economy entered a boom period as consumers went through an orgy of buying. In many ways, the American Dream came true as more Americans owned their own homes and immigrants rose on the social scale, a process reaching its climax when the son of an immigrant, John F. Kennedy, was elected president in 1960. But the American Dream turned out to be the American Nightmare. The homes Americans lived in were situated in the blighting conformity of Levittowns, and civil rights for blacks were systematically ignored by the White Citizens Councils in the South. Material prosperity did not bring happiness either to parents or children, and parents who had waited so long to acquire membership in the "right" country club found themselves being criticized by their children who had not experienced their parents' earlier deprivations.

This material prosperity is, of course, best symbolized by the huge growth of suburbs during the 1950's. In 1950, 69% of Americans lived in urban areas while in 1960 that number had risen to 75%, but that growth masks the fact that more and more Americans chose to live in suburbs next to the cities rather than in the cities themselves. Suburbs were nothing new, of course; probably the earliest and most famous was Brooklyn to which New Yorkers began to flee as early as the mid-nineteenth century. New styles of architecture, like the cottages pioneered by Andrew Jackson Davis, and new street designs which abandoned the city grid pattern in favor of twisting thoroughfares called "lanes" or drives," characterized these new suburbs. Yards emerged which were no longer strictly utilitarian, but rather ornamental; perfectly manicured green swaths separated and protected the home from the corrupt world beyond. But these islands of security could be afforded only by the relatively well-to-do until the development of the balloon frame house, the availability of cars, and, especially after 1950, mass production techniques borrowed from the automobile industry dramatically lowered the cost of suburban homes.

Balloon framing actually appeared in 1833 in Chicago, but did not become widespread until the late nineteenth century. Instead of using heavy timber framing whose posts and beams required specialized labor skills and expensive tools, the balloon frame used cheaper 2x4 studs to frame the house, and required only a few simple carpentry tools; such a home could be erected quickly by two men where a heavy timber frame required 20. Moreover, the use of machine made nails, as opposed to the more complicated mortise and tendon joints, also lowered costs; such nails cost less than 5% of the older wrought iron nails. Balloon framing proved its stability on the open prairie where it withstood wind and severe weather, and the technique dramatically lowered prices, but the balloon frame house had to be accessible to the city in order for the middle class to move out.

The first suburbs were connected to the cities by public transit systems like the trolley and especially the commuter railroad. Both such systems, however, required a large population density to be profitable, and suburbs, with their lower population densities, were frequently not sufficiently profitable for rates to drop very low. As a result, once again, only the relatively well-to-do could afford the suburbs. However, the development in the early twentieth century of mass production on a moving assembly line helped reduce the price of a Model T from $950 in 1908 to $290 in 1924, and cars became available to the middle class for the first time. By 1923, Kansas alone had more car registrations than France or Germany! The Federal Road Act of 1916 as well as the later Federal Highway Act of 1956 created eventually thousands of miles of paved highways, and made it possible for people to live farther from their work in the city. A possibility, but not a reality, for there were still very few homes in suburbia the average middle class family could afford. As late as 1933, cars were used primarily for discretionary travel with over one half of Americans either walking or taking public carriers to work. The development of the 1950's suburbias, therefore, required one more element to bring the price down low enough to allow even the average middle class family to escape the city.

That element was the adoption of methods first pioneered by the meat packing industry but made famous by Henry Ford in the automobile moving assembly line. Following World War II, when the demand for affordable housing soared, houses were simplified and standardized as the Model T had been before them, and they were built in groups called "developments" which benefitted from economies of scale. Among the first ,and certainly the most famous to adopt this system, was the Levitt family whose Levittown on Long Island became the model for such developments. Dispensing with expensive cellars in favor of a poured concrete slab, these houses were all Cape Cod style, varied only by the exterior color, and set down on a bulldozed stretch of land from which all impediments like trees had been removed. In time, new trees and shrubs grew up to relieve the original monotonous impression, but at least the young families who bought them had homes of their own at a price they could afford. Some discovered, however, that the blighting conformity of these artificial non-towns bore down heavily on their children, some of whom escaped into delinquency as *Rebel Without a Cause* so clearly portrays.

According to the wisdom of the time, however, juvenile delinquency was not only the product of the blighting conformity of such suburbs as Levittown, but also of the insecurity bred of the Cold War which likewise pervaded the seemingly serene 1950's. In 1949, the Soviet Union acquired the atomic bomb, and the development of Inter-Continental Ballistic Missiles (ICBM's) obliterated the security which America's geographical isolation had previously provided. While Americans joined country clubs, they also increasingly built individual bomb shelters in their back yards. In the planetarium scene in *Rebel*, for example, the end of the world is portrayed as a giant fire ball. Hiroshima had in fact been consumed in a ball of fire when the United States leveled the city with an atomic bomb in 1945. Although the insecurity was real, the etiquette of the period demanded the fear remain unspoken; politicians like Adlai Stevenson who voiced concern over the outcome of the arms race in 1956 were soundly defeated by father figures like Dwight Eisenhower, who significantly, had been Supreme Allied Commander in World War II when the first atom bombs were dropped. People like Jim's parents who refused to recognize their children's problems likewise forced themselves to forget about the threat of nuclear annihilation--at least until the launching of Sputnik in 1957 displayed the technical advances made by our Russian adversaries and prompted a nation-wide campaign to find out why Johnny couldn't read but Ivan could.   And John Kennedy made the supposed missile gap between the United States and the Soviet Union, a gap supposedly in the Russians' favor, an issue which helped him win the presidency in 1960.

To be fair, *Rebel Without a Cause* stresses the perils of prosperity as the causative factor of the juvenile delinquency problem and ignores Cold War insecurity except for a fleeting reference to it in the planetarium incident. Once having explained how juvenile delinquency developed, however, the film also tries to suggest what could be done about it, but the solution offered to the problem is rather simple-minded and overly optimistic. If only parents would be more involved with their kids and more sensitive to their needs, the film seems to say, nice kids would not go wrong. The model offered, of course, is the only sympathetic adult in *Rebel*, the juvenile court cop whose name, Ray, is the same as that of the film director, Nicholas Ray. He lets Jim release his frustration early in the film by letting him pound the desk; as Jim says to Ray, "You can see right through me, can't you?" It is Ray who orders the lights extinguished at the planetarium showdown when Jim requests it, and it is Ray who tells Jim to come by anytime he has a problem. But it is exactly here that the difficulty emerges. When Jim does go to Ray after Buzz's death, Ray isn't there, and the other officers tell Jim to come back tomorrow. And when the lights are extinguished, the policeman whom Plato had shot at cannot determine who is exiting from the planetarium door and so has the lights turned on again.   Then, when Plato is frightened by the lights and flees, he is shot. One good cop does not a good society make. Individual solutions to a group problems, therefore, do not seem overwhelmingly convincing.

Moreover, the film begs the question of how many individuals can change their ways and how long-lived these changes might be. For example, can all individuals be rehabilitated? It is hard to see any regeneration for Crunch, the sociopath who hunts Jim down following Buzz's death. Likewise, Plato had been abandoned by his parents and lives in a fantasy world as a result ,and that in spite of psychoanalytic treatment. After all, Plato was brought to the police station in the first place for shooting puppies. Although we are encouraged to believe that Jim's parents have stopped their bickering, we never see Judy's family reach any kind of awareness. Moreover, the action in the film is so compressed and fast-paced--all of it takes place in one day--we cannot know how long-lasting the effects of everyone's conversion may be. Jim's parents look at one another knowingly as the film ends, but what will happen the next time they have to decide between going to the club and caring for their son? If the society which produced juvenile delinquency was sick, as the film suggests, how possible is it to change the Levittown culture by changing a few of its members and how sincere is their conversion in the first place?

Even more disturbing in terms of the film's proposed solution is its reinvocation of traditional sex roles as crucial to recovery. If Jim's father would just stand up to his mother and put her in her place, all would be well, the film seems to say. But women in the 1950's were different from women in the thirties to a large degree because of the liberation of the World War II experience when women joined the labor force in huge numbers, replacing men soldiering overseas. When men returned from the war, they wanted their old jobs back in spite of the fact that 95% of working women also wanted to continue in their jobs. Many women were fired to be replaced by returning veterans, but the image of Rosie the Riveter helping to rid the world of fascism remained long after Rosie herself had joined the unemployment lines. Women's position in the economy and by extension in the family had been remarkably improved. In Rebel, Jim's mother may indeed be a shrew who forces her husband to serve her dinner, but modern audiences must question the film's assumption that by helping his wife with her chores her husband automatically becomes a poor father figure to his son and thus drives him into juvenile delinquency. Perhaps it could be argued that a boy needs a strong father figure to achieve adulthood, but then surely a girl should have a strong mother figure for the same reason. However, Judy's mother appears warm and sensitive and is certainly supportive of her husband, and yet her daughter too attends chickee runs with stolen cars and ultimately runs away. One must doubt, then, whether the reestablishment of traditional male/female roles would prevent juvenile delinquency or render unnecessary the violence which pervades the film.

It is of course that violence which galvanizes the adult world into action at the end of *Rebel Without a Cause* and causes Jim's parents to change their ways, but while adults viewed the violence with horror, teenagers worldwide used the film as a textbook to formalize or even ritualize juvenile violence. One kid insulting another or even slugging him was nothing new, but the use of switchblades and chickee runs substantially upped the ante; a punch can get one hurt while a switchblade can get one killed. The film portrayed the elaborate etiquette of a swtichblade fight and explored the almost chivalric quality of the chickee run. The lesson was learned too well by some. The United States experienced an enormous upsurge in teenage violence, and in Japan the samurai sword replaced the switchblade with deadly effect. The film caused such fear among authorities in Spain that it was banned for four years, and in the interior of England where cliffs were scarce, inventive English teenagers found ways to adapt the California chickee run to winding English roads. *Rebel* not only formalized such violence, but it presented violence as an attractive rite of passage from adolescence to adulthood. The idea of testing one's manhood by risking one's life had an almost atavistic quality to it which teenagers worldwide eagerly embraced. Not only did such young people copy and improve upon the etiquette of violence portrayed in the film, but they also copied Dean's mannerisms and dress. To be cool meant to be tough, and to be tough meant to wear jeans and a sulky expression. James Dean became a cult figure, the more so since he died as he had lived when his Jaguar crashed in October, 1955, just a few days before *Rebel* was released. Ironically, then, a film Nicholas Ray made to condemn juvenile violence ended up encouraging it.

While the movies could portray violence, their arch-rival television could not. By 1952, television was sufficiently widespread to begin to cut into movie box office receipts. The great studios had remained profitable to a large degree because they manufactured large numbers of serials and Grade-B films which filled the second spot on a double feature, and because they earned large profits from distributing their own films through theater chains they owned themselves. But by 1955, neither of these situations existed any longer. In 1952, the Supreme Court ordered the great studios to divest themselves of their theater outlets and forced them also to stop obliging theater owners to buy blocks of films which included the good with the bad. As the movie industry reeled from the financial losses this court decision produced, it was also being hurt by the competition from television which increasingly took over the Grade-B movie subject matter for its own broadcasts. Desperate to create a new audience in order to bolster profits, the industry began to specialize in big, spectacular movies filmed on location and in violence which television could not bring into middle America's homes during prime time. *Rebel Without a Cause* is part of this second movement. But Hollywood could not just portray violence on the screen without showing that violence would be properly punished. Thus, only lawmen could shoot first with impunity. Gangsters were out and G-men were in. Even safer for Hollywood was to put the violence in the past, such as in *The Robe*, which dealt with Biblical times. Rarely was violence shown in a contemporary setting, and even more rarely was there any suggestion that that violence was not absolutely justified.

The movie industry's glorification of the law was part of its reaction to the upheavals caused by the House Un-American Activities Committee's (HUAC) investigation of Hollywood and the terrors of McCarthyism which followed it. In the hysteria of anti-communism which gripped the country in the period following World War II, communist influence both real and imagined was thought to exist everywhere, even in Hollywood. The HUAC launched an investigation of the movie industry, and when the notorious Hollywood Ten refused to testify before the Committee, claiming the Fifth Amendment, many assumed they were guilty of being communists and thus potential traitors. To correct the image that Hollywood was somehow un-American and part of the communist conspiracy, many movie personalities, among them Walt Disney and Ronald Reagan, came forward to condemn communism, or like Elia Kazan, to admit membership in the party and willingly to identify other party members. Those who refused to "name names" or who sought to defend themselves were usually blacklisted by the Hollywood studios. For those working behind the scenes such as script writers or cameramen, the effects of blacklisting were inconvenient but not completely destructive; many continued to work under assumed names or worked for much less than they had before the HUAC reared its ugly head. On the other hand, for those who were actors, and whose identities could therefore not be camouflaged, blacklisiting usually meant the end of a career.

The HUAC never proved that anyone who found his "name named" in the Hollywood investigation had actually committed treason or tried to subvert the government of the United States. Indeed, most of those accused had joined the party during the depression years when communism seemed a viable alternative for ending the economic woes then facing the country. During World War II, when the Soviet Union was our ally, many had written and produced films like *Mission to Moscow* which portrayed our communist allies as noble, albeit bear-like, patriots. As the Cold War settled in, however, youthful association with or praise of Russia or communism came back to haunt many in the movie industry just as it would those in the State Department. What the HUAC did in investigating Hollywood, Senator Joe McCarthy did in investigating first the State Department and ultimately the United States Army. Both McCarthy and the HUAC merely created a climate of fear in which innuendo and unsubstantiated charges could and did wreck people's careers.

Hollywood reacted to this climate of fear by producing a series of big-production musicals and other escapist fare, especially genre pictures or westerns set in faraway times and places. Almost any film dealing with contemporary social issues was bound to involve some criticism, and since criticism had been confused with sedition, most filmmakers shied away from the here and now. There had been a spate of "message films" like *Gentlemen's Agreement*, which dealt with anti-semitism, produced in the relatively open years after World War II, but they had virtually ceased by 1952 when McCarthyism enjoyed its heyday.   Beginning in 1954, however, the year of the ill-fated Army-McCarthy hearings which led to the Senator's downfall and ultimate censure by the Senate, a new series of serious films began to make their appearance.   No longer remakes of literary classics like *The Great Gatsby*, these films were set in the present and provided criticism of the society they saw.   Drug addiction was addressed in *The Man With the Golden Arm*, labor racketeering in *On the Waterfront*, and juvenile delinquency in *Rebel Without a Cause*, just to mention a few of the themes Hollywood now felt bold enough to explore.

But the influence of the atmosphere of fear could still be detected in that these films had a "happy ending." The protagonist always sees the evil of his ways, and the problem is always corrected before the theater lights go back up.   The hero may be bloodied during the film, but emerges triumphant as it ends.   By contrast, note the despair prevalent in more recent films like *Serpico* in which the hero is almost killed, and yet precious little change occurs either in the New York police force or the New York underworld.   By the 1970's, the problems facing America seemed almost unsolvable, at least according to the evidence of most Hollywood films.   The War Against Poverty launched by Lyndon Johnson seemed no more winnable than the war in Vietnam.   In this context, the happy ending of *Rebel Without a Cause* is bound to seem simple-minded and overly optimistic, but at least it offered hope.   In more recent films, as perhaps in contemporary life, hope is in short supply.

Rebel Without a Cause - Instructor's Guide

1. Was there really a rise in juvenile delinquency in the 1950's? Why or why not? Define your terms and cite specific examples.

2. How is the rebellion of youth in the fifties the same as or different from the rebellion of youth in the 1960's?   In your answer you should consider all the following:

    1. Which involved violence, of what kind and why?
    2. Which was more political?
    3. The campaign for president of Barry Goldwater in 1964 and George McGovern in 1972
    4. the pivitol role of John Kennedy, the Peace Corps, and Vista

William H. Chafe, *Unfinished Journey: America Since World War II* (1986) is a useful source.

3. Write a brief biographical sketch and assess the significance of any or all of the following:

1. James Dean
2. Jack Kerouac
3. the University of California at Berkeley riots and demonstrations
4. Elvis Presley
5. the Beatles

4. Account for the rapid development of suburbs following World War II and the depression thirties and assess the signficance of suburbs in the realm of politics and social development. A helpful source is Kenneth Jackson, *Crabgrass Frontier* (1985).

5. Write a book report, indicating the author's hypothesis and relating events in the film to events in the book, in any or all of the following:

1. William H. Chafe, *The Unfinished Journey: America Since World War II* (1986)
1. Bruce Cook, *The Beat Generation* (1971)
2. Scott Donaldson, *The Suburban Myth* (1969)
3. J.K. Galbraith, *The Affluent Society* (1958) third edition, 1976
4. Kenneth Jackson, *Crabgrass Frontier* (1985)
5. Jack Kerouac, *On the Road* (1957)
7. David Riesman, *The Lonely Crowd* (1950)
8. Irwin Unger, *The Movement: A History of the American New Left, 1959-1972* (1974)

6. Discuss how Hollywood movies emphasized the virtues of conformity and taught fear of foreigners, especially in the spate of horror movies produced during the 1950's. Peter Biskind, *Seeing is Believing* (1983) is an excellent source.

On the Waterfront - The Gang's All Here

Released in 1954, *On the Waterfront* explores the relationship between organized crime and labor unions, a connection which first came to public notice following the 1950-1951 investigations of Senator Estes Kefauver. The exposés of the Kefauver committee were part of an attack on labor unions generally, an attack which had begun as early as 1947 with the Taft-Hartley bill, and was designed to reduce the power of one of the key elements in Roosevelt's New Deal Coalition. The abuses the film decries were addressed and mostly corrected after the formation in 1955 of the AFL/CIO under George Meany, who worked diligently to rid labor unions of violence and unethical practices. The major exception to Meany's efforts, however, were the Teamsters to which the Longshoremen's Union of the film belongs. The Teamsters displayed a violence and gang organization which owed much to the Mafia, an Italian import, and shows that once crime elements enter a labor union, it is difficult, if not deadly, to get rid of them. If, then, the events upon which *On the Waterfront* was based were real, it is nonetheless true that the film is a dramatized rendering of real life, and as such, it introduces a new style of acting associated with Marlon Brando. More important, the film presents a new kind of hero with limited goals; demanding the right to be a contender, not a champion, this hero's ideals underlay the developing civil rights movement and eventually the Great Society of Lyndon Johnson.

Between 1950 and 1951, Senator Estes Kefauver from Tennessee led a Senate committee which investigated the relationship between organized crime, labor unions, and big city political machines. The evidence the committee produced clearly showed that crime elements had penetrated both unions and political machines. "Bosses" frequently ran unions to benefit themselves, and used a private army of thugs to enforce their decisions. In *On the Waterfront*, Johnny Friendly is the boss, and the film begins with his using Terry, played by Marlon Brando, to lure a would-be defector up to the roof so his thugs can kill him. Later, Friendly has Terry's brother, Charlie, killed when Charlie disobeys orders; he also has Dugan, another would-be defector killed, and he openly threatens Terry himself after he gives testimony to the Crime Commission. Events like these were real, everyday occurrences at the time, and the Kefauver committee sought to expose them.

That would not be easy, however. Not only did the bosses threaten men like Terry and Dugan who came forth to testify, but the bosses also were adept at legal maneuvers which made prosecuting them difficult. For example, in the film, the bookkeeper of Friendly's gang explains to the Crime Commission that he cannot discuss the union's financial arrangements because their books were, conveniently, stolen the night before. So it appears were the books of all the union locals due to testify that day. Without evidence, the Commission must rely on personal testimony like Terry's. Such testomony, however, must be corroborated before conviction can take place; as viewers, we are led to believe that others will come forward to testify against Friendly and so convict him of murder. Friendly himself certainly fears for his life: "They're dustin' off the hot seat for me," he wails. But will the other union members really come forward? Is it, as the film so confidently suggests as the door closes in the finale, really "The End?"

Not necessarily. The other union members have repeatedly shown no willingness to buck the bosses. Pop, Joey's father, refused to fight them although he suspected they were behind his son's death. Even Terry agreed to testify mostly because his brother has been killed and because Friendly ordered him to throw a fight; these are personal reasons, however, not a conviction based on abstract principles of justice. Moreover, what will keep Friendly and his "pistoleros" from returning once the glare of publicity has dimmed? As long as the armed thugs stick together, intimidation is always a strong possibility when they compete against unarmed civilians.

In fact, most real gangsters who went to jail were convicted on technical charges, like income tax evasion in the case of Al Capone, or they were murdered by fellow gangsters, like "Dutch Schultz" Flegenheimer in 1935, or "Buggsy" Siegel in 1947. Some, like Lucky Luciano, simply left the United States. Murder is a serious charge, and proving it is correspondingly difficult. Thus, while Capone stopped profiting from his ill-gotten gains when he went to jail, he was not executed, although he had clearly been responsible for the murders of many. And Lucky Luciano continued to live in splendor in Italy! We have an imperfect justice system in which it is easier to convict a man of a lesser charge with a lesser sentence than to deal out harsh justice for major crimes. In *On the Waterfront*, Friendly is humiliated at the end, but alive, still presumably wealthy, totally unrehabilitated, and with continued access to the guns which made his reign of terror possible.

Why would otherwise decent people have tolerated Friendly's organization in the first place? His "racket" includes charging men a couple of dollars a week in kickback money, and obliging them to borrow money at exorbitant rates even though they don't need it and can't pay it back. One reason, as the film rightly points out, is fear of losing their jobs. In real life as in the film, the longshoremen are not well educated and basically constitute unskilled labor. Such workers can easily be replaced by other brawny newcomers if they prove recalcitrant, and in the early twentieth century, when masses of new immigrants deluged the United States, there were plenty of newcomers to hire. To cut down on this flood of immigrants and hence to stabilize the labor pool and raise wages, labor unions acquiesced in the restrictive immigration policies of the 1920's such as the Immigration Act of 1921 and the Johnson Act of 1924. Labor unions saw little benefit from this legislation, however, for by 1930, the country was sinking into the Great Depression, and there were so many unemployed people willing to work for any wages that once again the labor pool was enlarged and wages fell.

Roosevelt's New Deal vigorously aided the unions through the National Recovery Act's section 7a, which provided for collective bargaining, and later by the 1935 Wagner Act. More important, the CIO or Congress of Industrial Organizations was formed by John L. Lewis in 1935. It concentrated on organizing unskilled or semi-skilled laborers like miners and longshoremen, and was different from the AFL or American Federation of Labor, formed in 1887, which was exclusively for skilled laborers like cigar makers and garment workers.

As a result of the New Deal and such organizations as the CIO, labor union membership climbed to 8.5 million ,or about 23% of the labor force ,by 1940, but these figures are misleading. For one thing, as *On the Waterfront* shows, being a union member did not necessarily guarantee work; the men not chosen to work by Big Mac are all union members. Moreover, in 1940, 11 million people remained out of work in spite of the New Deal's programs, and the labor pool was accordingly still too large. Easily replaced, unskilled workers still feared for their jobs. Only in World War II, when the country experienced full employment, could unions guarantee a job and a living wage to their members.

When World War II veterans returned from overseas in 1946, however, the same problem of too many unskilled workers vying for too few jobs occurred again. Workers who had stayed at home when any labor was scarce refused to give up their large wartime paychecks and job security. Accordingly, in the spring of 1946, a series of strikes swept the country. Over 4.5 million workers stormed off the job. One of the most critical was the strike by railroad workers which paralyzed the nation's most effective method of transportation and which consequently delayed demobilized veterans who were trying to return home. Even worse, when the bituminous coal miners walked off the job, their strike threatened to bring all of American industry to a standstill, because without coal to fuel them, factories could not operate. As a result of such disruptions, antagonism to labor unions reached new highs; 69% of Americans in one 1946 poll held an unfavorable opinion of John L. Lewis.

President Truman reacted to such labor unrest in a confused, almost contradictory way, which managed to antagonize everyone:organized labor condemned him when he threatened to draft railroad workers into the army to stop their strike; consumers were outraged when he permitted businessmen to pass on the cost of new labor contracts which contained large pay increases; and Congress was furious when he blamed them for weakening wartime wage and price controls while he offered nothing else to replace them. When Truman vetoed a bill to continue wage and price controls in 1946, claiming it was so mangled by compromises it was worse than no bill at all, prices of scarce consumer goods were free to skyrocket. Americans, who had had no money in the Depression thirties and then few consumer goods to buy during the wartime forties, were willing to pay these high prices, and they had the moeny to do so. Thus, $136 billion dollars in personal savings built up during the war were abruptly released at a time when industry had not yet retooled for a peacetime economy. Too many dollars chasing too few consumer goods resulted in classic inflation; prices rose 18% in 1946 alone. The Republican campaign slogan of 1946 was simple and devastating: "Had enough?" In November, the Republicans gained control of both houses of Congress for the first time since 1930.

They moved quickly to curb what they regarded as excessive labor demands and the coddling of labor unions when they passed the Taft-Hartley act in 1947 over Truman's veto. This bill did not destroy labor unions as the President feared it would, but it did sharply curtail their power. The bill forbade the closed shop in which no one could work who was not a union member, obliged union leaders to sign non-Communist oaths, and provided for a 80-day cooling off period before a strike could be called which might endanger national health or safety. In effect, the bill simply redressed the balance of power between labor unions and management which since the 1935 Wagner Act had been clearly in favor of the unions, and placed the government in a more neutral position between the two.

The Taft-Hartley Act was in part a reaction to previous strikes, but it was also a direct challenge to one of the basic elements in Roosevelt's New Deal coalition. Labor unions had consistently supported the New Deal during the thirties, mostly because they had nowhere else to go. Communists and socialists were such a tiny fragment of the American population, that they could not realistically produce constructive legislation, and Republicans were openly hostile to organized labor. Not that Roosevelt himself ever personally showed any real affection for labor; John L. Lewis' thundering rhetoric in the 1938 steel strike merely caused Roosevelt to sniff, "A plague upon both your houses!" Yet in spite of the verbal sparring, Roosevelt's New Deal programs, such as section 7a of the NRA and the Wagner Act, helped unions directly, while New Deal relief programs such as the WPA and PWA aided union members indirectly as poor Americans. Unlike earlier Progressives who had prided themselves on their even-handedness, FDR was willing to aid one side more than the other in labor/management disputes. No longer simply a protector of labor unions, the New Deal had become their advocate. Thus, when the Republican-inspired Taft-Hartley Act restored Washington to a more neutral position in regard to labor, the effect was to weaken the Democratic New Deal coalition Truman would need to get reelected in 1948.

In spite of Republican hopes and a three way split in the Democratic party, Truman trounced Thomas E. Dewey, 303 electoral votes to 189, in 1948, but labor unions did not benefit much from this victory. Truman's Fair Deal, including measures such as national health insurance and federal aid to education which would have helped labor union members, did not become law when the president called Congress into special session after November. Some of the measures were regarded as simply too radical. Moreover, Truman erred when he sent all the legislation to Congress at the same time; unable to digest such a vast number of bills through its complicated committee system, Congress simply gagged. Finally, powerful conservative southerners who controlled the very committees through which Truman's proposed legislation had to pass refused to support it, and thus insured its defeat. Many of these southerners had been angered when the president embraced Hubert Humphrey's civil rights plank for the Democratic platform in 1948. As a result, Strom Thurmond and other southerners had bolted the Democrats to form the States' Rights party, or Dixiecrats as they were known. Thurmond, running as the Dixiecrat candidate, won 4 southern states and 39 electoral votes in the presidential election. Even though he lost to Truman, Thurmond was in no mood to pass the Fair Deal, especially when the centerpiece of the new legislation involved a federal anti-lynching bill and prohibited discrimination in federal housing projects!

Union workers could not benefit from the Fair Deal because it never passed Congress, and their economic condition became precarious once more when a recession engulfed the country in 1949. Again, unskilled labor like the dock workers in *On the Waterfront* found less and less work sought after by more and more men. With their jobs insecure, workers were willing to pay protection money, kickbacks, and outrageous interest charges in order to safeguard their livelihood. Gangsters like Johnny Friendly thrived in such conditions.

The abuses portrayed in *On the Waterfront*, then, were real, and after the Kefauver committee among others publicized them, labor moved to clean its own house. The rival AFL and CIO merged in 1955 following very complex negotiations. Under the leadership of George Meany, a Bureau on Ethical Practices was established which set guidelines for union behavior. Those unions which did not abide by these guidelines were ousted from the AFL/CIO. The most powerful union to be removed was the International Brotherhood of Teamsters, or Teamsters for short, a union which had organized predominantly unskilled workers in the transportation industry. Longshoremen like those in the film were also Teamsters. This union demanded members pay a substantial part of their wages into a pension fund, and organized crime found such huge sums of money invaluable for financing their illegal activities from gambling to prostitution to drugs. In 1957, Teamster boss Dave Beck had to invoke the Fifth Amendment 209 times to avoid telling a Senate investigating committee what he had done with $320,000 in union funds. He later went to jail for embezzlement. Then, in the early 1960's, Attorney General Robert Kennedy declared war on organized crime, and zeroed in on Jimmy Hoffa, the president of the Teamsters. After years of investigation, Hoffa was convicted of income tax evasion and sentenced to prison. The Teamsters as a whole, however, did not mend their ways, and when Hoffa returned from prison to reform the organization, he mysteriously disappeared and is presumed dead.

The crime organization in the Teamsters bears an uncanny resemblance to the Mafia. To understand these similarities, it may be helpful to review briefly the history of the Mafia and organized crime in the United States.

Born in Italy in the early nineteenth century, the Mafia (Maffia in Sicilian) was a response to the lawlessness created by the Napoleonic invasions. Southern

Italy had never been well governed by the Bourbon family anyway, but the upheavals created by Napoleon's rearranging of Europe's map meant that effective, impartial justice all but disappeared. Groups of vigilantes organized to administer a rough form of justice, settle land disputes, and provide peace. These groups later coalesced to form the Mafia as we know it today. Criminals and thugs found employment in the organization, and used terror to enforce its decisions.

Italy was finally united under Victor Emanuel II only in 1871, and he and his chief minister, Cavour, insisted that all of the country, including Sicily, abide by the progressive constitution they had established. Accordingly, attempts were made to suppress the Mafia, with mixed results; mostly, the organization was simply driven underground, but some lower echelon mafiosi were forced to emigrate. Many came to the United States where they quickly found a niche, dispensing justice and order through terror in the almost ungovernable American cities of the late nineteenth century. As cities began to reform themselves under the influence of muckrakers like Jacob Riis and aristocrats like Theodore Roosevelt, however, ex-Mafiosi sought new employment.

They found it thanks to the labor unrest of the period. Industrialists had set themselves against labor unions in any form, claiming they were examples of godless socialism. To break strikes, the businessmen began using private "security guards" like the Pinkerton detectives who did not hesitate to battle strikers. In 1892, for example, workers at the Carnegie Steel plant in Homestead, Pennsylvania, fought a mini-war against 300 Pinkerton guards, a battle in which 10 died and 60 were wounded. The government too, attacked strikers at will; in the Pullman strike of 1894, President Cleveland had called out the army to force workers back to their jobs. His Attorney General, Richard Olney, arrested the strike's leader, Eugene Debs, claiming his union was a "combination in restraint of trade" and hence illegal under the 1890 Sherman Anti-Trust Act. When, in 1895, the Supreme Court in *In re Debs* upheld the conviction, the government had a free hand to use the injunction powers of the Sherman Anti-Trust Act against labor unions, rather than against big businesses for which it had obviously been intended. Faced with the physical violence of the Pinkertons and the legal intimidation of the injunction, union leaders welcomed the services of the ex-Mafiosi.

The hired guns of labor now faced the hired guns of management, and inevitably violence resulted. For example, 1905 saw the formation of the International Workers of the World or IWW which accepted a conscious program of industrial sabotage against big business. In 1910, the *Los Angeles Times* newspaper offices were blown up, and when suspicion fell on McNamara, a union organizer, the AFL stepped in to pay for his defense by Clarence Darrow. Businessmen met violence with more violence; in 1914, in Ludlow, Colorado, state militia and mine guards charged a tent city of coal strikers, killing 26 people, mostly women and children.

In this environment of industrial violence, criminals found employment easily. Looking for men willing to use some "muscle" to protect their lives and those of their families, labor union leaders sometimes turned, perhaps unwittingly, to these violence prone immigrants. Thus, many of the gangsters who would become famous in the prohibition twenties got their start as labor enforcers before World War I.

Back in Italy, Mussolini and his fascists came to power after the March on Rome in 1922, and the Duce was determined to root out the Mafia once and for all. Believing that "There is nothing against the state, outside the state, or above the state," Mussolini would not permit extra-legal vigilantes to dispense justice anywhere. His crackdown resulted in a massive migration of criminals, many to the United States, where they quickly found jobs in the crime empires being created by liquor-running gangsters like Al Capone in the Prohibition era.

Newcomers quickly discovered, however, that the older crime figures had perfected a much more modern, professional organization than they had known in Italy. Basically using monopolistic schemes pioneered by big business the century before, criminals in America had developed sophisticated methods to control the manufacture and distribution of the product. As Capone saw it, "Prohibition is a business. All I do is supply a public demand. I do it in the least harmful way possible." In short, Capone controlled liquor the way Rockefeller had controlled oil with his Standard Oil Company. And like Rockefeller, Capone prospered; he did $27 million worth of business in 1927 alone.

Ruthless and eager to make a place for themselves in this country, however, the newcomers challenged the older immigrants for dominance, and gang wars erupted, like the 1929 St. Valentine's Day Massacre. To limit the loss of life and so reduce government interference, the rival gang leaders were persuaded by Meyer Lansky to meet in 1933 to divide the United States up into separate spheres of influence. Everyone agreed not to meddle in anyone else's area.

Since gangsters could not expand into someone else's territory, they had to increase their profits by increasing business in the territory they had been allotted. Especially when the 21st Amendment did away with prohibition, criminals had to find new sources of income other than running liquor, and they found them in prostitution, gambling, drugs--and labor unions. Union dues were a steady source of funds which could be used to finance other illegal operations and pay for the criminal "staff." Thus, as the 1930's progressed, unions were increasingly infiltrated by gangster elements, like Johnny Friendly.

Were all American gangsters Mafiosi? Of course not, but there are clear similarities between the two which *On the Waterfront* explores. The Mafia believed in *omertá*, from the Sicilian *omu*, meaning man. Manly, correct behavior meant never attempting to get justice from legally constituted authorities, nor to help them in the detection of crime. Most important, silence about Mafia activities was to be observed at all times when dealing with the outside world. On the American docks, *omertá* became "D and D," deaf and dumb in the face of illegal activities. Note in the film how no one, not even Joey's father, seeks help from the police to find his son's killers. When Edie, Joey's sister, tries to get help, even she significantly turns to the priest, Father Barry, not the police. The union members also refuse to testify before the Waterfront Crime Commission because to do so would violate the "D and D" rule, and so invite retaliation from the "pistoleros," an Italian word for gunslingers. Loyalty to the crime "family" must replace real family ties; when Charlie attempts to save his brother Terry's life against the orders of Johnny Friendly, Charlie is brutally murdered by the gang. Note, however, that Friendly is not of Italian descent--his name is Scully--that Terry is Polish, and Dugan, Irish. While many of the pistoleros are Italian, as we learn when they give their real names before the Crime Commission, not all the criminals are. In real life, too, the Mafiosi from Sicily may have brought with them their techniques of intimidation and organization, but their "expertise" was quickly appropriated by other ethnic groups and used to their own advantage.

The events described in *On the Waterfront* were real, then, but the film itself is a dramatized account. One reason for its intense impact is the presence of the young Marlon Brando, who pioneered a new style of acting. Sometimes called "method" acting, the technique was taught most fully by Lee Strasburg in New York City. American actors before the 1950's had for the most part approached their characters from the outside in, so to speak. That is, actors tried to mimic externally what the character had to be feeling internally; if the character was sad, the actor forced himself to cry, and might even try out sad facial expressions in the mirror. By contrast, method actors approached their characters from the inside out: they tried to "become" their character, to feel what the character had to be feeling, and assumed the outside facial expressions would take care of themselves. Strasburg also emphasized body language. A character expressed emotion not only on his face and through his words, but in how he moved and held his body.

Brando became the first nationally known and certainly the most famous method actor. Note how in *On the Waterfront* he moves his entire body freely to express emotion, much as modern dancers from Martha Graham onward learned to move not just arms and legs, but the back as well. Terry, the character Brando plays, is poorly educated and inarticulate; thus Brando has Terry stumble through his lines, stammer, and speak sometimes in machine-gun-like bursts of words. Not much for flowery rhetoric, he communicates physically, not only when he breaks down the door into Edie's apartment and kisses her--that was written in the script--but when he asks her to dance at the wedding. He says, "Do you, ah, want, ah...," and then he executes a few elaborate dance turns with his arms held out, and only finally finishes, a little sheepishly, with "dance?"

Brando's physicality reenforces the gritty realism Elia Kazan sought to achieve in *On the Waterfront*. The film is obviously shot on location, for example. Steam rises from subway vents when Edie and Terry meet in a vest pocket park, and a rooftop bedecked with television antennas serves as Terry's pigeon hutch. Furthermore, when people get hurt, they show it; at the end of the film, Terry is beaten up by Friendly's thugs, but unlike Clark Gable or even Humphrey Bogart, Brando's Terry is bleeding, his eyes are partially closed, and he staggers to the loading dock.

For while Brando is the hero of the film, he is not heroic, at least not in the tradition of Gable or Bogart. Gable never even perspired, let alone bled. He also got what he wanted. Even in his most famous role, as Rhett Butler in *Gone With the Wind*, he is financially successful, and at the end has even acquired Scarlet's love and respect, although by that time he doesn't care anymore--"Frankly, my dear, I don't give a damn!" Bogart's Sam Spade is closer to Brando's Terry, in that Spade too gets beaten up and associates with known criminals. But in *The Maltese Falcon*, when Peter Lorre clobbers Bogart on the back of the head, Bogart displays no blood, and simply holds his head for a moment before rushing out to continue his investigation. By contrast, Brando' s Terry is vulnerable both physically and emotionally.

Brando's Terry is unlike previous heroes in yet another, more important way. Heroes like Gable, Jimmy Stewart, or John Wayne not only avoided showing pain, but they also succeeded. When the theater lights came back up, these men had the girl, the money, and the admiration of their peers. But Terry does not. He has Edie, to be sure, and the admiration of his peers, but he certainly does not have the money and he has even lost the fight with Friendly's thugs. Success for Terry is not the unrealistic rags to riches, but rather defined by very limited goals; all he wants is a steady job as a longshoreman and a loving family. In fact, all he wants is a *chance* to succeed, not the guarantee of success itself. As Terry says to Charlie, "I could have been a contender."

This is the same philosophy which underlay the civil rights movement of the 1950's. In 1954, the same year that *On the Waterfront* was released, the Supreme Court in *Brown vs. the Board of Education* took the first step towards insuring that all children would have the right to be a "contender;" declaring separate but equal schools unconstitutional, the Court outlawed school segregation. The next year, Martin Luther King's support of the 1955 Montgomery, Alabama, bus boycott helped overturn the humiliating "back of the bus" segregation laws which had hamstrung blacks in their drive for success. In 1957, President Eisenhower chose to enforce the Supreme Court's decision when he federalized the National Guard to preserve peace during the desegregation of Little Rock, Arkansas schools. Like Terry, the early civil rights movement sought only the *access* to success, not the guarantee of success.

Bringing everyone, especially the young, at least to the starting line in the race for life continued on into the 1960's. John Kennedy argued this same way when he defused the religious issue in the presidential election of 1960; was it fair, he argued, to deprive almost 50% of the American population from running for President merely because they were Catholic? The desire to let everyone have a chance probably reached its highest expression in Lyndon Johnson's Great Society programs passed between 1963 and 1965. The Office of Economic *Opportunity* (my italics) administered a variety of programs like Head Start, for example, which tried to ready underprivileged children for elementary school. The Job Corps attempted to train high school dropouts for vocational jobs.

These programs tried to provide everyone with a chance to succeed, without having artificial, arbitrary barriers put in their way. In *On the Waterfront*, Terry has a promising career as a boxer until Johnny Friendly orders him to throw a fight, thus ending his chances for success in the ring. This arbitrary decision so angers him, that Terry is willing to risk his life by testifying against Friendly before the Crime Commission. He admits he might not have been able to win a championship fight, but he demands at least the chance. Brando's Terry, then, was part of the generation which asked less to be champions, than the opportunity to be contenders.

On the Waterfront - Instructor's Guide

1. Write a brief biographical sketch and assess the historical significance of any or all of the following:

    1. International Brotherhood of Teamsters
    2. Industrial Workers of the World (IWW)
    3. George Meany
    4. Marlon Brando
    5. John L. Lewis
    6. Lee Strasburg
    7. Al Capone

2. Write a book report on any of the following, giving the author's hypothesis and relating events in the film to events in the book:

    1. Melvyn Dubofsky and Warren Van Tine, *John L. Lewis: A Biography* (1977)
    2. Walter Galenson, *The CIO Challenge to the AFL* (1960)
    3. Ray Ginger, *Eugene V.Debs: A Biography* (1962)
    4. Eric F. Goldman, *The Crucial Decade--and After, 1945-60* (1961)
    5. Joseph Bruce Gorman, *Kefauver: A Political Biography* (1971)
    6. John Laslett, *Labor and the Left: A Study of Socialist and Radical Influences in the American Labor Movement, 1881-1924* (1970)
    7. R. Alton Lee, *Truman and Taft Hartley* (1966)
    8. Harold C. Livesay, *Samuel Gompers and Organized Labor in America* (1978)
    9. William H. Moore, *The Kefauver Committee and the Politics of Crime, 1950-1952* (1974)

10. Joseph G. Rayback, *A History of American Labor* (1966)
11. Joel Seidman, *American Labor From Defense to Reconversion* (1953)

3. Choose one of the books above and find the scholarly reviews of it in two or more of the following journals:

1. *The American Historical Review* (published by the American Historical Association)
2. *Journal of American History* (published by The Organization of American Historians)
3. *History Teacher*
4. *History, Review of New Books*
5. *Choice*

Compare and contrast the reviews. What did the reviewers like and dislike and why?

4. Describe the developing organization of Prohibition era crime syndicates like that of Al Capone.

5. Show why and how the AFL and CIO merged in 1955, and evaluate the results.

6. Explain why there was an upsurge of criminal violence after World War II. Cite specific examples.

7. Write a brief history of the Industrial Workers of the World (IWW), explaining who formed it and why, whom it tried to organize and why, and why it failed. Melvyn Dubofsky, *We Shall be All: A History of the Industrial Workers of the World* (1969) is a useful source.

8. According to Bert Cochran in *Labor and Communism: The Conflict That Shaped Americsn Unions* (1977), what role did communist ideology play in the formation and history of the American labor movement, especially after 1945. How did unions react to the World War II American alliance with the Soviet Union, to the "loss of China" in 1949, and to the early period of McCarthyism?

9. What exactly was discovered in the Kefauver committee hearings of 1950 to 1952, and how did Truman react to these disclosures? A useful source is William H. Moore, *The Kefauver Committee and the Politics of Crime, 1950-1952* (1974).

10. Describe the theory behind what became known as "method acting." Where did this new style of acting develop, who was instrumental in its development,

and how did it influence the careers of Marlon Brando, Paul Newman, and Lee Strasburg? What became of the movement in the 1960's?

Dr. Strangelove - Laughing at Armageddon

Dr. Strangelove, or How I Learned to Stop Worrying and Love the Bomb, released in 1963, is a black comedy about nuclear holocaust. It was produced the year after the Cuban Missile Crisis brought the world to the brink of World War III, and when the so-called "missile gap" in the Soviets' favor was shown never to have existed. Americans had been nervous about their defense since the launching of Sputnik in 1957, which revealed for all the world to see that the much vaunted American technological superiority was not all that superior. The ability of the Russians to shoot down a supposedly invulnerable U-2 reconnaissance plane in 1960 further damaged American self-esteem, and the collapse of the super power summit that summer, along with the building of the Berlin Wall in 1961, seemed to show the Russians were indeed the aggressive bullies anti-communists had long portrayed them to be. Against this background of increasing perceived Soviet menace both to American self-esteem and security, President John Kennedy inaugurated the "space race" to beat the Russians to the moon, and began the tentative steps which would carry this country into the quagmire of Vietnam.

Dr. Strangelove repeatedly plays with the idea of a missile gap, the idea that the Soviets have more missiles than does the United States. By the end of the film, when the crazed Dr. Strangelove has suggested that survival might be possible in deep mine shafts, the concept has metamorphozed into the "mine shaft gap," by which the Russians would have access to more mine shafts than we would. Many Americans believed until 1962 that a missile gap really did exist, and that the American government had deliberately permitted it to occur.

The idea of a missile gap developed following the Russian launch of Sputnik, the first artificial sattelite, in October, 1957. This successful launch was a public relations disaster for the United States which had prided itself on its technological superiority to the Russians. Looking for the culprit which would have permitted the Russians to do what the Americans could not, people in this country began an agonizing reappraisal of our school system following the publication of books like *Why Can't Johnny Read, While Ivan Can?*; they discovered woeful inadequacies, and the federal government passed the National Defense Education Act to help train teachers of both sciences and the humanities. Congress created the National Aeronautics and Space Administration in 1958 to compete with the Russians in the "space race." But while Sputnik damaged American prestige, more frightening was the thought that our security had been dramatically reduced.

Although Sputnik itself was of no military signficance--all it did was beep--the missile that put it in space was of enormous significance. It was a large rocket, large enough to launch a huge payload into space, and this meant that the Russians now had the capability to reach the United States with missiles from bases within the Soviet Union. Thus, the reaction time to a Soviet strike would be reduced from a matter of several hours, during which negotiations like those in

Dr. Strangelove were possible, to a matter of minutes before the missiles hit this country. With every second now counting, American government officials would have no choice but to launch an immediate American counterstrike on the mere *suspicion* of a Soviet launch. "Use 'em or lose 'em," as the conventional wisdom went.

While Sputnik seemed to show the Russians did have reliable missiles, by contrast, the United States did not. Indeed, American long range missiles, like the *Atlas,* were so unreliable that most blew up on the launching pad before they ever got off the ground, and those that actually flew usually went off course. Some newspapermen joked the missile should be called the "At Last." Although lacking good long range missiles, this country did have good short and medium range ones. In fact, the United States was actually able to reach targets in the Soviet Union using such missiles, because we had countries friendly to us, like Turkey, sufficiently close to the Russians to permit limited range missiles to be effective. The problem was these missiles were fueled with liquid oxygen, so highly flammable a substance that it could not be loaded into the missile until just before launch, and, since it took at least 20 minutes to fuel each missile, they were very vulnerable. As a result, Americans relied, as *Dr. Strangelove* makes clear, upon warheads delivered by B-52 bombers.

At the time, many Americans believed that a missile gap had been opened in the Russians' favor, that they had more and better missiles than we did. One who criticized the Eisenhower administration for permitting a missile gap to be created was Senator John Kennedy, and his criticisms increased when the president refused to panic and build a whole generation of these virtually useless liquid oxygen fueled missiles. But Eisenhower had discovered that Sputnik did not really represent a threat to American security, because, although the Russians certainly had long range missiles capable of launching a huge payload, these missiles were not reliably targetable. Although they could lob a satellite into orbit, their guidance systems were not precise enough to permit them to hit targets within the United States with accuracy. There was no missile gap; the Russians, like the Americans, would have to rely on long-range bombers. The reaction time was still a matter of hours, not minutes.

Unfortunately, Eisenhower's explanation that there was no missile gap sounded suspiciously lame, and the president could not give specific reasons for his views without compromising American intelligence gathering operations. As a result, Kennedy continued his criticism of the president for permitting a missile gap to grow, and he used that argument with devastating effect when he ran against Eisenhower's vice president, Richard Nixon, for president in 1960. Kennedy accused Ike's administration of mismanagement, lack of enthusiasm, and failure of will.

One event which played into Kennedy's hands was the downing of Gary Power's U-2 reconnaissance plane in May, 1960. U-2's flew very high and very fast, so much so that Russian fighters were not supposed to be able to catch up with them. Powers brought his plane down a little for a better view, however, and suddenly found Soviet MiG's on his wings. He ejected to safety, but he had to slow the plane down and bring it even lower to do so. As a result, when the plane crashed, the wings fell off, but the fuselage of the plane remained intact, and was recovered by the Soviets as was Powers. American authorities knew the plane was missing, but assumed the pilot had blown up the plane and himself, according to standard orders. The United States, therefore, put out a cover story that the missing plane was doing weather reconnaissance. After four days, the Russians sprung the trap, displaying both Powers and the intact fuselage of the U-2. For several days, the Soviets had had access to secret American codes and to secret American spying equipment. If Sputnik did not represent a threat to American security, the U-2 incident did! Worse, the United States government had mishandled the incident by not changing the codes the instant the plane went down, and by blithely assuming that the plane and pilot were destroyed without checking to determine if that was so. Moreover, Ike's administration had lied publicly about the purpose of the flight.

The Russians had known about the U-2 flights for some time, but they chose to make an issue over the shooting down of Power's plane for several reasons. For one thing, they were vying with the Chinese for leadership of the communist world, and they could not, as a result, be seen to be "soft" on capitalism. For another, Khruschev was engaged in a very delicate balancing act between the hawks in his government who wanted a sterner policy toward the Americans, and the doves who wanted peaceful coexistence; since the doves had been placated by the Soviet leader's trip to our country in September, 1959, the hawks now demanded Khruschev's attention, especially since the U-2 incident involved such a blatant violation of Russian sovereignty. Most important, the Russians hoped to disrupt a summit conference between Khruschev and Eisenhower which was set for the summer of 1960. If he threatened retaliatory measures for the U-2 incident vigorously enough, Khruschev thought he could frighten our European allies sufficiently that they would pressure the United States into compromising at the summit on such issues as the disposition of Berlin and Cuba. The western allies held together, however, and, having taken so extreme a position, Khruschev could not compromise without losing face before his comrades in the Politburo, so the Soviet leader permitted the summit to collapse. Eisenhower could not, therefore, demonstrate that his restraint with the Russians had produced the peace he longed for, and the way was left open for others to be more aggressive toward the Soviet Union.

Such a man was elected President in 1960. John F. Kennedy squeaked to victory over Richard Nixon in November. Kennedy had a "can-do" mentality; he believed all problems were capable of solution if enough willpower were exerted. He was also a highly competitive man, who encouraged a rivalry between the State and Defense Departments to develop creative solutions to difficulties overseas. Unfortunately, the State Department had been crippled during the McCarthy years between 1950 and 1954, when the best and the brightest had left government service in disgust, and the former Secretary of State, John Foster Dulles, had not seen fit to rebuild it. Moreover, since the military promised results more quickly than the diplomats, Kennedy came to rely increasingly on military rather than diplomatic solutions. To do so, he would have to increase the size, variety, and firepower of the American armed services. Thus, the man who came to office pledging peace supervised the most massive buildup of American weaponry since World War II.

Kennedy's idea was "flexible response," a concept vastly different from that of the Eisenhower administration which preceded him. In an effort to contain costs, Ike had relied increasingly on air power and nuclear weapons to achieve his objectives. Dulles called it "massive retaliation," that is, the firm threat to retaliate immediately with nuclear weapons in case of American displeasure. The Soviet invasion of Hungary in 1956, however, called our bluff, and the United States was forced to choose between no response at all and starting World War III. Kennedy, by contrast, believed the president should have a variety of responses available to him, including nuclear weapons, but including also a variety of conventional forces. Thus, the president expanded the Special Forces, or Green Berets, an elaborately trained counterinsurgency force. Moreover, he prepared to add 5 combat-ready divisions and 3 air wings while keeping 10 divisions in reserve, at a cost of $6 billion in 1961 alone. But while such moves to revamp the conventional forces of the United States concerned the Soviets, they were not unduly worried, for their Red Army would have remained clearly superior in numbers even with Kennedy's proposed changes.

What did terrify the Russians, however, and what led to a dramatic upsetting of the world's balance of power was Kennedy's massive buildup of nuclear weapons and delivery systems. Once in office, Kennedy learned what Eisenhower had known for some time, that there was no missile gap in the Russians' favor. In fact, by 1961, the United States actually had a small advantage. Since Sputnik, we had developed solid-fueled rockets which, because the fuel was already in them, were not as vulnerable as the early liquid fueled missiles had been. Moreover, American missiles were relatively accurately targeted, meaning they could be launched from this country and come close to their targets in the Soviet Union thousands of miles away. We had 16 ICBM's (Intercontinental Ballistic Missiles) already. In spite of this information, however, Kennedy insisted a missile gap remained, and using that excuse he began creating an awesome nuclear arsenal which gave the United States first strike capability. He authorized the construction of 1000 Minutemen ICBMs (five times the number Eisenhower had felt necessary) and a fleet of 32 Polaris submarines (up from the two Ike had possessed) capable of delivering 656 warheads. With the submarines, missiles, and a fleet of over 600 B-52 bombers, the United States would have had a 4 to 1 advantage in warheads over the Soviet Union. Now there was indeed a missile gap, but in the Americans' favor.

Knowing they had such a lead encouraged Americans to be provocative; although the official position of the United States government was that we would never launch a first strike, some in the administration began talking about fighting--and winning--a nuclear war. This is what *Dr. Strangelove* satirizes so brilliantly. A mad Air Force general, Jack D. Ripper, devises a plan which will force the United States to use its superiority: he will order his wing to attack the Soviet Union, make it impossible to call them back, and, since this government knows the Soviets will retaliate with nuclear weapons, the United States will be forced to send everything we have for a massive, unprovoked first strike. That is exactly what General Buck Turgidson, played by George C. Scott, argues. We have a five to one missile superiority, he says, and with a first strike could destroy 90% of Russian retaliatory capability. With what they had left, the Russians could kill only "20 million civilians, max!"

Only there's a hitch. The Soviets have developed a Doomsday device which, if ever any missile explodes in their country, will automatically create such radiation that all life on earth will be killed. When asked why anyone would build such a horrendous machine, the Russian ambassador explains his country could not keep up with the expense of the arms race, trying to match Kennedy's vast appropriations for weaponry. Furthermore, his countrymen learned through the *New York Times* that the United States was building such a device, and could not allow a "Doomsday gap" to be created.

Dr. Strangelove is fiction, of course; the United States neither launched a first strike nor did the Soviet Union create a Doomsday device--but the Soviets did begin a massive arms build-up of their own. Moreover, the Soviets worked quickly and brutally to defend what they regarded as their legitimate security interests. For example, the flow of skilled workers from East to West Berlin damaged Soviet prestige and robbed the East German regime of precisely the people it would take to compete well with the West. Khruschev demanded Kennedy give up West Berlin when the two met in June, 1961, telling him frankly he intended to sign a separate peace treaty with East Germany and that West Berlin could not be defended. Kennedy, hoping to impress Khruschev with his resolve, and knowing he had that vast nuclear arsenal, engaged in "brinksmanship"; he called up 150,000 National Guardsmen, began a crash program of fall-out shelters, and promised to spend $3 billion more on defense. Unable to bully the young president, and aware the United States could destroy his country with nuclear weapons, the aging Kremlin leader had to back down. On the night of August 13, 1961, the Soviets sealed off East Berlin by building a wall which armed guards patrolled. The flow of refugees stopped abruptly, but the Soviets had suffered a humiliating loss of face, and they now desperately looked elsewhere for a quick way to right to balance the power with the United States, and so be able to protect themselves.

Their eyes turned to Cuba. Fidel Castro had brought Cuba increasingly into the Soviet orbit, enough so that in the 1960 presidential campaign, Kennedy had criticized the Eisenhower administration for allowing a "Communist satellite" to be created on "our very doorstep." Once in office, the new president ignored the warnings of many advisors and congressmen, like Senator Fulbright, Chairman of the Senate Foreign Relations Committee, who urged a diplomatic solution to our difficulties with Cuba. Instead, he chose a military option, and in April, 1961, permitted the Bay of Pigs invasion to go forward. It was a disaster: all the CIA-trained Cuban refugee invaders were either killed or taken prisoner. Nonetheless, the United States had clearly signaled our unhappiness with the Castro government, and had shown we would consider invading Cuba to overthrow it. The Soviets now saw a chance both to redress the strategic balance between the two super powers, and at the same time, to protect Cuba from another American invasion. Taking a desperate gamble, Khruschev began moving missiles into Cuba in the summer of 1962.

By October, American planes had confirmed the introduction of 24 medium range and 18 intermediate range missiles into Cuba. Kennedy ordered Khruschev to take them out, and, in a thinly veiled threat, announced he would hold the Soviet Union, not Cuba, responsible, meaning that the United States would retaliate against the Russians, not the Cubans. The president then threw a naval blockade around Cuba, and waited for the Soviets to respond.

Khruschev was under intense pressure from members of his own government. Some urged accommodation with the United States to avoid having this country use its massive first strike capability against the Soviet Union, wiping out Soviet defenses. Others urged, however, that the Soviets stand up to the Americans, and use Cuba as we had long used Turkey, as a forward staging ground from which to launch otherwise useless short and medium range missiles against the enemy. With Cuba only 90 miles off the coast of Florida, American cities could be hit within eight minutes of launch. There would be no time to react, let alone negotiate as in *Dr. Strangelove*. The Soviets would have acquired first strike capability, not by building expensive new weapons, but by putting existing weapons where they would do the utmost damage. The missile gap, in the Americans' favor, would have been decisively closed. In the end, Khruschev decided the risk of total annihilation was unacceptable. Had more of the missiles in Cuba been operational, perhaps he would have done otherwise, but the Soviet leader agreed to remove the missiles in return for a pledge from the Americans never to invade Cuba.

Kennedy's brinksmanship prevailed in the Cuban missile crisis, and at first the incident appeared to vindicate the president's massive arms build-up; it was generally conceded that Khruschev had to back down because of the certainty of massive American retaliation. The Democrats won big in the off-year elections in November. Moreover, the Russians proved more conciliatory when they offered to accept a "hot line" which would permit instant telephone communication between Washington and Moscow in times of crisis, and when, in 1963, they signed the Nuclear Test Ban Treaty which outlawed the testing of nuclear weapons in the atmosphere.

But the long term negative effects of the Cuban missile crisis plunged the world into a new arms race. The Soviets vowed never again to be caught in the position of having to surrender because the United States possessed a 4 to 1 nuclear advantage over them. As a result, they began a crash program to build up their nuclear arsenal, and within five years actually had more ICBMs than we did. Moreover, they began to experiment with defensive systems, or ABMs, which would shield their major cities from nuclear attack by shooting down incoming warheads. The Americans responded with MHRVs, or multiple headed reentry vehicles; these devices allowed the missile not only to carry multiple warheads, which had been done for some time, but to target each one individually, meaning that one rocket could deliver as many as 10 warheads to different places. Not content with improving their missile capabilities, the Soviets also began to expand their navy dramatically. Not only did they add new submarines capable of launching nuclear warheads, but they also managed to pressure Turkey into opening the Dardanelles, that narrow passage out of the Black Sea, so as to allow Russian naval power into the Mediterranean. How effective that presence was was shown clearly in 1973, when Egypt attacked Israel; the latter found her communications with her forward positions being jammed by Russian radios located on naval vessels off the coast.

Finally, if the Soviets would not be held hostage by American nuclear power, they certainly would not stand by and allow a hostile neighbor to develop delivery systems for nuclear weapons. Thus, when the Chinese, with whom the Russians share a 2000 mile long, almost indefensible, border, exploded a nuclear device in 1964, the Russians watched closely as Chinese air power and missile capabilities improved. Afraid, they secretly asked the United States in 1969 whether this government would condone a Soviet preemptive strike against China. Fortunately, the Americans wisely chose not to respond at all; to have permitted such a strike would have obliterated a potential ally against the Soviet Union, and to have refused to sanction such a strike would have put the United States in the position of defending a country with whom we did not even have diplomatic relations.

The American nuclear superiority which Kennedy had built up, therefore, and which had allowed him to settle the Cuban missile crisis so obviously in his favor did not produce the peace he sought. Instead, the Russians began their own buildup which produced in the long run global instability. Worse, some Americans looked back fondly to the glory days of the Cuban missile crisis when this government had been able to dictate to the Soviet Union, and sought, at enormous cost, to reachieve that superiority. There will always be, as *Dr. Strangelove* so frighteningly portrays, the General Buck Turgidsons, who, although professing that "Peace is our Profession," in fact contemplate obliterating the Soviet Union with a first strike, and will blithely call the 20 million civilian American casualties which would result from Russian retaliation "acceptable." Indeed, recently members of the Reagan administration actually suggested that a few feet of soil over one's head would suffice as a bomb shelter, a notion which sounds suspiciously like the mad German scientist, Dr. Strangelove's, insistence that survival was possible in deep mine shafts, providing people stayed down there for 100 years during which time, carefully selected, genetically pure specimens would breed prolifically to repopulate the earth, a sort of Nazi dream come true.

The probably impossible dream of reachieving, and then using, American nuclear superiority is only one response to the anxiety the arms race has produced. At the opposite pole are those who claim we have nothing to fear from the Soviet Union, and who urge disarmament as a result. Since it is highly unlikely the Soviet Union would voluntarily disarm herself too, especially after the devastation she has endured in two world wars in this century alone, American disarmament would give nuclear superiority to the Russians, and there is no reason to believe they would act with any more foresight or restraint than we did when, for a brief moment, we enjoyed that position. Sanity suggests, then, a rough parity between the super powers is the position most conducive to peace.

The debate should focus on how and when parity is achieved, but to answer that question, we must first understand that the defense needs of the two super powers are vastly unequal. Diplomats joke that the Soviet Union is the only major power completely surrounded by hostile countries, but to a real extent that statement is true. The Soviets not only have to protect themselves from us, but from their supposed "allies" as well. About one third of all Soviet short and medium range missiles are targeted on China, not the United States. This should show that the Soviets cannot trust their allies. To put it another way, NATO works, but its Eastern equivalent, the Warsaw Pact, does not. When the Soviets invaded Czechoslovakia in 1968, the Roumanians, allies of the Russians, sent troops to aid the Czechs! Thus, in determining how much defense is "enough," Americans can add their military strength to that of their allies, while the Russians must subtract from their vast arsenal the weapons and men held in reserve to defend against their neighbors.

Still, as *Dr. Strangelove* so forcefully suggests, the possibility of a mistake exists. The number of crazed generals, like Jack D. Ripper in the film, are virtually non-existent, and the attack order must come from the president anyway. Nonetheless, when split-second decisions are needed, computers must do quickly what humans do slowly. The possibility of a computer malfunction is significant; several times within the last decade, the computer at NORAD, the government agency in charge of North America's security, has failed. Computer malfunction is the premise behind the recent film, *War Games*, in which a willful computer plays thermonuclear war as a game.

Moreover, the results of such a "mistake" could be devastating for the entire planet. Modern scientists suggest the possiblity of a "nuclear winter"; so much debris would be thrown up into the air following a full nuclear exchange that the sun would be blocked, the temperature of the planet correspondingly decreased, and life not killed by the blast or radioactivity would die off. Dr. Strangelove notwithstanding, even if life were possible in deep mine shafts, the survivors and their descendants would reemerge to a dead planet.

Psychologists tell us that the best remedy for tension and anxiety is sometimes laughter. Anyone living through the tense instability of the post-Sputnik age, which culminated in the near miss with war of the Cuban missile crisis, might have found the black humor of *Dr. Strangelove* appealing. Although dealing with a frighteningly grim possibility of nuclear holocaust, the film's savage humor is therefore ultimately very healthy.

Dr. Stangelove - Instructor's Guide

1. Write a brief biographical sketch and assess the historical significance of any or all or the following:

   1. Werner Von Braun
   2. Nikita Khruschev
   3. Andre Gromyko
   4. Alexei Dobrynan

2. Write a brief history of the Cuban missile crisis, indicating

   1. When the missiles were discovered and how
   2. Why the missiles were in Cuba
   3. What options Kennedy had, which he chose and why
   4. What the long term effects of the crisis were on American and Soviet policy

3. Write a book report on one of the following, indicating the author's hypothesis and relating events in the film to events in the book:

   1. Elie Abel, *The Missile Crisis* (1966)
   2. Desmond Ball, *Politics and Force Levels: The Strategic Missile Program of the Kennedy Administration* (1981)
   3. Freeman Dyson, *Weapons and Hope* (1984)
   4. Henry Fairlie, *The Kennedy Promise* (1973)
   5. Robert Kennedy, *Thirteen Days: The Cuban Missile Crisis* (1969)
   6. Henry Kissinger, *Nuclear Weapons and Foreign Policy* (1957)
   7. Henry Kissinger, *Problems of National Strategy* (1965)
   8. Michael Mandelbaum, *The Nuclear Question: The United States and Nuclear Weapons, 1946-1976* (1979)

9. Alva Myrdal, *The Game of Disarmament: How the United States and Russia Run the Arms Race* (1982)
10. Glen T. Seaborg, *Kennedy, Khruschev and the Test Ban* (1981)
11. Peter Wyden, *Bay of Pigs* (1980)

4. Describe how Henry Kissinger views nuclear weapons as part of American defense. His book, *Nuclear Weapons and Foreign Policy* (1957), is an excellent source. Would Kissinger have approved of the Nuclear Non-Proliferation treaty? Why or why not?

5. Using recent magazine articles, discuss the relative strength of the United States and Soviet nuclear arsenals, conventional armies, and navies.

6. Show why and how the Nuclear Non-Proliferation treaty was passed. What major powers refused to sign it and why? How many nations now have nuclear capability?

7. Show the role of conventional forces in American defense policy, especially in regard to the defense of Europe, and evaluate how successful the current NATO defense mix would be in carrying out that defense. Steven E. Miller, editor, *Conventional Forces and American Defense Policy* (1986) is a useful source.

The Autobiography of Miss Jane Pittman - Stride Towards Freedom

Released in 1973, *The Autobiography of Miss Jane Pittman* tells the story of Jane Pittman, a black woman from Louisiana, from her days as a slave in 1862, to her eventual participation in the civil rights movement in 1962. Jane's recording her memories of her long life reminds us of the famous WPA slave narratives collected in Franklin Roosevelt's New Deal, and her recollection of white violence against blacks vividly recreates the years of lynching and terror at the turn of the century. Moreover, the characters in the film remind us clearly of the numerous occupations blacks held in the American economy. Most important, however, is the film's presentation of the early civil rights movement of which Jane becomes a part, for Jane's actions reflect the moderate program of Martin Luther King rather than the more confrontational approach of Stokely Carmichael or Malcolm X. Jane's stand on human dignity, symbolized by her drinking from a Whites Only water fountain, then, is characteristic of the first stage of the civil rights movement, before the advent of busing to achieve school desegregation, before affirmative action and the resulting reverse decrimination suits, before the riots born of frustrated hopes, and before the mushrooming American involvement in Vietnam fragmented and slowed the drive to civil rights King had begun.

The Autobiography of Miss Jane Pittman is based on the premise that a young white reporter wants to record the life of an elderly black woman of no special historical importance. In fact, a similar thing actually did occur in the 1930's under the New Deal program called the WPA. Passed in June, 1933, the Works Progress Administration was part of Roosevelt's First Hundred Days (or First New Deal) and was mandated to put the "unemployables" to work. While the Civilian Conservation Corps took young people out of cities and put them to work in constructive conservation programs, and while the Public Works Administration built dams or hospitals, the WPA worked with writers, actors, landscape designers, and artists among others to improve the life of Americans in the Great Depression. For example, troops of actors performed stage plays in towns that had never seen such things before, and artists like Jackson Pollack painted pictures to adorn the inside of public buildings. Parks were built or expanded, and free pools were constructed.

Among those who found themselves "unemployable" were young historians who were paid by the WPA to interview the surviving slaves, asking them about life under slavery as well as their life since that time. Many of those interviewed were quite elderly and, in the catastrophe of the Depression years, may have softened somewhat their memories of youth under slavery, but these narratives remain among the few recollections of slavery described by black people themselves. Within a few years, most of these black ex-slaves would be dead.

Many people, especially southerners, disagreed vigorously with the collection of such narratives. They argued that it was unnecessary and hence a waste of government money. Moreover, who would want to know anything about the lives of worthless ex-slaves anyway? Finally, to conservative southerners, even the collection of the slave narratives seemed to violate a tacit agreement they felt they had with the President.

When Roosevelt was inaugurated in March, 1933, he knew at once that he would have to work with the conservative southerners in order to pass his desperately needed New Deal through Congress. Since the South was effectively a one party region at the time, southern Democrats once elected tended to be reelected indefinitely. This gave them seniority in Congress which in turn gave them control of the important committees through which Roosevelt's legislation had to pass. Roosevelt used charm and guile to woo these powerful democrats, but he had to agree not to raise the issue of civil rights in return for their support.

The lack of a major civil rights bill is the gaping hole in the otherwise far-sighted, compassionate New Deal programs. Nor were southern blacks the only minority group who found their rights ignored in the New Deal period; hispanics, for example, saw their average wage dip from 35 cents an hour to 14. New Deal programs generally provided for a separate, and lower, pay scale for women, and married women especially were discriminated against in hiring and promotion.

Southerners in Congress, however, were mostly concerned with southern blacks, and stoutly opposed any organized, legal government help for them. To avoid endangering the entire New Deal, Roosevelt had no choice but to agree to their demands. Therefore, although blacks changed their political affiliation from the party of Lincoln, the Republicans, to the party of Roosevelt, the Democrats, they did so less because of specific programs targeted for them, than because of symbolic acts performed by Franklin and ,even more so, Eleanor Roosevelt. For example, Franklin named a black, William Hastie, to the Interior Department, and Eleanor arranged for the black contralto, Marian Anderson, to sing at the steps of the Lincoln Memorial in Washington in 1939, after the Daughters of the American Revolution refused to allow her to sing at Constitution Hall because of her race.

Significantly, *The Autobiography of Miss Jane Pittman* never mentions either Franklin or Eleanor Roosevelt. Jane is illiterate and by her own admission has children read her the sports news and comics only. A down-to-earth woman, Jane is less concerned with symbolic political acts than she is with practical results: her hero is less Franklin Roosevelt than Jackie Robinson, the black second baseman for the Brooklyn Dodgers.

While Jane ignores the New Deal, by contrast she remembers vividly the day she "got her freedom," the day a meek Master Bryan read out Lincoln's Emancipation Proclamation, and she recounts with simple dignity the horror of violence against blacks in the post-Civil War period. In the film, white vagabonds attack and kill most of the group of freedmen leaving Bryan's plantation, while a terrified Jane and Ned watch from their hiding places, and Jane is verbally abused by a poor white woman who blames blacks for the deaths of her husband and son in the war.

Violence indeed did stalk blacks in the post-Civil War period, in part because of traditional race hatred, in part because of the bad economic situation of the period, and in part because of a breakdown of law and order. Technically, federal troops were to preserve order until the states could be reconstructed and new state governments formed. These troops, however, were not sufficiently numerous to do the job, and after 1868, even this insufficient force was steadily reduced. As a result, "law and order" frequently stopped at the outskirts of the larger towns these federal troops occupied. Since most blacks lived on isolated plantations and farms in the Deep South, they were thrown on the not-so-tender mercies of their former masters. Those freedmen who sought to travel, like Jane and her friends, literally risked violence and death as they passed through the chaotic, ravaged southern countryside.

Southerners attempted to control freedmen first by law and then by terror. In 1865, for example, soon after Appomattox, southern states instituted the "black codes," laws which severely restricted the ex-slaves' new freedoms. To counter these black codes, an infuriated Congress instituted Radical Reconstruction, which saw the passage of the 14th and 15th Amendments designed to protect black voting rights and hence insure Republican supremacy in the otherwise solidly democratic south. Many southerners struck back by forming the Ku Klux Klan (1866) or similar vigilante organizations. Originally something like a social club, by 1868, the Klan became more violent, and sought to push blacks back into subservience by terror if not by law. In Louisiana where the film takes place, for example, in 1868 200 people were killed or wounded in two days, and a pile of 25 bodies was found half buried in the woods. The scene in *The Autobiography of Miss Jane Pittman* where masked riders invade a black school, burn the school, and hang the teacher is eloquent testimony to this period of racial violence.

The Klan effectively died out by 1872, in part because its job of intimidation was so thoroughly accomplished. The black subservience to which it dedicated itself, however, could not survive forever. Especially in the very late nineteenth century, educated blacks began challenging white restrictions. Whites once again struck back with organized violence against blacks, and, as the film makes clear, these attacks reached a crescendo after the War of 1898.

The incident in *The Autobiography of Miss Jane Pittman* in which Ned returns to Louisiana after his distinguished service in the black 10th Cavalry and opens a school for his race may be fictitious, but it represents a real historical trend. Blacks educated at Booker T. Washington's Tuskeegee, at Hampton Institute, or at other colleges were urged to return to the south and educate their race. As a result of their efforts, illiteracy among blacks dropped from 45% in 1900 to 30% in 1910 and eventually reached 23% by 1920.

These gains were made in spite of southern states' segregated school systems which the Supreme Court declared constitutional in 1896, with *Plessy vs. Ferguson*. This decision permitted separate schools for blacks and whites, provided they were "equal." But southern legislatures were reluctant to fund black education properly; South Carolina, for example, spent $13.98 annually for each white child but only $1.13 for each black youngster.

Even this crippled black education, however, was opposed by southerners, partly because educated blacks rendered the premise of black racial inferiority more difficult to maintain, and partly because educated blacks could defeat some of the legal obstructions put in the way of their voting. Although the majority of black males continued to vote until the 1880's, by the turn of the century black voting in the South was drastically reduced: in Louisiana where *The Autobiography of Miss Jane Pittman* takes place, for example,130,000 blacks voted in 1896, but only 5000 in 1900. In the late 1890's, southern legislatures began requiring voters to pay a poll tax few poor blacks could afford, or to pass literacy tests which forced would-be black voters to read and interpret part of the constitution. Education would do little to solve the problem of poll taxes, but it struck at the heart of literacy tests. Coupled with simple race-hatred, fear of black literacy caused whites both north and south to lash out at blacks.

Between 1900 and 1914, over 1100 blacks were lynched. Many more were killed or injured in racial violence. A particularly brutal race riot in Springfield, Illinois in 1908, for example, which resulted in the lynching of two blacks, one 84 years old, led to the formation of the NAACP (National Association for the Advancement of Colored People) in 1909. Dedicated to improving the lot of blacks, the NAACP's journal, *The Crisis*, was edited by W. E. B. DuBois, who abandoned Booker T. Washington's apparent willingness to accept second class citizenship for blacks in favor of equal rights for all races. In 1911, the Urban League, also formed with DuBois' help, attempted to help blacks find jobs in the northern black ghettos.

Both the NAACP and the Urban League, however, met with only limited success. The economic position of blacks did not noticeably improve, and violence did not diminish either. In 1917, for example, a race war in East St. Louis killed 9 whites and 40 blacks. The end of World War I produced an orgy of violence, with 63 blacks lynched in 1918 and over 72 in 1919; in July, 1919, as Wilson returned with his Treaty of Versailles, over 50 blacks were killed in one month in race riots. Moreover, black demands for equal voting rights were met with intimidation and violence, symbolized in the film when the Cajun Albert murders Ned.

Worse was yet to come, for 1915 saw the appearance of the second Ku Klux Klan. The second Klan, unlike the first, was not only anti-black, but anti-Catholic, anti-immigrant, and anti-semitic as well. It was part of the rural attack on the cities, city ideas, and city dwellers characteristic of the Roaring Twenties. The Klan flourished both north and south of the Mason-Dixon line, and by clever advertising grew to have 5 million members by 1923. In the beginning, it enjoyed at least the tacit support of many whites; after viewing *Birth of a Nation*, for example, which glorified the formation of the first Klan, even the progressive president, Woodrow Wilson, said it "was like seeing history written with lightning."   Wilson, after all, also introduced rigid segregation into federal programs.   In spite of the NAACP and Urban League, therefore, legal and extra-legal subordination of blacks increased.

It is important to note that Ned, who is murdered by Albert, had been in the army, in the segregated 10th Cavalry in the Spanish-American war, for this reminds us that blacks held many positions in the American economy.   In fact, 10% of the Union army was black, although they fought, as they would until the Korean war, in segregated units.   The black Ninth and Tenth Cavalry helped to subdue the indians on the Great Plains, helping to capture Geronimo in 1886. Known as "buffalo soldiers," blacks comprised 20% of the entire American cavalry between the years 1865 and 1890.   One out of four cowboys was, like Joe Pittman, black.   Blacks were politicians like Blanche K. Bruce, educators like W. E. B. DuBois, poets like Langston Hughes, and musicians like Scott Joplin.   They were electricians and plumbers, although they frequently earned less than their white counterparts.   Some, especially in urban areas, owned stores.

While many blacks like Jane remained mired in rural poverty, thousands seeking greater opportunity "voted with their feet," and left the south.   In 1879, for example, thousands of blacks left for Kansas in a mass exodus.   Ned, we learn from the film, was one of them.   Even more significant were the mass migrations of southern blacks to the north in the early decades of the twentieth century, a process World War I only accelerated.   Between 1890 and 1910, for example, 200,000 blacks migrated to the north, while in the war years, between 1916 and 1918, over 450,000 blacks left the south.

Those blacks who left the south soon discovered that, although their lives might be more secure and they had more money, anti-black prejudice was as strong north of the Mason-Dixon line as it was in the south.   Still, the humiliating segregation laws which blighted the lives of southern blacks became the chief target of the early civil rights movement.   So it was that, following World War II, the black leaders of the NAACP and Martin Luther King turned their attention to winning basic human dignity in the south, and the civil rights movement, of which Jane Pittman becomes a part, was born.

One aspect of this segregation which blacks concentrated on was the deplorable conditions in the separate but unequal black schools.   The drive for education to which Ned had sacrificed his life received enormous impetus when, in 1954, in *Brown vs. the Board of Education*, the Supreme Court reversed the earlier *Plessy vs. Ferguson*, and declared separate but equal facilities for the races unconstitutional.

Blacks appealed to the Supreme Court in part because passing desegregation laws through a hostile Congress would have been almost impossible.   After all, only a few years before in 1948, Strom Thurmond of South Carolina at the head of the Dixiecrat party had challenged Truman for the presidency with a program vehemently opposed to any civil rights for blacks, especially to a federal anti-lynching law Truman's ally, Hubert Humphrey, had proposed. Strom Thurmond lost the election, but he and his fellow southerners remained in powerful positions in Congress, and they worked to sabotage Truman's civil rights bill which was presented to the legislature as part of the president's Fair Deal. Although Truman remained devoted to civil rights and desegregated the armed services by executive order in 1949, he could not directly affect segregation in schools which were under state and local jurisdiction. With Congress hopelessly stalemated on the issue of desegregation, and southern state legislatures openly hostile to reform, black leaders appealed to the Supreme Court where they would not have to persuade over 250 people to support a bill, but only five justices. The NAACP, which had filed suit in *Brown vs. the Board of Education of Topeka*, was delighted, therefore, when the Court ruled unanimously in 1954 that desegregation must take place "with all deliberate speed."

But Eisenhower's executive branch was hesitant to enforce the Court's ruling, in part because Eisenhower felt the court had overstepped its legitimate sphere of activities. The President only moved to support school desegregation in 1957, when he reluctantly called in the National Guard to preserve order when nine black students attempted to enroll at the all-white Central High School in Little Rock, Arkansas. Eisenhower proposed a mild civil rights bill which Lyndon Johnson, the senator from Texas, weakened considerably before it passed Congress in 1957. Obviously the executive and legislative branches moved very slowly to protect the civil rights for blacks the Supreme Court had granted in its landmark 1954 decision. One can safely say, then, that civil rights weren't "given" to blacks; instead, blacks seized their own rights and obliged others to respect them.

The name most closely associated with the black civil rights movement is, of course, Martin Luther King, whose birthday recently became a national holiday. King first came to national prominence at the age of 27 in 1955 during the Montgomery, Alabama, bus boycott. Ms. Rosa Parks had been ordered to give up her seat on a bus to a white person in accordance with a law which separated the races on public conveyances. She sought and received the support of the NAACP and other blacks in the area who together boycotted downtown white merchants and refused to ride the city's buses. King exerted his leadership to keep the protest peaceful, for he had been inspired by the career of Ghandi whose ideas on passive resistance had met with such success in India. But while King was willing to remain peaceful, others were not. The boycotters were harrassed legally and suffered from sporadic violence. King persevered, however, organizing car pools to take blacks around town, thus cutting revenues of Montgomery's bus system by 65%. In 1956, the Supreme Court ruled that bus segregation, like school segregation, was unconstitutional; the buses were desegregated, and the boycott ended.

The Montgomery bus boycott resulted in a surge of black pride which stiffened their resolve to contest those humiliating Jim Crow laws mandating separate rest rooms, separate lunch counters, and, as we see in *The Autobiography of Miss Jane Pittman*, separate water fountains. More important Martin Luther King created a new organization in 1957, the Southern Christian Leadership Conference, to press for peaceful change. Inspired by King and the SCLC, four black students in Greensboro, North Carolina began a "sit-in" at a downtown Woolworth's lunch counter, beginning a movement which within two years had involved 70,000 people, and had effectively desegregated over 100 southern cities. By 1961, "freedom riders," both black and white, traveled the south, and courted arrest so as to test the validity of segregation laws in court. In spite of the violence sometimes visited upon them (one bus was burned in Anniston, Alabama, and they were set on by a mob in Birmingham), they continued their peaceful but direct confrontation.

The film makes clear she was not the first to challenge this law; remember that a young
This is the stage of the civil rights movement Jane Pittman becomes involved in when, in 1962, she drinks from a Whites Only water fountain. The film makes clear she was not the first to challenge this law; remember that a young black girl had done so several days before, and she and Jimmy's group had been arrested for this "crime." Jimmy feared that violence would erupt if the young girl broke the law, and had earlier urged "Miss Jane" to do the deed instead, for given her age and the universal respect accorded to her, she would not be molested. She refuses, however, saying she would wait for "God to give her a sign" before getting involved. A few days later we learn Jimmy has been shot in jail under mysterious circumstances, and, perhaps haunted by guilt (the crusading Ned too had been murdered), Jane decides to throw her prestige in on the side of the desegregationists. She goes to Bayonne, Louisiana, even though the white man on whose land she lives warns her not to and subtly threatens to have her evicted if she does. At first helped to walk, this frail woman soon dispenses with such aid and slowly, almost painfully, strides up to the water fountain to drink.

The film ends here, but the civil rights movement did not. As viewers we are led to believe that all will be well, and indeed the humiliating Jim Crow laws such as those mandating separate water fountains did fall relatively quickly in the south. It is also fair to note that desegregation of southern schools in the border states proceeded rapidly and with little violence. But the Deep South staged massive resistance to school desegregation through the White Citizens Councils, and as late as 1961, only 1% of black children in the Deep South attended integrated schools. Some cities like Birmingham remained almost completely segregated, and blacks were systematically denied jobs.

These last bastions of segregation were challenged in the 1963 Birmingham affair which shocked the nation and brought President Kennedy out into the open in favor of civil rights. Attempting to desegregate Birmingham's downtown facilities and to create more job openings for blacks, King and others staged sit-ins and peaceful demonstrations. The Police Chief, "Bull" Connor, arrested them, and when 6,000 schoolchildren marched in their stead, Connor set upon them with dogs and fire hoses. These events were broadcast on television to a horrified American audience, and the outrage thus produced encouraged Kennnedy to lend public support to King.

Elected in 1960, Kennedy understood his legislative program required the help of those southern conservatives with whom Franklin Roosevelt had had to deal in the 1930's. Although he supported civil rights for blacks and secured the release of King from a jail in Georgia during the 1960 campaign, Kennedy had to move with caution to avoid antagonizing southern conservatives without whom his plans for a tax cut, a Peace Corps, VISTA, etc. would fail. The consensus on civil rights which Kennedy had been waiting for was forged in the Birmingham incident, and Kennedy as a result moved to aid black leaders. He arranged for a peaceful solution to the Birmingham confrontation which granted blacks most of their demands, and in June, clearly endorsed civil rights. "We are confronted primarily with a moral issue," he pronounced. "It is as old as the Scriptures and is as clear as the American Constitution." Even more important, Kennedy proposed a civil rights bill which would outlaw discrimination in public facilities and give the Attorney General the right to intervene in legal suits to speed up desegregation, and which threatened to withhold federal money from state programs which engaged in discrimination.

Partly inspired by Kennedy's embrace of civil rights, 200,000 of King's supporters met in a peaceful demonstration at the foot of the Lincoln Memorial in August, 1963, in what is known as the March on Washington. Here King delivered his famous "I have a dream" speech which ended stirringly, "Free at last! Free at last! Thank God almighty, we are free at last!"

But they weren't. Kennedy did not forcefully fight for passage of the civil rights bill, and in November, 1963, he was assassinated. Then, the situation began to look a little better. Capitalizing on Kennedy's death, for example, the new president, Lyndon Johnson, pressed for passage of the same civil rights bill which finally became law in 1964. In addition, Johnson's Great Society programs helped poor people, many of whom were black, to achieve better educational and economic opportunities. The Voting Rights Act of 1965 banned literacy tests in states in which less than one-half of the population had voted in 1964, and provided federal registrars to insure black voting. In less than a year, black registration in Mississippi alone skyrocketed 400%, and by 1970, 65% of all eligible black voters were registered. By 1965, two years after the March on Washington, black civil rights leaders had been aided by massive federal legislation which helped them both as members of a race and as poor Americans. But then came the summer of 1965.

The Civil Rights Act and the Great Society programs raised expectations without satisfying them. In fact, blacks had actually fallen behind whites in disposable income since the 1950's. They could vote, but they couldn't eat. King's moral superiority had won him many followers, but younger, more impatient black leaders like Stokely Carmichael and Malcom X were less interested in self-denial than in self-defense. Black anger and frustration exploded in 1965 when rioting broke out in the Watts area of Los Angeles which resulted in 34 deaths and almost 1000 wounded. 1967 saw major riots in Newark and Detroit with over 60 deaths. The assassination of King in 1968 produced an explosion of violence in more than 100 cities.

The rioting alienated many whites from the civil rights movement, even though they were not directly hurt by it. The Kerner Commission, empowered by Johnson to investigate the causes of these disturbances, quite rightly pointed out that the rioting existed almost exclusively in black ghettos, that those killed were almost exclusively black, and that the property damage was limited exclusively to black areas (Watts alone suffered 200 million dollars in losses.) Still, whites were angered, especially when white firefighters sent to battle the fires were shot at or pelted with rocks and bottles. Feeling blacks were dangerous as well as ungrateful, many whites came to resent what they regarded as "favoritism" in affirmative action programs which gave special consideration to minority applicants, and they struck back at court imposed quota hiring systems as "reverse descrimination." "Busing" to achieve racial desegregation in ghetto schools especially infuriated whites, and led to disturbances in Boston, Pontiac, Michigan, and several other northern cities. Worse, urban school systems experienced a dramatic reduction in the number of enrolled white children as their parents "fled" to the suburbs or chose to put their children in private school. While white flight accellerated, cities found their tax base shrinking while the demand for social services for the poor grew inexorably. Finally, especially after changes in the draft system in 1969 brought more middle class white kids into danger of being drafted for the war in Vietnam, white middle class parents abandoned the civil rights movement and in increasing numbers entered the anti-war movement.

Not only did whites desert the civil rights coalition, but the coalition itself splintered by 1966. The Student Non-Violent Coordinating Committee (SNCC), an outgrowth originally of King's Southern Christian Leadership Conference, was taken over by Stokely Carmichael, who was tired of King's call for patience and turning the other cheek. "I am not going to beg the White man for anything I deserve. I'm going to take it." The black civil rights movment had to be "black-staffed, black-controlled and black-financed." Black power was born. In June, 1966, the split between King's moderate program and SNCC's more confrontational approach came out into the open when King's supporters, singing "We Shall Overcome," were drowned out by Carmichael's supporters chanting, "We Shall Overrun." King's denunciation of the growing Vietnam war cut him off from the more conservative NAACP and Urban League, but was not made soon enough to satisfy younger, more radical men like Carmichael, who pointed out that a disproportionate share of the body bags returning from the war contained blacks. Then, in April, 1968, a white assassin shot King in Memphis, Tennessee. With King dead, the civil rights movement fragmented, the mushrooming American involvement in Vietnam, and white disenchantment with

Black Power, progress in civil rights slowed to a crawl.

Perhaps it was just as well that Miss Jane Pittman died soon after making her protest in Bayonne in 1962 , for had she lived she would have seen many more Neds and Jimmys die, some from racial violence and others in a faraway war. Nonetheless, her simple but courageous act symbolizes the early stage of the civil rights movement in which King called for peaceful, non-violent demonstrations, and moral right was easier to determine. As Jane makes the long, painful journey up the courthouse path to the Whites Only fountain, the camera dwells on her shaky feet and cane. We are reminded of the title of Martin Luther King's own story, *Stride Towards Freedom*. King had in mind a program for a brave new world where blacks and whites would live together in freedom, and he urged blacks to march boldly into this future. Belatedly, somewhat reluctantly, in 1962 a frail black woman in Bayonne, Louisiana, began her more modest stride toward freedom.

The Autobiography of Miss Jane Pittman - Instructor's Guide

1. Write a book report indicating the author's hypothesis and relating events in the film to events in the book:

   1. Numan V. Bartley, *The Rise of Massive Resistance: Race and Politics in the South during the 1950's* (1969) on southern reaction to civil rights movment.
   2. Stokely Carmichael and C.V. Hamilton, *Black Power: the Politics of Liberation in America* (1967)
   3. Clayborne Carson, *In Struggle: SNCC and the Black Awakening of the 1960's* (1981)
   4. Richard Dalfiume, *The Desegregation of the United States Armed Forces* (1966)
   5. John C. Donovan, *The Politics of Poverty* (1973)
   6. David R. Goldfield, *Promised Land: The South Since 1945* (1987)
   7. David Lewis, *King, A Critical Biography* (1970)
   8. Martin Luther King, Jr., *Stride Towards Freedom* (1958)
   9. Richard Kluger, *Simple Justice* (1976), history of Brown vs. Board of Education
   10. Malcom X, *Autobiography* (1966)
   11. James T. Patterson, *America's Struggle Against Poverty, 1900-1985* (1986)
   12. Harvard Sitkoff, *The Struggle for Black Equality, 1954-1980* (1981)

2. Choose one of the books above and find the scholarly reviews of it in two or more of the following journals:

1. *The American Historical Review* (published by The American Historical Association)
2. *Journal of American History* (published by The Organization of American Historians)
3. *Black Scholar*
4. *Journal of Southern History*
5. *History Teacher*
6. *History, Review of New Books*

Compare and contrast the reviews. What did reviewers like or dislike and why?

3. Discuss how and why Truman desegregated the armed services of the United States. What effect did desegregation have on combat abilities, morale, and military organization. Richard Dalfiume, *The Desegregation of the United States Armed Forces* (1966) is an excellent source.

4. Write a brief biographical sketch and assess the historical significance of any or all of the following:

1. Martin Luther King, Junior
2. Stokely Carmichael
3. Malcolm X
4. Huey Newton

5. Discuss how and why black men became cowboys. Show where they operated, what conditions they put up with, and assess their significance both for the cattle industry and for their race. Joe B. Franz and Julian E. Choate, *The American Cowboy: the Myth and Reality* (1955) is a useful source.

6. Discuss the roles played by blacks in the economic life of late nineteenth century America. Robert Higgs, *Competition and Coercion: Blacks in the American Economy, 1865-1914* (1977) is a useful source.

7. Discuss the role of President John Kennedy and his brother (and Attorney General) Robert Kennedy in the civil rights movement. In your answer, you should discuss:

1. Why Kennedy delayed support for the civil rights leaders?
2. How each man used the court system to address civil rights concerns?
3. How and why Kennedy supported King following Birmingham in 1963?
4. How the Kennedys reacted to the 1963 March on Washington?

8. Discuss the development of the Great Society programs designed to reduce

poverty in the United States. What happened to the Office of Economic Opportunity (OEO) and the other anti-poverty programs following Lyndon Johnson's presidency? An useful source is James T. Patterson, *America's Struggle Against Poverty, 1900-1985* (1986).

Deer Hunter - Hard Hats with Hard Choices

Deer Hunter, released in 1978, deals with the Vietnam war experience both in Vietnam and in America. Indeed, the film explores the close association between American industrial might and the devastation of the war. *Deer Hunter* does not concern itself with the causes of the conflict, but it does graphically portray the brutality of the war and depicts how this brutality radically changed the lives of relatively naive soldiers. Further, the film explores how the enormous lack of understanding on the part of those who remained behind rendered the soldiers' changed lives more difficult. Finally, by inviting comparison with an older concept of heroism developed in the early nineteenth century in the novel *Deerslayer*, the film raises disturbing questions about the nature of heroism in the age of industrialized war.

Deer Hunter begins with a long shot of a steel factory on a gray morning, and throughout the film this factory reappears frequently as background. Grimy and unromantic as it is, the factory nonetheless reminds one constantly of the American industrial might capable of producing refrigerators and cars, but just as capable of producing artillery and armored personnel carriers. For example, one of the opening scenes shows a river of molten steel attended to by robot-like men in visors which conceal their identify. Later in the film, when Micheal, played by Robert de Niro, goes back to rescue his friend as Saigon falls, the Mekong river is depicted as a river of fire which the weapons of steel from the mill has produced.

Historically, the United States has relied on this industrial capability to keep American military strength potential, rather than actual; instead of staffing a huge army on the European model, until World War II the United States relied upon a small elite of trained soldiers whose numbers would be rapidly increased through conscription and volunteers in case of national emergency. As late as 1900, for example, with 100,000 men, the United States army ranked 15th largest in the world, on a par with the Persian army. By contrast, the Russian army of the same period numbered over 800,000. So it was that the Germans in World War I feared less the military capability of the United States than they did American industrial capacity made possible by the steel mills we see in *Deer Hunter*.

Although small in time of peace, the army in time of war was theoretically to be enlarged quickly, but in reality that process could take time. In World War I, for example, even after American entry in 1917, it took this country over a year to raise, train and transport an army to Europe. Furthermore, these troops were transported on European vessels because we had no ships under American registry large enough to be troop carriers, and they were equipped with French guns because we did not have a sufficiently large arms industry. In fact, the Germans were counting on a long delay before the Americans could make much of a difference militarily, and that was one reason they were willing to risk unrestricted submarine warfare even though they knew it would bring the United States into the war; as far as they were concerned, we were helping the allies about as much as we could with our industrial and agricultural products, and with such a tiny army, our military significance, even if we entered the war on Britain's side, would be negligible.

The debate continues even today about how much of American defense should be actual and how much potential. The controversy over the reinstatement of the draft, for example, basically involves the question of how much of a standing army this country needs in order to maintain military credibility. This argument becomes more intense as our industrial base decays, and thus our ability to be the "arsenal of democracy" is called into question. The steel mills in *Deer Hunter* which produced the materials for the guns, trucks, missiles, and planes of Vietnam are closing daily in the face of stiff foreign competition. Without those mills, or with imported steel which could be cut off in time of emergency, can we still afford the luxury of a small army which necessarily takes time to be brought to full fighting strength, or do we need a huge army like the Russian Red Army to be ready in case of any emergency? And if we opt for the latter, can we afford it?

Twentieth century industrial advances, made possible by the steel mills in *Deer Hunter*, guaranteed a more technologically sophisticated war as weapons became more efficient and powerful, but these weapons also guaranteed a more brutal war where mass destruction became almost inevitable. Simply put, more people can be killed by a machine gun than with a single-shot rifle. Ironically, this fact of modern war led to a central paradox of the Vietnam conflict.

Although the United States possessed an enormous industrial advantage over the North Vietnamese and Viet Cong, America could not use this superiority effectively to crush the opposition. Take, for example, the B-52 bombing raids. The Americans dropped thousands of tons of bombs on North Vietnam. Because the planes made a great deal of noise, the enemy usually took cover, with the result that these raids killed perhaps 100 of them a year. However, a certain percentage of bombs never went off; at least 27,000 tons of unexploded bombs were left in Vietnam during the course of the war. The North Vietnamese and their Viet Cong allies became skilled at extracting the explosives from these bombs which they used to make booby traps which killed over 1000 Americans a year. The air raids inflicted approximately 600 million dollars of damage in North Vietnam, but the cost to the United States in airplanes alone was 6 billion dollars. In short, the bombing cost us 10 times as much as it cost the enemy, and may have killed more of our soldiers than it did theirs. The American attempt to use our vast industrial capacity as we always had was unsuccessful, and led to great frustration in this country.

As the war dragged on inconclusively, a premium was placed on killing off the enemy rather than on "liberating" areas from enemy control. For example, reporting on World War II, newsmen used maps to show how many square miles had been captured in a given assault; in Vietnam, however, newmen emphasized body counts, usually inflated, of enemy dead. Such a strategy was bound to create a brutal war, demoralizing both for combat soldiers and politicans at home, but for the politicians this brutality was embarrassing while for the combat soldiers it was life-threatening and immediate.

No more harrowing scenes exist in American film than those Russian roulette scenes in *Deer Hunter* which symbolize the suicidal pointlessness of the war and the role of pure chance in surviving it. To the best of our knowledge, Russian roulette was not a favorite pastime of the enemy in Vietnam, but the game does portray in graphic terms the brutality the war produced. Human life is cheap when people can bet money on the outcome of pulling a trigger. Michael survives, and also manages to save his friends, by manipulating a game of chance. By having three bullets inserted in the gun, he increases his own risk of dying, but at the same time improves his chances of escaping. Moreover, as the film suggests, brutality can become a habit. Nick, played by Christopher Walken, goes AWOL, and remains in Vietnam earning his living by becoming a famous player of the game in Saigon's back streets.

Deer Hunter not only graphically depicts the brutality and degradation of Vietnam, but it also suggests that Russian roulette is merely an extension of an all-pervading violence typical of the society which produced both Michael and Nick. In the scenes set in America before their departure for Vietnam, the group of friends of which Michael and Nick are a part, engaged in relatively open aggression almost constantly. Verbal abuse, pushing, shoving, practical jokes, hunting--all characterize their relationship. Nor is risk-taking either strictly a product of Vietnam. Early in the film, for example, Michael takes bets on his car's ability to pass a truck and risks his life and those of this friends to win the bet. What Vietnam represents, then, is an extreme point on a continuum of violence and risk-taking, but it is a point so far removed from the realm of possibility of the soon-to-be-soldiers' world that their exposure to it shatters the weakest of the three and makes it impossible for the other two to communicate with those left behind once they return to "the World."

The brutality of the war deeply affects the three soldiers. Steven, played by John Savage, has his legs amputated, and Nick becomes a professional Russian roulette player who repeatedly risks his life in that potentially deadly game. Only Michael returns physically unscathed ,but he is withdrawn and uncommunicative. While the violence of Vietnam would be sure to affect anyone profoundly, at least some part of the trio's emotional change can be attributed to the naiveté with which they went to war. *Deer Hunter* makes clear that the would-be soldiers contemplate going to war as a kind of adolescent adventure, something like going on an extended hunting trip The community in which they live prepares an elaborate party both to celebrate Steven's marriage and to send off the trio of enlistees. This party takes place in the VFW hall and is supervised by veterans of previous wars. Yet at no point does anyone mention the possibility of dying or even of being hurt. Instead, the young trio of steelworkers are bathed in the glorious rhetoric of war more reminiscent of Audie Murphy Grade-B World War II movies than the reality of Vietnam being portrayed on virtually every nightly news show. Nor is it clear that the trio have any idea of why the United States is fighting in Vietnam to begin with. Issues of national security, let alone anti-communism, are remarkably absent. No one even discusses reasons like duty to the country or patriotism. The prospective soldiers cannot comprehend the hostility and isolation of the veteran Green Beret they meet by chance at the bar as he systematically drinks himself into oblivion. If anyone could have prepared them for Vietnam, this officer could have, but he, like everyone, chooses not to. In short, the young men go to Vietnam decidedly ignorant about why they are going or what they can expect when they get there.

Although the film does not address the issue of why the United States fought in Vietnam and the would-be soldiers have only a vague idea themselves, it might be helpful to review the history of the conflict, for it was indeed a confusing war in which the issues were not clear cut. Vietnam had been taken as a colony by the French in the late nineteenth century, and they retained control of it following World War I in spite of their unenlightened administration and in spite of President Wilson's commitment to "self-determination" for former colonies. At the Paris Peace Conference which ended that war, a young Vietnamese nationalist, Ho Chi MInh, addressed the conference, arguing in favor of independence for his country, but he was ignored. He stayed on in Paris and later traveled to the Soviet Union as his commitment to Communism grew. Back in Vietnam, the French found themselves badgered by small cadres of Vietnamese fighters who staged occasional hit and run attacks, but colonial rule was easily maintained until the Japanese attacked Vietnam in 1940. The French quickly abandoned the country almost without a fight, and it was Ho's fighters, not the French, who struggled against Japanese occupation. They were encouraged to do so by the French, who suggested, although they did not promise, that Vietnam would be granted her independence after the war. Moreover, Franklin Roosevelt, the president of the United States, had taken a firm, public stand against colonialism, a policy he applied not only to British India but to French Indochina as well. Expecting, therefore, to create an independent Vietnam when World War II ended, Ho set up an administration which in fact formed a government in the North immediately following Japanese surrender in 1945.

This government, however, was not recognized by the western powers. Britain helped France regain control over French Indochina, just as she struggled to regain control over British India, and the United States acquiesced in order to strengthen the western alliance against what we perceived to be the growing threat of the Soviet Union. The fact that Ho had ties to both Stalin and Mao guaranteed he would not find aid and comfort among the western allies. After all, the United States, in order to preempt Mao and strengthen our non-Communist Chinese ally, Chiang Kai Chek, had airlifted Chiang's troops to northern China to accept the Japanese surrender in 1945. Anti-Communism, combined with a resurgent neo-colonialism, therefore, worked against Ho Chi Minh, and the government he had formed was swept aside in favor of a new Vietnamese emperor who was, in fact, a puppet of the French.

Ho began a resistance movement against the French whom, he felt, had reneged on their promise of independence. Called the Viet Minh, Ho's resistance fighters made life miserable for the French. Finally, at Dienbienphu in 1954, the French suffered a humiliating defeat when 10,000 French soldiers were obliged to surrender. Looking for a face-saving way out, the French called an international conference at Geneva, which developed a two stage solution to the Vietnam problem. First, the country would be temporarily divided at the 17th parallel, with Ho forming a government to the north, and the non-communist Ngo Dinh Diem forming one in the south. Second, within two years, elections would be held both north and south, and the winner would reunite Vietnam under a single government. Everyone knew that if such elections were held, Ho Chi Minh would win, for he was better known and honored for his long history as a Vietnamese nationalist struggling against colonialism.

The promised elections, however, never took place, because the Diem government in the south refused to hold them. Diem was a Vietnamese Catholic in a country predominantly Buddhist, and he was associated with the former French colonial masters. Moreover, he ran the south almost as a dictator, handing out political plums and government monopolies to his family while ignoring land reform. By no stretch of the imagination could he be considered democratic, although he was was anti-communist, and by harping on that issue was able to win the support of the United States which sent Diem economic, but not military, aid. The American president, Eisenhower, was unwilling to become involved in a land war in Asia which he considered unwinnable and unnecessary in the first place; concerned with strengthening the NATO alliance in Europe, Eisenhower considered Vietnam a peripheral interest at best.

Back in Vietnam, the Viet Cong, a group of southern resistance fighters financed and aided by Ho's North Vietnamese government, began a guerrilla war in the south by the late 1950's. These attacks encouraged John Kennedy, who became president in January, 1961, to extend not only economic but military aid as well to the Diem regime in order to avoid a communist takeover. Thus, American military "advisors" began training the South Vietnamese army, and the United States made saving the south from a communist takeover a measure of its resolve worldwide. Although Kennedy was willing to accept a neutralist coalition government for Laos, in Vietnam to the east he refused to accept communist participation in the government, and instead staked American prestige on preserving a non-communist south. The Viet Minh attacks, however, combined with Diem's dictatorial tactics, sparked a series of revolts among the South Vietnamese by 1963; several Buddhist priests set themselves on fire to protest Diem's attacks on their pagodas. Diem had become an embarrassment to the United States because of his obvious unpopularity in Vietnam, but he refused to go quietly in spite of American pressure: the tail was wagging the dog, or, as the conventional wisdom of the time had it, the puppet was pulling his own strings.

With the war against the communist insurgents going poorly and American displeasure obvious, Vietnamese generals planned a coup to remove Diem. They asked for and received American blessing for this coup, with the understanding that Diem and his family would not be harmed. However, during the coup in November, 1963, Diem and his brother, the head of the secret police, were both assassinated. The hostility to Diem and his family was so great our government should have been aware that, once American support was removed, Diem was doomed. Three weeks later, in what appears to be an unrelated development, Kennedy was himself dead of an assassin's bullet.

Thus, Lyndon Johnson became president of the United States in November, 1963. In Vietnam he faced a series of revolving door governments, most led by generals, and all ineffective in the struggle against the north. To support the south and stave off defeat, Johnson increased their military aid. In August, 1964, he acquired the authority he needed to prosecute the growing war in Vietnam when Congress passed the Gulf of Tonkin resolution which authorized the president to "repel North Vietnamese aggression by any and all means." This resolution came after two supposedly unprovoked attacks on American warships in the waters off the coast of North Vietnam; historians now dispute that the second "attack" ever occurred, and the first was hardly "unprovoked," since the American navy had regularly been aiding South Vietnamese attacks on the North's installations, and American vessels were in what North Vietnam considered her territorial waters. Even though he knew this information, Johnson chose to present the Gulf of Tonkin incident as an unprovoked attack on American ships, and used the incident to prove his "anti-communism" during a heated presidential campaign against Barry Goldwater.

Once safely elected, Johnson decided to force the north to stop aiding the Viet Cong and to bring the north to the bargaining table. In March, 1965, Operation Rolling Thunder launched B-52 raids over the north. Not only were the raids of questionable effectiveness, but the huge planes at the Danang airbase were attacked on the ground, and so in April, 1965, Johnson ordered the first American ground forces into Vietnam to protect the planes. The American escalation of the war which would see eventually 500,000 Americans in Vietnam and which would cost over 55,000 American lives, had begun.

Some soldiers volunteered for the war like the trio in *Deer Hunter*, but many more were drafted. Until 1968, however, the draft system discriminated against those with less education or less money. If a young man were a student in college, he could defer his being drafted, and so, many white middle class kids stayed in school while poorer minorities were taken into the armed services. As a result, a disproportionate number of minorities served in combat duty in Vietnam. After 1968, to correct this problem, a new draft based on a lottery and which eliminated the student deferment created a fairer draft sytem, but also brought more middle class parents into the anti-war movement as their sons were now being sent overseas.

Whether volunteer or draftee, there had to be an abrupt change from civilian to military life. This change is reflected in *Deer Hunter* by the radical shift from the enclosed, quiet atmosphere when the group gathers in the bar after their hunting trip and the open, noisy reality of the assault on a Vietnamese village. In the bar, the steelworkers share a moment of peace and profound friendship which binds them together after the divisive jostling on the hunt. They are relaxed and confident in the dark, cave-like bar lit only by artifical light. In the next scene set in Vietnam, however, the soldiers are unprotected, out in the open, under the full glare of the bright semi-tropical sun. The thundering noise of helicopters and artillery fire drowns out civilized conversation, and speech is useless anyway when one is fighting to survive. The audience watching *Deer Hunter* is meant to feel in a small way what the combat soldier felt viscerally: that war and peace are profoundly different and that the rhetoric of war does not correspond to the reality of war as they experience it.

The young soldiers, then, rapidly discover what Vietnam combat is like, but significantly those who remain at home preserve the naiveté the soldiers had enjoyed before their departure. For example, when a group of his buddies throws a party to welcome Michael home, they festoon his trailer with red, white, and blue bunting and American flags in a recreation, although on a smaller scale, of the celebration the town provided before he left. While these icons of patriotism may have been acceptable to the naive would-be soldier, to the combat veteran they are a travesty, far too simple-minded to do justice to his battle experience. Michael chooses to avoid the entire situation, ducking down in his taxi while ordering the cabbie to drive on, and Michael only returns home in the morning when the party has broken up. Moreover, his friends find Michael changed and aloof once they finally do get together. When they all go hunting again, their high spirited hijinks and clowning anger him whereas before his departure for Vietnam, Michael had been willing at least to tolerate their games.

In fact, Vietnam veterans frequently had trouble reintegrating themselves into American society. Much younger than World War II soldiers, whose average age was 26, the Vietnam vets, average age 19, had not yet made a place in the world for themselves before they left. More important, Americans were deeply divided about the wisdom of the war they were fighting as they had not been in World War II, and many condemned anyone who would fight in it. Moreover, the tactics of the war, with its emphasis on body counts instead of liberating territory, made any sense of accomplishment rare; platoons would be brought into an area, fight a bloody firefight, and be withdrawn, only to have to go back a few days later. Sacrifice appeared to be in vain. Unable to tell supporters from adversaries, American soldiers sometimes shot at anything that moved as in the My Lai Massacre in 1969, and frequently suffered pangs of guilt later. Finally, after serving their 365 day tour, soldiers were simply boarded on planes and flown to the States, without any decompression time. No wonder many had trouble getting back to civilian life.

In *Deer Hunter* the community finds it hard to reintegrate Michael, the "conquering hero," and it is totally at a loss to deal with those severely wounded physically and psychologically. We learn only when Michael returns home that Steven, whom he saved in Vietnam, has had his legs amputated, probably as a result of his fall from the rescue helicopter. This young man has retreated to a VA hospital and is refusing to come home to his disbelieving and unsupportive wife and baby. Even his mother, with whom his wife now lives, cannot understand her son's psychological trauma. Significantly, it is Michael, the man who has experienced Vietnam, who takes his friend home, the first step towards reintegrating him into the community. And it is from his friend that Michael learns that Nick is still alive when he guesses that the money Steven has been receiving has been sent by Nick. Thus, the Vietnam veterans form a subset of the community; able to communicate with one another, they nonetheless remain outsiders in their own hometown, unable to share their experiences with friends and relatives who can't or won't understand and who are impatient with the veterans' inability to simply pick up their lives where they left off before going to war.

When a form of reintegration does take place, it is a bitter-sweet reunion following the funeral of Nick who died playing Russian roulette as Saigon fell. The amputee attends church services for his friend, the first time we see him back home. Significantly, he has returned to the church which throughout the film has served as a symbol of community. After all, it is at the elaborate Orthodox Church wedding that the entire community congregated before the trio left for Vietnam. When the group comes together at the bar following the funeral, they literally break bread together in a secular reenactment of the communion they have just attended at church. Moreover, for the first time, women have become part of this small group of previously all male buddies. Not only is the community reintegrating the veterans, they are integrating the women who will have to support emotionally their returning warriors and who have traditionally been identified with home and hearth. At a loss for words and deeply affected by the death of their friend, they sing "God Bless America." Only by reaffirming their naive patriotism can they deal with the agony of Vietnam.

This patriotism and the values of honor and heroism associated with it are quite different from the earlier concept of heroism in the novel to which the film invites comparison, James Fenimore Cooper's *Deerslayer*, written in 1841, in the heyday of American Romanticism. *Deerslayer* recounts the coming of age of Nattie Bumppo, a hero typical of early nineteenth century America. Nattie had been raised by indians and has absorbed from them a profound respect for nature as well as the finely honed skills of a woodsman and warrior. Michael, on the other hand, has not been raised by indians, but he does share with Nattie a respect for nature and a feeling that nature is more pure and morally preferable to civilization. When Michael goes hunting early in the film, for example, it is he who insists on the purity of the hunt, carefully tracking the deer indian-fashion rather than shooting from behind a blind while the deer are driven toward him. When he returns from the war, Michael again goes hunting and again carefully stalks the deer, but by the end of the film, Michael has become a *Deer Hunter*, not a *Deerslayer*; he deliberately lets the deer live by shooting wide of the mark. Michael has rediscovered what Nattie knew all along, that while the killing of animals for food conforms to the laws of nature and is therefore morally acceptable, slaughtering animals for sport violates the laws of nature and is therefore morally unacceptable. He has acquired a more profound and mature respect for life in all its forms after his war experience. Though Michael as a soldier killed to survive, he has drawn a distinction which enables him to reintegrate successfully into his community when others could not.

Interestingly, the novel *Deerslayer* is set in the French and Indian war even though it was written almost 100 years later, and, although Nattie Bumppo is engaged in a guerrilla hit and run operation much as Michael and his friends are in Vietnam, the view of the enemy in *Deerslayer* is remarkably different from that in *Deer Hunter*. Nattie respects indian ways, and while carefully noting that he is a white man with white man's ways, he can appreciate indian civilization and standards of bravery. Indeed, his best friend is a Mohican, Chingachgook. By contrast, the enemy in *Deer Hunter*, whether North Vietnamese regulars or Viet Cong, are portrayed as evil incarnate, playing Russian roulette with prisoners' lives and throwing a grenade into a group of hiding women and children. Nowhere does Michael or anyone else express any sympathy for or understanding of the Vietnamese people To be fair, Nattie does occasionally draw a distinction between good indians like Mohicans and Delawares, and bad indians like the Iroquois, but according to the film, there is precious little difference between the North Vietnamese playing Russian roulette in some remote village and the South Vietnamese playing Russian roulette in the back streets of Saigon. Indeed, the nasty portrayal of all Vietnamese earned the film a great deal of criticism from American liberals who thought the it too one-sided.

This view of the enemy may help to explain *Deer Hunter*'s view of heroism, a view apparently shared by many returning veterans. In the morality of the film, a hero is one who survives by using his wits. In a brutal war in which even one's allies are corrupt, dying for some noble cause in meaningless, and grand gestures of defiance ridiculous. While a hard-headed realist might contend that such is always true of war, signficantly, in movies this view is relatively recent. In *Fort Apache*, for example, noble sacrifice is extolled as soldiers go willingly to certain death under their vainglorious leader, but in *Deer Hunter*, Michael takes risks only for his friends and for the most part tries to stay alive by any means necessary. This more limited view of heroism may correspond to a nation-wide, more limited view of the need and usefulness of American involvement overseas. Sometimes dismissed as mere neo-isolationism, such behavior is really more of a hard-headed nationalism which sees the need for risk taking ,but not willy nilly in the support of every cause. Perhaps Vietnam has profoundly changed the way

Americans view war and its possibilities. In any case, *Deer Hunter* offers a very different concept of war and heroism from the one normally seen in American films, and in so doing has begun to come to grips with the effects of the Vietnam war.

Deer Hunter - Instructor's Guide

1. Describe the development of the Vietnam conflict from the emergence of Ho Chi Minh in the 1930's to the American escalation of the war in 1965. In your answer, you should discuss all the following:

    1. World War II and the Japanese
    2. Dienbienphu
    3. 1954 Geneva accords
    4. Diem
    5. Gulf of Tonkin resolution (1964)

2. Discuss how the conflict in Vietnam did or did not advance American national security. Cite specific examples. Two useful sources are Earl C. Ravenal, *Never Again* (1978) which argues against the war, and Norman Podhoretz, *Why We Were In Vietnam* (1982) which defends the war.

3. Using recent magazine aticles, describe the problems many Vietnam veterans have experienced upon their return to the United States. You should consider the following in your answer:

    1. delayed stress syndrome
    2. Agent Orange
    3. differences between World War II and Vietnam veterans.

4. Show how and why a large portion of American public opinion turned against the war in Vietnam. In your answer, you should consider all the following:

    1. Tet offensive of 1968
    2. the presidential election of 1968
    3. role of the Vietnam conflict in the civil rights movement
    4. My Lai
    5. Cambodian incursion
    6. demonstrations at home.

5. Why did President Nixon begin Vietnamization and what were its results? Cite specific examples.

6. Write a brief biographical sketch an assess the signficance of any or all of the following:

1. Ngo Dinh Diem
2. Daniel Ellsberg
3. Eugene McCarthy

7. Write a book report, indicating the author's hypothesis and relating events in the film to events in the book, for any or all of the following:

1. Larry Berman, *Planning a Tragedy* (1982)
2. Leslie Gelb and Richard Betts, *The Irony of Vietnam: The System Worked* (1979)
3. David Halberstam,*The Best and the Brightest* (1972)
4. George Herring, *America's Longest War* (1979)
5. Roger Hilsman, *To Move a Nation* (1967)
6. Arnold Isaacs, *Without Honor: Defeat in Vietnam and Cambodia* (1983)
7. Stanley Karnow, *Vietnam* (1983)
8. Gunther Lewy, *America in Vietnam* (1978)
9. Thomas Powers, *The War at Home* (1973), reprinted 1984
10. Wallace Terry, *Bloods: An Oral History of the War by Black Veterans* (1984)
11. Kathleen J. Turner, *Lyndon Johnson's Dual War: Vietnam and the Press* (1985)

8. Choose one of the books above and find the scholarly reviews of it in two or more of the following journals:

1. *The American Historical Review* (published by The American Historical Association)
2. *Journal of American History* (published by The Organization of American Historians)
3. *History, Review of New Books*
4. *History Teacher*
5. *Choice*

Compare and contrast the reviews. What did the reviewers like and dislike and why?

9. Describe what exactly happened in the Gulf on Tonkin in August, 1964, and how it was presented to the American people. The following are useful sources:

1. Joseph C. Goulden, *Truth is the First Casualty: The Gulf of Tonkin*

Affair (1969)
2. Stanley Karnow, *Vietnam: A History* (1983)
3. Kathleen J. Turner, *Lyndon Johnson's Duel War: Vietnam and the Press* (1985)

10. According to Richard Nixon in *No More Vietnams* (1985), why was the United States in Vietnam and what could have been done to win the war?

All the President's Men - It Can Happen Here

All the President's Men, released in 1976, portrays the *Washington Post's* investigation of White House connections with the break-in into the National Democratic Party's headquarters in the Watergate complex. The June 17, 1972 break-in was one of a series of clandestine, illegal operations coordinated by the White House and financed by cash contributions to President Nixon's campaign. The film creates an atmosphere of fear and claustrophobia, made all the more sinister by the fact that these events really did happen. The break-in and the cover-up which followed, events collectively known as Watergate, may be usefully viewed as the end game of the "imperial presidency," that growth of presidential power from the accession of Theodore Roosevelt to the presidency in 1901. Likewise, Watergate may also be seen as the product of the political stalemate which has bedeviled Congress since the collapse of the New Deal Coalition between 1937 and 1938. However, the clandestine activities and the cover-up which followed are also the product of a particular president, one with a history of vicious campaigning and a reputation as a " hatchet man" for the Republican party. Most important, Watergate was not like scandals in previous administrations, in large part because Watergate did not involve mere graft and corruption, and because the president himself was deeply and personally involved.

All the President's Men portrays a sinister, nighttime world of intrigue and claustrophobia. Note, for example, how almost all the scenes take place in artificial light, either the blinding light of the *Washington Post* composing room, or the poorly lit streets and interiors of Washington, D. C. With very few exceptions, action takes place indoors where walls and furniture create small "living spaces." This claustrophobic effect is heightened by filming indoors at night with the illumination of only one table lamp which creates a tiny pool of light even in a large room. The best example of this intrigue and claustrophobia is of course the meetings between Bob Woodward, the *Washington Post* reporter, and Deep Throat, his White House contact; these meetings take place in a cave-like, underground garage, with Deep Throat photographed in shadow.

The low level functionaries of the Committee for the Reelection of the President (CREEP) simply radiate fear. Some fear for their jobs, especially the political appointees, but others, like the bookkeeper, choose silence out of a sense of loyalty to their employers. She too, however, is at least partly motivated by fear. She warns Woodward and Bernstein , his reporter colleague from the *Post*, when they show up at her home that "They'll see you," although she never explains who the "they" are nor how the "they" could possibly watch the homes of everyone with knowledge of Watergate. Simple events take on frightening possibilities in this atmosphere of fear and intrigue. When Bernstein is talking to his source at the Justice Deaprtment, a man waiting in line to visit the White House takes pictues which might include Bernstein and the source. His source rapidly disappears. This fear is also infectious. When Woodward meets Deep Throat in the garage, a car suddenly starts and speeds up the ramp, tires squealing. Deep Throat disappears mysteriously and Woodward ends up running out of the garage, obviously quite scared.

The fear of losing jobs or even of criminal proceedings is, of course, justified to some degree, but the film does tend to sensationalize this problem. At the end of the film, Deep Throat warns Woodward his life may be in danger and his phones and house bugged. While the latter is a real possibility--after all, the Nixon administration did tap the phones of Daniel Schorr, a CBS correspondent--the first alternative that lives are in danger seems less plausible. In spite of the inflated, macho rhetoric of the Watergate participants, such as Chuck Colson's office motto, "When you've got them by the balls, the hearts and mind will follow," the fact is that no one was killed or even physically injured in any of the clandestine operations or the cover-up. Nonetheless, the climate of intrigue the White House created obviously convinced many, including Woodward and Bernstein who were certainly not naive, that threats to their lives really did exist.

The film heightens this sinister atmosphere by injecting elements of realism which make the other more frightening events of the film seem more plausible. Television and radio broadcasts provide a backdrop of almost mundane factuality. The language of the newspapermen, their interruptions of one another, the gritty realism of the daily grind of putting out a newspaper--all seem to mirror life as we would expect it to be. Although Bernstein, played by Dustin Hoffman, and Woodward, played by Robert Redford, are obviously heroes, even they are not without flaws; Woodward sleeps through an interview with Deep Throat and Bernstein devises such a complicated scheme for confirming the story that H. R. Haldeman controlled the slush fund that his source becomes confused and unintentionally misleads him. To demonstrate how effective this use of realistic elements is in lending credibility to the story, one might compare *All the President's Men* with *Ragtime* where historical accuracy is sacrificed to plot exposition. Ultimately, of course, the viewer of *All the President's Men* knows that the plot Bernstein and Woodward are exposing actually did take place and that many of the men portrayed in the film confessed their guilt and served prison sentences. For while *Ragtime* is a fictional story based on real historical events, *All the President's Men* portrays a real historical event which caused the resignation of a president and challenged the rule of law and order as contained in the Constitution.

Why were the burglars, whom Bernstein and Woodward investigate, in the Watergate complex to begin with? To answer that question, we must understand a bit more about the history of the Nixon White House and the time the events took place. The Nixon White House was obsessed with secrecy, and perhaps because of that fact, was plagued with "leaks" to the press which were embarrassing if not really dangerous. If the leaks had really compromised national security, Nixon could have ordered in the FBI, which would have presented probable cause to a judge who in turn would have ordered a legal wiretap. But Nixon did not have sufficient probable cause, because the leaks he was disturbed about were simply embarrassing and annoying rather than real threats to national security. Therefore, since he could not use the FBI, the Nixon White House put together a group of ex-CIA men called the "plumbers," so-called because they were there to stop "leaks." The plumbers were responsible for a number of illegal operations, financed by republican money, about which they reported to Chuck Colson or John Ehrlichman in the White House.

The most famous of these operations was the illegal break-in into Daniel Ellsberg's psychiatrist's office in Los Angeles in 1970. Ellsberg had taken what became known as the Pentagon Papers and given them to the *New York Times* to publish. These papers dealt with the American involvement in the Vietnam war before Nixon took office in 1969, and showed clearly that the American people had not been told the truth about the Gulf of Tonkin incident and that the American government was implicated in the overthrow and perhaps even the assassination of Diem. Deeply embarrassing, these papers nonetheless did not hurt American national security, if for no other reason than the facts they contained were already known to our allies and our enemies, but Nixon went to court to try to stop them from being published anyway. The Supreme Court ruled, 9-0, that the president had not shown sufficient cause why the *Times* should not print the papers, and denied the president his suit. Thus, there was no way the papers themselves could be stopped, but perhaps the credibility of the man who took them could be compromised, and so the plumbers broke into Ellsberg's psychiatrist's office looking for damaging information to "smear" him with. Unfortunately, the Ellsberg file had been removed, and when the plumbers tried to make their break-in look like a burglary, they left such obvious clues that police knew something more was afoot.

In 1972, Nixon was running for reelection, and although there was no question he would be reelected, especially since the Democrats were in such disarray, the president wanted a huge electoral victory to vindicate his policies and to make up for the slim margin of defeat he had suffered in 1960 against John Kennedy and the slim margin of victory in 1968 against Hubert Humphrey. One way to win big was to run against the weakest Democrat, and so, in the spring of 1972, CREEP paid Donald Segretti to stage "dirty tricks" on the powerful democratic candidates. Some of these tricks were simply unfair, such as directing newsmen to the wrong hotel when an opposition candidate was speaking and thus effectively denying him press coverage, and some of the tricks were illegal, such as the letter written accusing Senator Scoop Jackson of being a homosexual and the father of an illegitmate child. The effect of these dirty tricks was to eliminate the most powerful democratic candidates, leaving the field open to George McGovern. But perhaps the Democrats had some secret campaign strategy, or worse yet, were communicating with the North Vietnamese during the sensitive peace negotiations. The first concern over strategy was simply none of the

Republicans' business, but had the second been true, a case could be made that this violated American security. If so, the president could have shown probable cause to a federal judge who would have ordered a wiretap of the Democrats' phones. But the second charge was not true, there was no probable cause to suspect the other party's loyalty, and so the White House resorted to the illegal plumbers once again. However, as the plumbers broke into the Democratic National Headquarters located in the Watergate complex on the night of June 17, 1972, they were caught by a security guard.

The plumbers agreed to remain silent, and the Nixon administration postponed their trial until after the November election. CREEP feverishly destroyed documents which would have linked it or the White House to the burglars. This is the frantic paper shredding captured in *All the President's Men.* The White House and CREEP prepared to "stonewall," that is to say nothing at all and let the mess blow over. By June 23, six days after the break-in, Nixon called off the FBI investigation of the incident on the grounds that CIA activities would be disclosed, although he had found out shortly before that indeed the CIA was *not* involved. Many suspected that there was more to the break-in than met the eye, but with the evidence destroyed, the burglars silent, and the FBI off the case, there was no proof.

That is where Bernstein and Woodward come in, for their investigation of the break-in suggested close links between the White House, CREEP, and the burglars. Although the film does not say so, however, they had no real proof, nothing that would stand up in court. They were investigators, not policemen and certainly not prosecutors. The documents law enforcement agencies could subpoena legally, the *Post* reporters could obtain only by stealth or unsworn testimony. Thus, Bernstein and Woodward's reports were damaging, but did not constitute sufficient evidence to prosecute.

The evidence which proved their assertions and which led to Nixon's resignation were contained in the taped recordings of White House conversations the president made himself. Originally designed to help Nixon write his memoirs and to help him recall exactly what was said in an interview, these tapes were voice activated and recorded almost everything said in the Oval Office and the president's office in the Executive Office Building across the street. The existence of the tapes was revealed during the Senate Watergate Committee's televised hearings in the summer of 1973, and were immediately subpoenaed by the Special Investigator, Archibald Cox, whom the president had appointed to look into the Watergate affair. Nixon refused to give up the tapes on the grounds of executive privilege, but the Supreme Court ruled the tapes had to be handed over to the Special Prosecutor. When Nixon complied, however, two tapes were missing, and one had an 18 and a half minute erasure at exactly the point where Watergate was discussed.

Nixon's tapes proved that he had been actively involved in the cover-up of the break-in and other clandestine activities, certainly as early as June 23, 1972, and they suggest the president may have had knowledge of these events before the Watergate break-in in June. The so-called "smoking gun" tape of June 23 has Nixon ordering the FBI to shut down the investigation of the break-in on the grounds that CIA activities might be exposed, although he already had been informed by the CIA that this was not so. The Watergate Grand Jury later cited Nixon as an "unindicted co-conspirator" on the basis of evidence presented to it. *All the President's Men* contrasts Nixon's taking the oath of office in January 1973, in which he pledges to "preserve, protect ,and defend the Constitution," with the increasingly obvious fact that he had violated his oath of office by permitting unauthorized wiretaps without clear evidence of danger to national security. Nixon's misuse of presidential authority later led the bi-partisan House Judiciary Committee to pass three articles of impeachment against him, and only his resignation on August 9, 1974, saved him from impeachment and trial in the Senate.

Watergate, then, was a momentous yet shabby event in the history of the United States, but how does Watergate fit in with that history? Watergate may usefully be seen as the end product of the "imperial presidency," that growth of presidential power since 1901 when an assassin's bullet elevated Theodore Roosevelt to the presidency. To be fair, no president in the twentieth century ever held the power that Lincoln did in the Civil War, but the near conviction in impeachment proceedings against his successor, Andrew Johnson, weakend the office so much that the late nineteenth century presidents are truly a forgettable lot. In the election of 1900, Theodore Roosevelt, a Republican reformer, was put on the ticket as vice president to kill him off politically, but the assassination of McKinley in 1901 made Roosevelt president instead. Mark Hanna, the kingmaker of the Republican party and one who wanted to muzzle Roosevelt, is reputed to have said after being informed of McKinley's death and Roosevelt's accession to the presidency, "Oh my God, that damn cowboy in the White House!" Once in power, Roosevelt dramatically resuscitated the power of the presidency. His settlement of the Anthracite Coal Strike in 1902 and his intervention in the Northern Securities Case of 1904 both show his commitment to an activist presidential role based on theories originally put forward by Alexander Hamilton. The power of the president, the size of his staff, and his dominant relationship with Congress has been growing in fits and starts ever since. Even the title of the film *All The President's Men* plays on that familiar phrase from the Humpty Dumpty nursery rhyme, "all the *King's* men."

One reason for this growth of presidential power may be that since 1901 the United States has fought two declared and two undeclared wars. During any war, the power of the Commander-in-Chief of the armed services naturally increases in the interests of national security. After every war, however, Congress has been quick to reassert its control , but it has never regained the power or influence it had before the war took place. Thus, one way of reading the Senate's failure to ratify the Treaty of Versailles after World War I is as a move on Congress' part to retrieve power from a wartime president by defeating his treaty. Likewise, the attack on the New Deal and the howl over the Yalta "sell-out" represents another attempt on the part of Congress to get power back from Truman following World War II. The Army-McCarthy hearings followed Korea, and Watergate followed Vietnam. As the power of the imperial president grew, Congress' attempts to whittle it down to size grew more desperate--and usually more unsuccessful. After all, since both Korea and Vietnam were undeclared wars, Congress never voted a resolution of war and as a result never had the control over the war it did in World Wars I and II. Indeed, the extraordinary power of Lincoln derives in part from the fact that the Civil War was also an undeclared war:because Lincoln regarded secession as illegal, he never asked for a declaration of war because to do so would have lent legitimacy to the Confederacy. As a result, he prosecuted the war strictly under his powers as Commander-in Chief. In a similar manner, Nixon handled the Vietnam war mostly under his vast powers as Commander-in-Chief, and when Congress tried in vain to reassert its control at least over the budget, Nixon impounded funds Congress had authorized. Thus, Watergate, which occurred just as the war was dragging to a close, may usefully be seen in the context of the growth of presidential power at least partly accelerated by wartime necessities, and Congress' desire once the war was over to reduce that presidential power.

Watergate is also the result of a stalemated Congress so difficult to work with that presidents have often preferred working in those areas of the federal government more clearly under their authority. Foreign policy is generally one such area; the CIA and FBI are two others. Both agencies technically have Congressional supervision, but in fact both report directly to the president and are part of the executive branch. At least as early as the administration of John Kennedy, the CIA was ordered to make several assassination attempts on foreign leaders, most of which, like those on Fidel Castro's life, were unsuccessful. Lyndon Johnson reportedly permitted the FBI to investigate Martin Luther King, Jr., the civil rights leader, not because he represented a threat to peace, but because the government hoped to find damanging information to use against him. The president's use of the FBI and CIA continued into the Nixon administration. As we have seen, the Nixon White House used ex-CIA operatives in their plumbers unit which, in addition to the Watergate break-in, also staged the break-in into the office of Daniel Ellsberg's psychiatrist after Ellsberg published the highly embarrassing Pentagon Papers.

If it is clear, then, that presidents increased their activities in areas under their control in part because Congress was so difficult to deal with, it is important to explain why Congress was as unwieldy and awkward in the first place. Since World War II, there have always been over 450 Congressmen, counting both House and Senate, and so its very size makes Congress difficult to work with. The weakening of seniority rules and the concommitant proliferation of Congressional committees has likewise created a complex mine field through which any legislation a president might propose must pass. A president like Woodrow Wilson used the caucus system, borrowed from England's House of Commons, to organize Congress and seek orderly passage of bills. Franklin Roosevelt mobilized his New Deal coalition which included powerful conservative southerners, who dominated most of the committees to begin with, to accomplish the same goals. But between 1937 and 1938, this New Deal coalition was hopelessly fragmented by the Supreme Court packing scheme, the "Roosevelt recession," and the unsuccessful attempt to purge the Democratic party, all of which alienated those powerful southerners. They were further angered by Truman's embracing of civil rights, even to the extent of running Strom Thurmond against Truman in 1948 at the head of the Dixiecrat party. Thus, Truman's Fair Deal failed to pass when the president called Congress into special session after the November, 1948 election, to a large degree because Truman could not reestablish the powerful new Deal coalition of Roosevelt's day, and especially because he had antagonized the southern committee chairmen. With the major exception of Lyndon Johnson's Great Society programs, Congess has failed to respond quickly or favorably to most presidential initatives ever since. No wonder most presidents under the full glare of publicity which demands quick successes desperately seek to display their expertise somewhere else than with Congress!

The fact that Lyndon Johnson was successful with Congress where others were not underscores a significant fact about our post-World War II presidents. Except for Kennedy and Johnson, no elected president since Truman had had any recent expertise with Congress before his inauguration, and many have had no experience at all in federal government. (Gerald Ford, who succeeded Nixon, was not an elected president.) Moreover, even Kennedy had been a lack-luster Senator who had not moved his legislation quickly through Congress. Like those who came before him, Nixon's inability to work effectively with Congress may be due in part to his ignorance of that venerable, though cumbersome institution; in 1972, when Watergate took place, Nixon had not been a senator for 20 years, and his most recent experience in federal government had been in the executive branch, either as vice-presdient from 1953 to 1961, or as president since 1969. Whether from ignorance or intent, however, he regularly ignored or defied Congress. For example, he invaded Cambodia in 1970 without telling Congress beforehand, and he repeatedly impounded funds authorized by Congress when they exceeded *his* but not *Congress'* budget. Scorning Congress as unwieldly, unreliable, and hopelessly addicted to "leaks," Nixon turned, as many presidents before him had, to those areas of government he could control more easily, areas such as the federal courts (federal judges are appointed by the president and then approved by Congress), foreign affairs (SALT I and the opening of relations with China), and the CIA and FBI. He became accustomed to having his own way, without the checks and balances between executive and legislative branches the founding fathers had prescribed.

If Watergate can be seen, then, as part of the growth of the imperial presidency and as a reaction to a stalemated, unwieldy Congress, it is nonetheless the product of particular president, a deeply insecure man who saw plots where none existed and who, in a desperate attempt to save himself and his reputation, stepped outside the law. Nixon's tapes reveal a "bunker mentality," a feeling of fighting the whole world which wrongfully and almost pigheadedly refuses to see things his way. He very much wanted to be popular, and it was this feeling which helped produce Watergate. To insure the president's reelection and his personal vindication, in 1972 CREEP financed the series of clandestine operations and "dirty tricks" we have alrady spoken of in order to damage powerful Democratic rivals, thus leaving the nomination to the politically impotent George McGovern. Although political campaigns have in the past descended to mud-slinging, what makes the '72 campaign different is that these "dirty tricks" were carefully coordinated by high officials of the Republican party, some of whom were in the White House, rather than being mere spur of the moment ideas of underlings.

Nixon himself had a long history of vicious campaigning and questionable use of campaign funds. In his 1950 Senatorial race against Helen Gahagan Douglas, Nixon accused her of being a communist sympathizer when she criticized Senator Joe McCarthy and questioned the premises of American foreign policy. His behavior in that race plus his earlier determined attack on Alger Hiss led the Republican party to nominate him as vice-president in 1952, when Dwight Eisenhower ran at the head of the ticket. The party feared that Eisenhower, who was almost above partisan concerns--after all he had been courted by both the Democrats and Republicans--would not use presidential patronage to reward the party's faithful, and so the Republicans put Nixon on the ticket to be the "hatchet man." Unfortunately, during the campaign, charges surfaced against Nixon, accusing him of benefiting from a private slush fund raised by his wealthy supporters, charges ironically which would be repeated 20 years later in Watergate. In 1952, Nixon turned to the new medium, television, and in a dramatic, nationally televised address, tried to clear himself. Known as the Checkers speech, the address sought to prove that Nixon had not benefited financially from his political career, proving, as one historian wryly noted, that Nixon was simply not a very good crook. Eisenhower accepted Nixon back on the ticket, and both were triumphantly elected in 1952 and again in 1956.

The history of Nixon's career before 1972, therefore, made him more likely to take advantage of the power, secrecy, and broad initiating policies which had grown up around the office of president since 1901, but significantly, the events collectively known as Watergate were not simply another example of the corruption which has from time to time plagued the presidency. Watergate was different from earlier scandals, in spite of the efforts of some Nixon supporters to make it appear otherwise. Most important, in Watergate the president himself was personally involved in the cover-up following the break-in and benefited personally and directly from the events which took place. Second, government agencies like the FBI and CIA which wielded enormous power were deliberately misused and involved in illegal activities clearly in violation of their charters--in some cases at the direct order of the president himself. For Watergate was no mere example of graft and corruption as had been the scandals of the Grant, Harding, and Truman administrations. Rather, it involved the sabotaging of constitutional guarantees of freedom of speech and freedom from unreasonable search and seizure. The President's oath of office binds him to protect such feeedoms, and yet in Watergate it was the president himself who violated such guarantees and permitted others to do so as well.

All the President's Men repeatedly explores the wide-ranging implications of what at first appeared to be an amateurish burglary of the National Democratic Headquarters. In many scenes, the camera starts with a close-up and then pulls back to reveal a larger picture. For example, in one scene in which Bernstein and Woodward drive out to question CREEP employees about the slush fund, the scene begins with a closeup of Woodward's beaten up Volvo, but as they drive off, the camera pulls back to reveal a large portion of downtown Washington, D. C. with the Washington Monument--dedicated, of course, to our first president--in the center. In the scene in the Library of Congress, the camera focuses first on the two reporters checking the files on White House withdrawals, but then pulls back to reveal the huge reading room in which Bernstein and Woodward are almost lost. Significantly, the desks in that reading room are arranged in a series of concentric circles, and Bernstein and Woodward sit at a desk in the very center. What the two reporters are investigating is the man who stood at the center of power in Washington, D. C., the President of the United States, a man who deliberately violated his oath of office by sabotaging those very freedoms the Constitution was designed to protect. Americans who pride themselves on the integrity and fairness of this government, as opposed to totalitarian governments overseas, would have to learn that "It can happen here"--and it did.

All the President's Men - Instructor's Guide

1. Write a book report on any or all of the following, indicating the author's hypothesis and relating events in the film to events in the book:

> 1. Carl Bernstein and Robert Woodward, *All The President's Men* (1974)
> 2. Carl Bernstein and Robert Woodward, *Final Days* (1976)
> 3. John Dean, *Blind Ambition* (1976)
> 4. Joe McGinniss, *The Sellng of the President, 1968* (1969)
> 5. Arthur M Schlesinger, *The Imperial Presidency* (1973)
> 6. Athan Theoharis, *Spying on Americans* (1978)
> 7. Theodore H.White, *The Making of the President, 1968* (1969) and *1972* (1973)

8. Gary Wills, *Nixon Agonistes* (1970)

2. Write a brief biographical sketch and assess the historical significance of any or all of the following:

1. Richard M. Nixon
2. "Checkers" speech (1952)
3. Edmund Muskie
4. John Dean
5. G. Gordon Liddy
6. John Mitchell

3. How are Nixon's activities in Watergate the same as or different from the events which preceeded the Checkers speech in 1952. Cite specific examples.

4. How is Watergate the same or different from the scandals of the late Truman administration? Cite specific examples. Consider in your answer all the following:

1. purpose of scandals
2. role of president
3. role of government agencies

5. Describe the sequence of events which led up to the resignation of President Nixon in 1974. Consider in your answer all the following:

1. the Break-in and cover-up
2. the role of John Dean
3. Senate Watergate Investigating committee (summer, 1973)
4. Saturday Night Massacre (October, 1973)
5. 18 1/2 minute erasure
6. House Judiciary Committee and articles of impeachment (summer, 1974)
7. resignation

Fort Apache, The Bronx - The War on Poverty--and Poverty Won

Fort Apache, The Bronx, released in 1981, portrays the disintegration of modern American cities and the despair of city dwellers on both sides of the law. The new frontier of the sixties is located not in the West, but inside older cities, and as in the earlier frontier of the West, in the South Bronx violence is pervasive and life cheap. The moral authority and non-violence of Martin Luther King has been abandoned in favor of confrontation politics as the Great Society programs fell apart from lack of funding and lack of success. The War on Poverty has become a shooting war where the victims are shot down with guns or shot up with drugs. Moreover, this film invites comparison with the 1949 classic directed by John Ford, *Fort Apache*, which began this film series. A comparison of the two, of course, reveals two very different societies. Nonetheless, *Fort Apache, The Bronx* shares with its famous predecessor a faith in the future, somewhat qualified to be sure, but real. A sincere belief that decency ultimately prevails makes this film typically American by reasserting our traditional values.

Fort Apache, The Bronx begins with a slow pan from the now famous skyline of Manhattan to the utter squalor of the South Bronx, and then immediately portrays the vicious murder of two rookie cops. The glamour, wealth, and culture of Manhattan may be only across the East River, but they might as well be across the continent. In the South Bronx, the streets are littered with garbage, the buildings are either decaying or being torn down, and almost every surface has been covered with grafitti. Violence stalks the streets, and old folks, women and children huddle at the precinct house as the only safe refuge in the neighborhood. The outgoing police captain explains some of this misery when he notes that 70,000 people are crammed into this 40 square block area with the worst unemployment, lowest income, and largest percentage of non-English speaking citizens in New York City. No matter what the cause, however, no one, alive or dead, is safe from this all pervasive violence. For example, when the police go to the rescue of a young man trying to commit suicide, they have to delegate someone to watch their car to keep it from being destroyed. And in one of the most telling scenes in the film, after the rookie cops are killed, a group of young people quietly rob their dead bodies. If Manhattan represented the best in American cities, South Bronx represents the worst, for it is a world in which civilization's rules have completely broken down.

The 41st precinct house, then, is a kind of lonely outpost in hostile territory, a Fort Apache, no longer in the Arizona territory, but in the Bronx. It is a new frontier, and shares with the Old West frontier many of the same vices. Many regarded the Old West as a place to get rich quick, and fortunes were indeed made by some in the mining or cattle industries. But violence was never far behind: claim jumping led to brutal murders, and cattle raising begot cattle rustling. In the South Bronx, fortunes can likewise be made, but only in activities outside the law and only if violence is quickly and effectively used. Thus, the South Bronx fortunes are made from prostitution and drug dealing. And violence is never far behind. A pimp beats up his prostitute for not bringing in enough money, and a drug dealer holding hostages in the hospital kneecaps a doctor just to get the attention of the police outside. Likewise, in the Old West, disputes were frequently settled privately without reference to the law and the same is true of the South Bronx; when a prostitute slashes a drug dealer, he doesn't press charges. He simply stabs her.

Loneliness and isolation characterize frontier life as much in the South Bronx as in Arizona of the 1880's. When the nurse Isabella staggers through the streets after taking a lethal drug overdose, no one comes to her aid until she falls down dead. We don't even know her name is Isabella until the movie is over and the credits roll, for though she is a central character throughout the film, no one ever called her by her given name. Surely, then, the two frontiers share many of the same vices, but do they have similar virtues?

The virtues of the Old West are rarely found in the Bronx. The sense of space captured is so many westerns in nowhere to be found. On the contrary, people are jammed into crowded tenements in tiny rabbit warren rooms. Furthermore, there is no deep respect for or awe of nature; in the South Bronx, people are dwarfed by huge buildings, not huge cacti, and a people's park is a gleam in a planner's eye rather than a reality. Finally, self-reliance, that frontier viture, is hardly encouraged by the present welfare system. Inner city ghettos like the South Bronx, then, share all the vices and few of the virtues of the older frontier of the mythic West.

However, while it is true that the South Bronx is a kind of frontier, it is not a *new* frontier in the sense that urban ghettos are not new. Indeed, squalid slums have marred American cities since such cities appeared in the seventeenth century. As a rule, though, such slums, and the crime and disease they fostered, were simply accepted as an unfortunate fact of life by most Americans. In the 1880's and into the twentieth century, however, under the twin influnces of the Social Gospel and Progressivism, many Americans first discovered the problem of urban poverty, and then decided to do something about it, much as reformers in the 1960's rediscovered urban slums and waged the war on poverty to eradicate them.

The problem of urban slums reached crisis proportions in the last part of the nineteenth century. In the 1860's and beyond, while the Old West frontier of Arizona and Utah was being opened for settlement, a huge influx of immigrants poured into ramshackle tenements in eastern cities, creating ghettos similar to the modern South Bronx. As a result, middle class New Yorkers, for instance, fled the lower East Side where the immigrants were settling for the safety of the brownstones much farther to the north at 20th St. With the development of reliable trolley and subway systems, the middle class population then leapfrogged the huge Central Park area and moved as far away from the immigrants as possible. The areas they left behind became slums; Hell's Kitchen and the Bowery became synonymous with filth, wretchedness, human depravity, and crime. By 1890, 1.4 million people lived on the island of Manhattan, and in the slum areas the population density approached 900 people per acre. The number of prison inmates rose 50% nationwide, but most of that growth was in the urban areas. The homicide rate doubled, and gangs, like the famous Hell's Kitchen gang, ruled the streets.

The squalor of the slums and the crime which accompanied it were blamed on the immigrants who lived in them, and the comforting belief that the immigrants were getting what they deserved at first absolved the wealthy from doing much to help. The plutocrats gave a little private charity from time to time, but they feared that a thorough government system to rid the cities of poverty or relieve its worst abuses would sap the moral fiber of those crowded into the tenements. Indeed, using Malthus' theories on population, many governmental and charitable organizations permitted the death rate in the slums to soar in order to correct what was perceived to be too high a birth rate. Men like Commodore Vanderbilt could and did justify this inaction on the grounds of Social Darwinism: the fit survive; the unfit do not. Assuming the "new immigrants" were responsible for their own wretchedness, moves were made to restrict immigration rather than to correct the problems of urban slums. The Omaha platform of the Populist Party in 1892, for example, called for immigration restriction, but did not demand a nationwide tenement law.

Poverty and slums were not invented, then, in 1890; they were merely discovered, much as they would be rediscovered later in our century. This discovery shocked many otherwise complacent Americans and galvanized them into action. Such exposés as Jacob Riis' *How the Other Half Lives* (1890) presented such an appaling view of slum life that many Americans began to support moves to improve life in the new urban ghettos. As a result, streets were paved and first gas and then electric lighting was introduced. New developments in architecture, especially metal framing, permitted buildings to grow in size and strength while at the same time improving their resistence to fire. Settlement houses, like Jane Addams' Hull House in Chicago, tried to integrate the immigrant into American life while at the same time providing a sanctuary from the crime and filth of the surrounding neighborhood, just as the precinct house in *Fort Apache, The Bronx* does. Laws were passed limiting the labor of women and children, and New York City in 1901 passed a new tenement house law with effective enforcement capabilities. The new law was not designed to clean up the slums which already existed, but rather to prevent the duplication of their worst abuses in the newly opening areas of the city like, ironically, the South Bronx.

The worst of the slums gradually disappeared, and urban life generally improved, but poverty was not erased and a huge gap still existed betwen the haves and have nots. Though alleviated, these problems did not go away. Rather, they were forgotten as America entered first World War I and then the boom period of the twenties. Likewise, the thirties Depression and World War II diverted

American attention elsewhere, and in the fifties, the release of pent up demand and savings produced a new boom similar in many ways to that of the 1920's. Disadvantaged groups still existed, of course, but they had not as yet forged themselves into a powerful political coalition. Beginning in the 1950's and gaining momentum in the 1960's, however, the civil rights movement did forge such a coalition, and taking advantage of the political stalemate in Congress which had been in effect since the collapse of the New Deal coalition between 1937 and 1938, civil rights leaders began to pressure government and the private sector to make major improvements first in civil rights and later in eliminating grinding poverty.

Martin Luther King was the leader of this movement. Emphasizing a non-violent approach, King supported the Montgomery bus boycott between 1955 and 1956. The 1954 Supreme Court decision of *Brown vs. the Board of Education* outlawed separate schools for blacks, and King and others pressed to end school segregation in the South and later turned their attention to de facto segregation in the North. Under President Kennedy, the Justice Department aided King's efforts by pressing federal courts to guarantee civil rights to blacks and other minorities. The culmination of King's drive occurred in 1964, when the Civil Rights Act outlawed segregation in public facilities. The 1965 Voting Rights Act furthered King's effort by providing federal support for his drive to reenfranchise blacks and other minorities. Within a relatively short time, then, legal discrimination against the disadvantaged was greatly reduced, but the problem of urban poverty and its resulting crime remained.

It was to deal with poverty that Lyndon Johnson's Great Society programs were introduced. The Economic Opportunity Act of 1964, for example, attempted to funnel federal funds into education programs for the poor (Head Start), into job training (the Jobs Corps), and into building up small businesses in poor areas. Urban renewal sought to replace vermin infested slums with new, clean highrise apartments. But the programs had only limited impact. Much of the money was wasted and some was stolen. Crime forced many small businesses to abandon the ghettos. Moreover, as the American economy became more technologically sophisticated, the unskilled jobs which immigrants and the poor had traditionally held became fewer in number. Finally, increasing concern over the Vietnam War and the demands the war made on the American economy shifted concern away from civil rights and the ghettos' problems. In spite of federal programs, poverty, especially urban poverty, remained intractable.

Moderates like King and the NAACP had staked their reputations on the success of programs like the Civil Rights Act and Economic Opportunity Act, and the failure of these programs caused moderates to lose control over the civil rights movement. More militant blacks like Malcolm X and the Black Panthers took advantage to urge more vigorous and sometimes even violent tactics to improve the lot of the disadvantaged. They pointed out the poverty fell most harshly on the non-white population. In 1960, for example, although non-whites were only

11% of the total population, a quarter of all poor people were non-white. Black anger exploded in a series of riots such as that in the Watts ghetto of Los Angeles in 1965, and the assassination of King in 1968 sparked rioting in 100 cities in which whole areas were completely gutted by fire.

The South Bronx was one of these, and *Fort Apache, The Bronx* depicts the devastation and demoralization the riots left behind. Indeed, even more rioting and demonstrations occur during the course of the film, but these riots, like those of the sixties, are very different from the earlier civil rights demonstrations led by King. For one thing, in the film, riots have become calculated media events which involve no moral position. Murphy, a 41st precinct cop played by Paul Newman, warns that the people of the South Bronx will stage a series of fires to capture the attention of media newsmen sent to cover the murder of the two rookie cops. Likewise, a young man threatening to jump off a building in protest will not jump until Tom Snyder, a reporter, is there to cover the event. Most importantly, however, the protests in the film are not quiet, organized demonstrations such as that led by King in Birmingham in 1963. In the South Bronx, people come equipped with baseball bats, and they pelt the police with rocks and garbage. And violence produces more violence. Although urged to remain calm and let the demonstrators get it out of their systems, the new captain, Connelly, orders tear gas to be used which is then followed up by truncheon-wielding police who proceed to break up the demonstration by force. The moral authority generated by King is totally absent from this mini-riot in which both sides rapidly resort to violence which achieves nothing.

The police and the South Bronx community are at war with one another as much as the United States Cavalry and the Indians were on the Old West frontier, and on this point everyone agrees. Murphy even wears United States Army fatigues when he goes out on a plain clothes patrol. It is over how to prosecute the war that disagreement emerges. Murphy, the cop on the beat, draws a basic distinction between victim and victimless crimes while Captain Connelly believes all crime and corruption must be rooted out. Hookers, bookies, and drug users violate the law, but Murphy deals leniently with them, reserving his time for really dangerous criminals like murderers and violent drug dealers. Murphy even offers to provide his girlfriend, the nurse Isabella, with the heroin which she occasionally uses. On the other hand, Murphy unhesitatingly kills a drug dealer who has taken hostages in a hospital. By contrast, Connelly insists on arresting prostitutes and fences, partly to get information about the murder of the two cops, and partly because he believes sincerely in trying to protect the decent people living in the district from every sort of criminal. Our sympathy is drawn to Murphy, in part because his distinction seems more realistic and in part because he is obviously the star. However, the film makes clear that this distinction between victim and victimless crimes is not all that neat. It was a hooker, after all, who murdered the rookie cops, and Isabella dies of an overdose on one of her occasional "vacations," as she calls them. The war on crime, like the War on

Poverty, seems unwinnable no matter what tactics are used.

It is the film's emphasis on warfare and its very title of course which cause *Fort Apache, The Bronx* to be compared to *Fort Apache*, John Ford's 1949 classic. When the two are compared, however, two very different social frameworks are exposed. In the original *Fort Apache*, there was great camaraderie among all the troops, while in *Fort Apache, The Bronx*, the camaraderie is restricted to just two police partners, Murphy and Correlli. The solidarity of a whole community is limited to a single friendship between two men, a reflection of the atomization of modern urban American and the loneliness of urban dwellers which results from it. Likewise, in the original film, while the troops may have drunk to excess occasionally and engaged in highspirited highjinks, real corruption was located in the Indian Bureau. By contrast, in *Fort Apache, The Bronx*, the corruption is inside the police force itself. His nerves frayed after being pelted by rocks, a policeman throws an innocent bystander off the roof of a building, and what is worse, he obliges his colleagues to cover up for him. Though it is true that not all cops are corrupt and that Captain Connelly is sincerely interested in rooting out corruption, in *Fort Apache, The Bronx*, the neat distinction between lawman and lawbreaker has broken down. Moral differences which were so clear in 1949 are considerably more hazy in 1981. Murphy struggles with his conscience trying to decide whether to testify against the cop who committed murder, and when he finally does so, he is reacting as much to Isabella's death as to the moral consequences of telling the truth. A cop himself, Murphy is well aware of the frustrations and fears which could cause a police officer to snap. As a result, he is not proud of his decision to testify; Murphy considers himself a stoolie because he has "ratted" on a fellow officer.

Equally striking is the different view of the "enemy" in these two films. In *Fort Apache*, the indian was regarded as different and dangerous, but also noble, and his behavior was explained as an understandable reaction to the perceived treachery of whites. By contrast, in *Fort Apache, The Bronx*, the "enemy," that is the criminals of the South Bronx, exhibit no nobility and almost no decency. To be fair, before the film's opening credits roll, a disclaimer on the screen advises the audience that, because the film deals with police work, it does not portray those decent, law-abiding citizens of the area or those who are trying to improve conditions. Yet the absolute lack of any such persons in the film casts doubt on this disclaimer. No one comes forward to finger the cop killer, and moreover, they rob the corpses of the dead rookie cops. When the police are summoned to protect firemen trying to put out a blaze, the inhabitants of the area pelt them with rocks and garbage and smash the windows of the patrol cars. The violence and lack of concern for one's fellow man are not just directed against the police, however. In one of the most telling scenes of the film, Murphy and Correlli are sent out to disarm a knife-wielding man. Murphy performs such crazy antics that the man gives him his knife, but not before he has slashed a young bystander. Our attention is directed to Murphy, but significantly, no one comes to the aid of the slashed young man who crumples up and falls, but who is obviously not dead. Likewise, when the nurse Isabella stumbles through the street in her nightclothes, no one goes to her aid although she is clearly unarmed and not dangerous. We are reminded of the famous Kitty Genovese incident in New York City in which a girl was stabbed to death outside her home although she called repeatedly for help and at least 27 people heard her screams. The view of the enemy in *Fort Apache, The Bronx* is similar to that in *Deer Hunter* which deals with Vietnam. Both belligerents and non-combatants in this war are indistinguishable and dangerous; both lack any concern for their fellow man. While the disclaimer may indeed be true, the view of the enemy in *Fort Apache, The Bronx* is one of total moral depravity; it is a universe in which all traditional moral values have broken down, and mere survival is the only imperative.

To survive one has to use one's wits. Playing by the rules means nothing and can even be dangerous when the other side does not honor the rules at all. The rookie cops, for example, do play by the rules and do not, therefore, draw their guns when the hooker, spaced out on Angel Dust, approaches them, and they are dead as a result. Murphy and Correlli, on the other hand, do not work "by the book." For example, they do not announce themselves as policemen when they raid the apartment of a suspected gun runner, because they fear the man may be standing behind the door with a loaded M-16 and will not hesitate to fire through the wooden door. Instead, they set a fire in a trash can, and the man comes out of his own volition, because he is convinced the building is on fire. In *Fort Apache, The Bronx*, then, not living by the rules insures survival whereas in the original *Fort Apache*, not living up to the bargain made by Cochise results in the slaughter of Colonel Thursby's forces. Rules are vital in 1949, but in 1981, rules exist only to be ignored.

In the dog-eat-dog world around the South Bronx police station, therefore, there appears little cause for hope in the future. Yet, by the end of the film, we are in fact encouraged to hope. In spite of the pressure on him not to, Murphy informs against the policeman who had killed the young bystander. He turns in his badge and prepares to leave the police force. Driving home, however, he encounters his partner Correlli, who cheerfully reveals he will testify with Murphy even though previously he had been unwilling to do so. As they drive along, they see the purse snatcher commit another robbery. At first, Murphy refuses to give chase, claiming he's a "civilian," no longer a combatant, but then he slams on the brakes and begins a mad dash to capture the young culprit. Early in the film, Murphy had chased this young man, but had had to give up the chase when the fellow outran him. Later, the young man had burgled his car, and Murphy did not even try to chase him, letting him escape instead. But now, at the end of the film, both Murphy and his partner try to chase the young purse snatcher down.

It is this chase sequence which gives the audience grounds for hope in spite of what we have seen in the film. First, of course, Murphy has decided not to give up. In his small way, he will not allow victimization to continue, either on the part of corrupt cops or young purse snatchers. Second, as they fly by a garbage dump, we see the rug-covered body of the hooker who had murdered the two rookie cops and who had herself been killed by an outraged drug dealer, who in turn had been killed in the hospital shootout. We are reminded that the two most overtly violent characters in the film are dead and that a rough justice has been done. As Murphy and Correlli race after the fleeing suspect, they pass a building which is being torn down by a wrecking ball. This building is not decaying; it is being destroyed deliberately, probably with a view towards erecting a new high rise in its place. Destruction here may beget construction. Finally, as Murphy and Correlli close on the young man, Murphy takes a wild leap with outstretched hand to capture him. At just that moment, the frame is frozen and the final credits roll. Murphy has not captured the young man yet. Indeed, it looks as though he may miss him, but he is trying.

In the original *Fort Apache*, the film ends with the entire troop of cavalry riding out triumphantly on patrol, but in *Fort Apache, The Bronx* the triumph is individual. Murphy is to be admired, not because he wins, but because he does not give up in the face of overwhelming odds. He is risking a heart attack to chase down the purse snatcher, not because he seeks personal glory, but because he is sworn to uphold the law. This is a much more limited view of heroism, but following the agony of Vietnam and Watergate and the mixed results of the Great Society programs, Americans had lowered their expectations on both the foreign and domestic fronts. Americans could not save the whole world, or even a small part of it like South Bronx. The faith here is in individual regeneration, but it is faith nonetheless. As the United States faces major challenges in the eighties and beyond, this faith, qualified and limited as it is, would stand the country in good stead.

Fort Apache, The Bronx - Instructor's Guide

1. Identify two or three programs from Johnson's Great Society package of programs and evaluate their success.

2. Write a brief history of the OEO or Office of Economic Opportunity.

3. Discuss the difference in philiosphy of civil rights between Martin Luther King, Malcom X, and Stokely Carmichael. For books which may help you with this project see:

   1. Martin Luther King, *Stride Toward Freedom* (1958)
   2. Malcolm X, *Autobiography* (1966)
   3. Stokely Carmichael and Charles Hamilton, *Black Power* (1967)

4. Describe in detail the conclusions of the Kerner Commission of Civil Disorders (1968) as to why the riots in black communities began and what can be doen to prevent future riots.

5. According to Jane Jacobs in *The Death and Life of Great American Cities* (1961), why are American cities in trouble and what can be done about it?

6. Write a brief biographical sketch and assess the historical significance of any or all of the following:

   1. Malcolm X
   2. Martin Luther King, Jr.
   3. Richard Wagner, mayor of New York City
   4. Eldridge Cleaver
   5. Stokely Carmichael

7. Give a brief history of the immigration of residents of Puerto Rico into eastern American cities.

8. Write a book report, indicating the author's hypothesis and relating events in the film to events in the book, for any or the following:

   1. Michael Harrington, *The Other America* (1962) reprinted 1971
   2. Jane Jacobs, *The Death and Life of Great American Cities* (1961)
   3. Martin Luther King, Jr, *Stride Toward Freedom* (1958)
   4. Oscar Lewis, *La Vida: A Puerto Rican Family in the Culture of Poverty* (1966)
   5. Malcolm X, *Autobiography* (1966)
   6. Dorothy K. Newman, *et. al., Protest Politics and Prosperity: Black Americans and White Institutions, 1940-1974* (1978)
   7. Gilbert Osofsky, *Harlem: The Making of a Ghetto* (1965)
   8. James T. Patterson, *America's Struggle Against Poverty, 1900-1985* (1986)
   9. Carol B. Stack, *All Our Kin: Strategies for Survival in a Black Community* (1975)
   10. William Julius Wilson, *The Declining Significance of Race: Blacks and Changing American Institutions* (1978) second edition, 1980

Garrison, Daniel H.

WHO'S WHO IN WODEHOUSE

ISBN 0-8204-0517-5   319 pp.   hardback $ 32.50/sFr. 48.75

Recommended prices – alterations reserved

A comprehensive prosopography or guide to the characters in the 74 novels and 234 collected stories of P. G. Wodehouse, 1881-1975. Based on Wodehouse's own descriptions of Bertie Wooster, his aunts, his valet Jeeves, the far-flung Mulliner clan, 44 members of the Drones Club in London, 70 butlers and their masters, 32 valets and *their* masters, a bevy of girls with tip-tilted noses and cornflower-blue eyes, the kith and kin of Blandings Castle, gangsters, movie moguls, English gentry, American millionaires – over 2100 of the funniest and bestloved characters in twentieth-century Anglo-American fiction.

Contents: A descriptive list of over 2100 characters in the fiction of P. G. Wodehouse, featuring Wodehouse's own language and point of view – Supplemented by a comprehensive list of Wodehouse titles and collections. The only full account of all Wodehouse characters from the schoolboy fiction of the early 1900's to the last Blandings novel, published posthumously in 1977.

PETER LANG PUBLISHING, INC.
62 West 45th Street
USA – New York, NY 10036

Iwe, N.S.'S.

THE HISTORY AND CONTENTS OF HUMAN RIGHTS

A Study of the History and Interpretation of Human Rights

American University Studies: Series 9, History. Vol. 11
ISBN 0-8204-0298-2   419 pp.   hardback $ 46.30/sFr. 81.00

Recommended prices – alterations reserved

What has been the fate and fortune of the fundamental rights of man in the course of history? What major historical documents have contributed significantly to the emergence of the concept of human rights? What is the essence and what are the implications of the basic natural rights of man? These are the central questions which Dr. Iwe has explored in this book, which highlights the contribution of Christianity, especially the Papacy, as the advocate of human rights in modern times. Dr. Iwe's book is important for its interpretation of natural law and Christian thought on human rights and for its emphasis on the socio-political significance of human rights for law and order in modern society.

PETER LANG PUBLISHING, INC.
62 West 45th Street
USA – New York, NY 10036

Jameson, John R.

BIG BEND ON THE RIO GRANDE
Biography of a National Park

American University Studies: Series 9, History. Vol. 18
ISBN 0-8204-0300-8   171 pp.   hardback $ 32.00/sFr. 48.00

Recommended prices – alterations reserved

Big Bend on the Rio Grande examines the history of Texas's possessive first national park from its origins 1930s through developments of the 1980s. It is a story of a unique landscape and its effect on people as well as the impact of human beings on the flora and fauna of a fragile desert environment. The story involves international intrigue and border incidents, conflicts over predators, and visitor and employee experiences in the Lone Star State's «last frontier». Other topics include publicity and fund raising campaigns, land acquisition, and development plans for the park. In addition, *Big Bend on the Rio Grande* provides a revealing case study of an important federal natural resource agency, the National Park Service.

Contents: The Quest for a National Park in Texas – Politics of Fund Raising – Publicizing the Park Movement – Land Acquisition – Visitor and Employee Experiences in the «Last Frontier» – Predator Incubator Controversy – National or International Park?

«John Jameson has a grasp of a broad range of problems in conservation and national park history, and he has provided us with a closely researched biography of Big Bend, one of the least known, most important parks. The sensitivity of his judgments will help provide a basis for generalizing to other, newer parks as well.»

(Robin W. Winks, Yale University)

PETER LANG PUBLISHING, INC.
62 West 45th Street
USA – New York, NY 10036